THE
RING
OF
DANCERS

SYMBOL AND CULTURE

A series edited by
J. Christopher Crocker, Peter Metcalf,
Michelle Zimbalist Rosaldo, Renato Rosaldo, and
J. David Sapir

Jonathan Wylie and David Margolin

THE
RING
OF
DANCERS

Images of Faroese Culture

Foreword by Einar Haugen

UNIVERSITY OF PENNSYLVANIA PRESS   1981
PHILADELPHIA

Library of Congress Cataloging in Publication Data

Wylie, Jonathan.
    The ring of dancers.

    (Symbol and culture)
    Bibliography: p. 169
    Includes index.
    1.   Faroe Islands—Civilization. 2.   Faroese dialect.
3.   Folk-lore—Faroe Islands. I.   Margolin, David,
joint author. II.   Title. III.   Series.
DL271.F24W94   949.1′5   80–50690
ISBN 0–8122–7783–X

Glymur dansur í høll,
Dans sláið í ring,
Glaðir ríða Noregsmenn
Til hildarting.

The dance resounds in the noble hall,
Form the dance in a ring,
Happy ride the men of Norway
To battle.

—traditional refrain

Plate 1. "The Ring of Dancers" ("*Dansiringur*"): detail of sculpture by Janus Kamban. (Photograph: Kalmar og Alan, Tórshavn)

FOR ALBERT LORD,
with appreciation

Contents

Illustrations

Figures

Plates

Foreword

Our plane was already late, and it looked as if it would be later. We might have to land in Iceland and not get to the Faroes at all. The peak of summer was past, and it was overcast enough for darkness to set in. We were hovering over the airfield at Sørvágur, the infinitesimal airstrip built between mountains by the British during World War II. We saw nothing but a sea of clouds between jagged peaks thrusting upward like guardian trolls on either side of the airstrip. Suddenly the pilot spied a rift between the peaks—invisible to us—and darted into the mist. Seconds later, while we held our breath, he was under the clouds, and a green valley opened before us. We just had time for a sigh of relief as the plane crunched down on the only landing field in this tiny Viking outpost in the middle of the North Atlantic.

We who landed so unceremoniously that evening in 1965 were a jolly crew indeed. Our flight, originating in Copenhagen, had flown via Stavanger in Norway, Stornoway in the Hebrides, and Kirkwall in the Orkneys on its way to the Faroes. Many of us were delegates to the Fifth Viking Congress, the first to be held in the Faroes. It proved to be one of the first scholarly congresses ever to be held in the islands, at least since they had become self-ruling. For all our sense of adventurousness, we were not real Vikings, only scholars devoted to the Viking Period, a palefaced band of professors and students specializing in the archeology and the philology of that last pre-Christian period of Scandinavian history. The professor from Oslo had broken out his bottle of Scotch, and by the time of arrival Irishmen, Scots, Englishmen, Danes, Swedes, Icelanders, and Norwegians were all on the best of terms.

As the only American I was a bit out of place, for membership in the congress was strictly limited to citizens of the British Isles and Scandinavia. By coincidence I had this year decided it was time for me, as a professor of Scandinavian languages, to visit the one Scandinavian nation I had not seen and to hear in its natural setting the one Scandinavian language I had never heard spoken. To be sure, I had met the leading Faroese scholar-poet, Christian Matras, while he was still professor of Faroese in Copenhagen, a *rara avis* indeed. In our evening of talk I had been struck by his having asked me for advice from America about the problems of teaching spelling. The standard orthography of Faroese, created in the mid-nineteenth century, was about as hard to learn for Faroese children as English is for Americans. To this day I do not know if my suggestions and references were of any help. To the average outsider, as I was then, it seemed a pity that the Faroese, when they had a chance to start writing with a clean slate, did not give themselves an easy, phonetic spelling. As I later learned, the problem is not as simple as that.

The authors of this book point out in chapter 4 the full complexity of it all. An orthography is an instrument of unification, a symbol of nationhood. In their etymologizing Hammershaimb orthography the Faroese had found themselves a national showpiece, what some might call "conspicuous waste," like royalty. But, as is also true of royalty—say in the folktales—the whole history of a people is compressed into this one symbol. The silent letters are tacit testimony that this land has a history, that its roots go back into the Nordic past, that its people are willing to put in some extra effort for the sake of a great perspective.

But here I was, my ears attuned to new and strange sounds, tape recorder poised to pick it all up. What I heard was surprisingly familiar. With a little good will on each side I could make out most of what I heard, and my Norwegian functioned as a viable instrument. This language of the Faroes, which on the printed page bristled with Icelandic-looking markers, had on the lips of its speakers the sounds of southwestern Norway, from which their ancestors had come a thousand years ago. The intonation, the flexible diphthongs, the burred *r*, the sharp consonant clusters—I had heard them before, from speakers of Sogn and Voss, Hardanger and Rogaland, even among immigrants in far-away America.

So communication was not a problem. The Faroese listened daily to the Norwegian national radio, and they had learned Danish in school. When they shifted from Faroese to their version of Danish, they sounded like West Norwegians trying to make out in urban speech. Oh, it was not "good" Danish, but why should it be? It was easier for a Norwegian to understand than the Danish of the Danes.

And compared with the Icelanders, with whom I had also learned to cope, these people seemed far more ready to talk; they were lively and free. Of all the Nordic countries it seemed the most southern in spirit.

Our authors have explored in depth some of the reasons for this spirit. Its roots are in the Faroese villages, those clusters of wind-swept houses where people have sought shelter over the centuries for mutual aid and protection. Icelanders are individualists, living on farms apart, by horse a day's ride from one's neighbor. An Icelandic theologian once gave this as the reason his people have never taken to revivalism: in the old days one simply couldn't get enough of them together in one spot to whip up mass emotion. He contrasted them with the tight little villages in the Norwegian fjords, where evangelism flourished. Whether valid or not, the idea seems to fit the Faroese as well. There is plenty of religious fervor here, along with the sin it is designed to counter. Yet the dances have miraculously survived: they are a communal activity that no amount of pietistic grumbling can suppress. The dances are ritual, they are—if one wants to see them in perspective—a cleansing ritual, closely associated with the whale killings so graphically described here in chapter 5. Unlike the modern couple dance, they are not sexual, but communal. Everyone takes part, from toddler to gray-beard, irrespective of sex, age, or occupation.

The Faroese dance is a warm, heartening experience, as we were to learn, carried along in the ring of the dancers. One is not an individual showing off one's skill, not a prima donna, but part of an intertwined, closely knit social order, member of a living, breathing organism of men, women, and children. It is an experience that modern urbanites can seldom enjoy in our fragmented society, unless it be in certain small religious communities.

But back to my Viking Congress. We were lucky to have landed well and safely—we heard tales of passengers marooned for days at the airport, waiting for the fog to lift or the storms to abate. Even the ride to Tórshavn was a long one that included several changes, one of them requiring a walk with our luggage around an unbuilt bridge. I was fortunate to have a room in a private home, where I could listen to Faroese and learn what I had come to learn.

The congress was coincidental, but it turned out to be central. Whether it was the location or the hospitality of the hosts or just something in the air, it was the most leisurely and entertaining congress I would ever attend—more of an extended picnic than a solemn conclave. The problem of nationality had been solved by enrolling me with the Norwegian delegation. I promptly switched my badge to "Vinland," the westernmost land entitled to recognition as part of the Viking empire, and just possibly locatable in Massachusetts, where I was a professor.

The papers given did not burden our days, and most of them did not deal with the Faroes, so we can pass them by and refer any interested reader to the published volume (*The Fifth Viking Congress, Tórshavn, July 1965*, edited by Bjarni Niclasen, published in Tórshavn, 1968). Only one very short paper is relevant here, the one given by Bjarni Niclasen, a teacher and the honorary secretary of the congress. He spoke of the lack of raw materials such as wood and metal in the islands and the necessity of replacing these with other products—for example, the ram's horns grown by the sheep that have given the islands their name. When these are boiled, they become flexible and can be shaped and cut to a number of purposes.

Niclasen illustrated one of these purposes by showing us a piece of horn shaped into a circle about four inches in diameter. This object had been chosen as the symbol of the congress, and has been so used ever since. He announced that each visiting member would receive one as a souvenir: he and his helpers had spent their free time all winter making up enough for each of us to get one. Then he conducted us into a nearby field to demonstrate its use. Two farmers in native costume stood ready and proceeded to use the ring as a loop or eye through which they threaded a rope. The rope was then twisted around a bale of hay, which one of the men could then hoist onto his back with the ring of horn holding the rope taut. It is called a *held* (from Old Norse *hǫgld*, plural *hagldir*) and is well known from other Scandinavian countries, but there it is usually made from wood (withes). In the Faroes it is more laborious and more permanent, and also more artistic, with a beauty that is best appreciated when one can hold it in one's hand. This ring, which was an implement of old-fashioned agriculture, has become the symbol of the grip of the circle of friendship, a reminder also of the ring of dancers.

Every congress has to have its excursions, but here they were special, being nearly all by boat. The weather around the islands made excursions problematic, and one day the program was suddenly switched around to make sure that we would see the famous bird cliffs, which are inaccessible by sea most of the year. A large motor launch conveyed us out to Mykines, the westernmost of the islands, where the bird cliffs tower up on the side that faces out to the North Atlantic. We threaded our way in and out among the cliffs, where myriads of birds were nesting, raucously angry at our intrusion, but quickly returning to their own concerns as we passed. Here we could see puffins, fulmars, guillemots, kittiwakes, and what they all are known as, these birds of the ocean. They have nothing to fear except Faroese bird catchers, who let themselves down the steep cliffs by rope to capture birds or eggs.

On our way to the bird cliffs we were treated to a view of an unpremeditated and unpredictable part of the island life: a whale kill or *grindadráp*. Not that we saw the kill itself; we arrived on the morning after. It was a bizarre sight: hundreds of dead whales stretched out on the sandy beach, each one twenty to thirty feet long and expertly marked with a number cut into its flesh; the highest number I observed was in the 550s. Every whale had been assigned to someone, from the appropriate authorities down to each participant in the kill. A grisly sight for the outsider, a marvelous piece of good fortune for the community, the occasion for all-night dancing by the participants. In the yards nearby fathers and sons were busy carving up their special whale. Modern technology was not much in evidence, but we were told that the meat is stored in freezers, and the surplus is carted away by truck to adorn the menus of Tórshavn the following day.

Birds and whales are delicacies; the staples are fish and mutton, for these are the chief income-producing foods. A generation ago the Faroes were almost entirely a country of villages, with sheep in the meadows and fish in the sea. Today a modest industry has made some of the villages into towns, and the capital, Tórshavn, is threatening to become a city. It still has its ancient harbor, with the meeting place of the old assembly (the *Thing*) on Tinganes jutting out from it. On this headland are the buildings of the government, wooden structures converted from the time of the Danish Monopoly, which had its offices here. We heard talk of tearing these down to create a modern center; one can only hope that no such plan will come to pass. For the town center has an old-fashioned charm that urban redevelopment can only succeed in destroying.

Tarred old wooden buildings with sod roofs, enclosing narrow streets and alleyways, climbing the amphitheater of its environs. New hotels were springing up, and there was a tourist office to attract visitors, all to see a charm that their very presence might soon destroy. It was and is a fragile charm that nothing but a firm stance by culturally conscious leaders can preserve. There were enough signs of prosperity around us: well-stocked stores, imported goods, plenty of taxis, handsomely dressed people—especially the women and men who turned out in native costume for the national holiday.

For in addition to everything else we were privileged to join the Faroese in celebrating 29 July (*Ólavsøka*, historically St. Olav's day), when the parliament opens its session. Streets are crowded, flags are flying (the only Danish flag was on the house of the high commissioner), bands are parading. My camera went click-click every minute, as endearing children in costume were held up by eager parents to have their picture taken. Again the weather was unexceptionable, as crowds swirled around the parliament house, marking the home rule that was granted to the islands in 1948 after so many centuries of dependence on Denmark. Not until this generation have the Danes come to realize that whatever benefits they may have conferred on the Faroes, they have also been their oppressors. They have had to learn that the Faroese are not second-class Danes, speaking a degenerate dialect of Danish. Yet the Faroese are deeply in debt to those Danes who helped open their eyes to their own culture and language: to scholars like Rasmus Rask, N. M. Petersen, Svend Grundtvig, and many others. The movement for Faroese self-rule originated in Copenhagen, where Faroese students at the Danish university gradually discovered that they were not and could never become real Danes.

As guests of the Faroe people we were royally treated, not only with excursions but also with banquets and entertainments. On the national holiday the residents had a choice: the newspapers announced revival meetings, "English" dancing (which at that time meant the Beatles), and Faroese dancing. All three seemed to be well attended, but we visitors found the Faroese dances the most attractive. No sooner was a dinner finished than the people would join together for dancing, and we visitors were drawn into the circle. Even if we did not know the words, we could quickly catch on to the refrain and join in the singing with the rest. One skillful song-leader was enough: he knew all the verses (and they could be many), and he led the singing. Not all the ballads were Faroese or even medieval in origin.

One night after a party we went past the national theater and looked into the dancing area, a room absolutely packed with people. My friend the runologist could not resist and slipped in to join the dancers, while I went off to catch up on needed sleep. Next day he told me that he had stayed until six in the morning, when the dancing finally broke up. The atmosphere was most intense on the last evening of the congress, when all the participants, some seventy to eighty strong, were benched in the medieval loft of Kirkjubøur, the seat of the ancient bishops and now the home of the uncrowned kings of the islands, the Patursson family. Speech after speech expressed the gratitude and admiration of the guests. After dinner, dancing went on in the tiny rooms, everyone clasping hands in a long chain of friendship, until the wee hours.

Other countries have ballads of the same kind as the Faroese: the Scottish and English ballads are famous, and some of them have spilled over into the American foothills. Denmark, Norway, and Sweden have their medieval ballads, written down, like the English, in modern times. We know that they also were danced to, but only in the Faroes have they been danced to continuously since the Middle Ages, when the oldest of them were composed. In the 1890s, when Scandinavians began perceiving folk dancing as a lost cultural treasure, students of the dance visited the Faroes to study the steps and the singing. The ballads were first committed to paper in 1773 by J. C. Svabo: this was the beginning of Faroese literature and of a written Faroese language. Even today, when the tradition has become self-conscious, and most of the longer ballads are learned from books, it is still a vital and compelling part of Faroese life.

For today books have become an important part of national life. There is a Faroese literature, grown from native soil and nurtured by influences from abroad. As a dependency of Denmark, the islands have had their writing channeled into and out of that country. Their school language, as well as their church and government language, was for a long time only Danish. Today Danish is still crucial for advanced work, but it is being pushed back step by step as Faroese takes over one sphere of life after the other.

There is one chapter of Faroese life that is still unwritten in this book: the story of their imaginative writing, and, for that matter, of the other arts. Svabo, who not only collected ballads but also wrote the first dictionary, did so in a purely antiquarian spirit. He was convinced that Faroese should learn Danish and forget their language, but he wanted to save it from oblivion before it was too late. It took, as we have seen, a new age and a new spirit to raise Faroese from a dying group of diverging dialects to a viable language, and thereby to implant the idea of nationhood and a national literature. A turning point came in 1891 with the publication of Hammershaimb's *Faroese Anthology* (*Færøsk Anthologi*), which comprised not only ballads and folklore but also original sketches of folk life written by himself.

The twentieth century has witnessed the rise of a native Faroese literature, some of it written in Danish. It seems like a minor miracle that a population of perhaps fifteen thousand at the turn of the century—now grown to about forty thousand, no more than an American small town—has produced a literature that includes masterpieces of international interest.

One of them is *Barbara*, which the author, Jørgen-Frantz Jacobsen, just managed to finish before his death in 1938. On its appearance in 1939, it quickly won fame as a masterly depiction of life and love in the Faroes. Barbara's story is based on a historical legend, but the novel stands on its own. She is the widow (and suspected murderer) of two pastors; in the novel she snares a third, but in the end this magnificent, generous female is left tragically emptyhanded. Another masterpiece is *The Lost Musicians* by William Heinesen, a bizarre and entertaining panorama of Tórshavn characters from the early part of this century. Published in Denmark in 1950, it was selected by the Council of Europe for translation into English in 1971. There is a whole flora of other writers whose poems, plays, short stories, and novels are noteworthy contributions to a newly founded literature. One of their warmest advocates is the American scholar and former Foreign Service officer Hedin Bronner, whose translations in *Faroese Short Stories* (1972) have made nine of them available in English, and whose critical study *Three Faroese Novelists* (1973) has provided analyses of Jacobsen, Heinesen, and the veteran Heðin Brú.

All this and much more was part of the memories of a Faroese fairyland that we carried away from our Viking Congress. No one who has walked among the old sod-roofed houses of Tórshavn harbor, strolled past the tarred buildings of Tinganes out to the anchor that seems to keep the Faroes from blowing away, or joined in the ring of the dancers to experience a real community of fellow beings will soon forget his impressions of the Faroes and the Faroese. In their literature he can relive his own experiences, recalling the bright, northern lights and imagining the raging dark seas of winter. He can appreciate the life of that community which this book so insightfully and engagingly presents to its readers.

Einar Haugen
Harvard University

Preface and Acknowledgments

The studies forming the bulk of this book were first written separately, as parts of larger efforts to understand the development of Faroese culture. Chapters 2, 5, and 6 were originally Wylie's work, while chapters 3 and 4 were Margolin's. We have thought it best to retain something of our separate personalities and styles of thought in the substantial rewriting necessary to give our studies the coherence of a single volume, but as rewriting requires rethinking, our ideas of Faroese society have become inextricably intertwined.

We welcome the opportunity to thank those who have made these studies possible. David Margolin was in the Faroes during the year 1970–71 and again during the summer of 1974. His research has been supported by the American Scandinavian Foundation, Fróðskaparsetur Føroya, and the National Institute of Mental Health Training Grant Program in the Social Sciences. Jonathan Wylie did field work in the Faroes in the summer of 1970, the year 1971–72, the summer of 1973, and the winter of 1974/75. His research has been supported by the Foreign Area Fellowship Program, the Comparative International Program in the Department of Social Relations at Harvard University, and the Woods Hole Oceanographic Institution Program in Marine Policy and Ocean Management. We are especially grateful to Professors Einar Haugen and James J. Fox for their encouragement and for offering an aegis under which to study the Faroes at Harvard. We are hopelessly indebted to the staff and students of Fróðskaparsetur Føroya, particularly Jóhan Hendrik W. Poulsen (who has also kindly let us use the picture of Jakob Jakobsen, plate 8), for their learning and their patience with brusque foreign ways, and to the kindness of Christian Matras and Niels W. Poulsen.

Too many friends, neighbors, hosts, and guides to the Faroese way of life have offered us advice and hospitality to thank in detail; but special thanks are due to Steinbjørn Jacobsen, Marius and Jóna Johannesen, Kristian and Sólvá Nielsen, and Klæmint, Heðin, and Maria Oknadal. On this side of the Atlantic, Roberto Da Matta, Peter Metcalf, and Susanna Kaysen have offered inspiration and criticism. We must thank Elena Wilson for her hospitality, Laurence Wylie for his unfailing encouragement and support, and J. David Sapir for his patient editorial assistance.

We alone, for all this, are responsible for the flaws in our vision of Faroese society and for errors of fact and emphasis.

We offer this book to Albert Lord on the occasion of his retirement, in appreciation—all too inadequate—of his teaching.

THE
RING
OF
DANCERS

1
Introduction

Illa er í Føroyum vorðið
tá ið aðrir stýra og ráða,
ofta óklár tíðindi eru
úr hesum landi at fáa.

It has gone badly in the Faroes
when others control and rule,
often unclear news is
to be gotten from this land.

—J. H. Djurhuus

The Viking Age may be dated, arbitrarily, from the sack of Lindisfarne in 793 to the death of Harald Hardradi at Stamford Bridge in 1066. Between these events Norsemen impressed themselves permanently on European memory, and for their own descendants created a Scandinavian heroic age—an age more memorable in the North, however, for exploration and internal strife than for the rapine and pillage recorded elsewhere.

The Viking Age did include a more peaceable movement of exploration and settlement across the northern rim of the Atlantic to the Faroes, Iceland, and Greenland. This book is about the culture of the Faroe Islands—Viking, perhaps, in origin, but selectively elaborated over less dramatic ages. In their traditional ballads Faroese may recall Olaf Tryggvasson's defeat and death in the year 1000 and the internal struggles which at about the same time brought Christianity and Norwegian tax collectors to the Faroes. But Faroese culture has been shaped less notably by Viking heroics than by the pattern of its bearers' dealings with the continent, and by

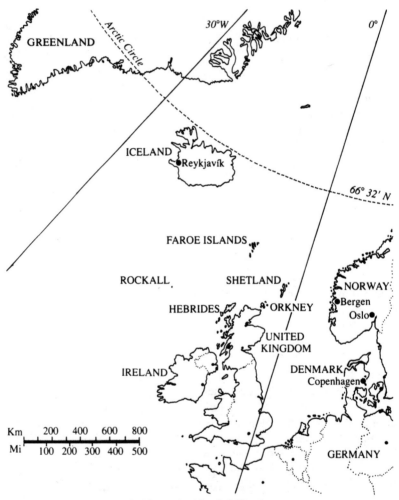

GREENLAND

30°W

0°

Arctic Circle

ICELAND ●Reykjavík

66° 32' N

FAROE ISLANDS

ROCKALL

SHETLAND

NORWAY
●Bergen
Oslo●

HEBRIDES

ORKNEY

UNITED
KINGDOM

IRELAND

DENMARK
Copenhagen●

| Km | 200 | 400 | 600 | 800 |
| Mi | 100 | 200 | 300 | 400 | 500 |

GERMANY

Figure 1. The Faroe Islands in the North Atlantic

continental events beyond Faroese control—for example the rise of Bergen, Norway's reversion of interest to the south and its subsumption under the Danish crown, the Reformation, the National Romantic movement and the liberalization of Denmark after 1830, and, most recently, a growing world demand for fish.

Little is known of Faroese society in the Viking Age. Scattered evidence suggests that the first Norse settlers came here early in the ninth century, mostly from southwestern Norway, but to some extent also by way of the Orkneys and other Scottish islands already under Norse control. The first Norsemen evidently killed, enslaved, or drove out Irish anchorites they found living in the Faroes.[1]

The Faroes were more or less democratically self-governing well into the eleventh century. The seat of government was (and still is) Tórshavn, where the yearly legal assembly, the Løgting, met on a rocky spit called the Tinganes. In about 1035, however, the Norwegian crown began to collect taxes regularly in the Faroes. The Faroes became Christian in about the year 1000, and around 1080 they were made a separate bishopric based at Kirkjubøur, a hamlet with good farming lands across the ridge from Tórshavn. The church and the royal administration had representatives on the Løgting, which, though it continued to be the highest court in the land, gradually had its prerogatives reduced to interpreting laws dictated by the Norwegian crown. Norwegian law was promulgated in the Faroes in the late thirteenth century, but it recognized local differences from continental practices.

Independent Norwegian hegemony over the North Atlantic islands was at its height in the middle of the thirteenth century. Bergen, founded in 1070 according to the sagas, was the center of a commercial and political confederacy embracing not only the Faroes but also Greenland and Iceland (which gave up their independence in 1261 and 1262, respectively), Shetland, Orkney, Man, and the Hebrides. But already Norwegian interests were reverting from the Atlantic to the Baltic, and were being overtaken by the commercial and political power of Copenhagen and the Hanse. The Hebrides and Man passed to Scotland in 1266, and in 1380 Norway itself was united with Denmark under the Danish crown. Norway's island dependencies grew less important. The Greenland colonies died out, and between 1468 and 1472 Orkney and Shetland became Scottish. Iceland and the Faroes survived in increasing isolation.

The Faroes are a poor land, and have always depended on imported grain, timber, and other commodities. The Faroese traditionally acquired these by exporting woolens and smaller quantities of such products as tallow, feathers, and dried fish. But only continental merchants owned the ships and had access to the resources upon which the Faroes' trade depended. Much of Faroese political and social history follows the development of trade relations with the continent. The Norwegian crown was regulating the Faroe trade as early as the late thirteenth century; by the sixteenth century a system had grown up whereby the king (now, of course, the king in Copenhagen) controlled it by renting out trading privileges to interested merchants, sometimes along with exclusive rights to collect taxes. This system did not become truly oppressive until after the Reformation.

The Reformation and its aftermath (ca. 1540–1620) had far-reaching effects on Faroese life. It established Copenhagen as the Faroes' point of contact with the continent, and severed virtually all their ancient ties with Bergen and the archipelagic confederacy. In 1557, the Faroes' bishop having been set aside, and the episcopal lands—about half the land in the Faroes—having been taken over by the king, the islands were reduced to a deanery under, first, the bishop of Bergen, and then, in about 1620, under the bishop of Sjælland. The episcopal school in Kirkjubøur was closed down, to be replaced in 1547 (rather inadequately, since it had likely been the home of an independent Faroese intellectual tradition) by a small "Latin School" in Tórshavn that offered preliminary training to candidates for the ministry. By this time Faroese was becoming a separate language—not yet so different from Norwegian or Icelandic, but very different from Danish. Danish was now the language of the church, of trade, and of the state. Faroese survived only as it was spoken. Far from destroying Faroese culture, the Reformation tended to preserve it in a more constraining mold. The economy remained based on landholding and traditional pursuits; royal policy and the self-interest of Danish officials and local men of substance kept it just viable enough that, for example, the Danish "priests" (Lutheran ministers) who came here could assimilate to Faroese society by control of substantial livings farmed in the traditional manner (Wylie 1978). Faroese society was not Danicized as Danish hegemony increased, but retained its own vitality—conservative, ingrown, and less and less recognized officially.

In the long run, perhaps the most important consequence of the Reformation was the progressive tightening of royal control over the Faroe trade. The Faroes' point of contact with the continent was finally moved from Bergen to Copenhagen in 1619, when the king chartered the Iceland, Faroe, and North-Norway Company. This monopoly was followed by one managed by the courtier Christoffer von Gabel and his son Frederik from 1655 to 1708. They controlled not only the Faroes' communication with the outside world, but also their local government, the administration of justice, and the collection of rents and taxes. It was a bleak, bitter, and often hungry time. When Frederik von Gabel died, the king took over the trade; it was run as a royal monopoly until 1856.

This Monopoly was not, on the face of things, so harsh, but its maintenance entailed the Faroes' continued economic stagnation and the survival until well into the nineteenth century of a society essentially unchanged since about 1620. At most, several ships a year called in Tórshavn, where they discharged imports and took on goods for export. Faroese bought and sold at fixed prices. The Monopoly warehouse in Tórshavn was the only commercial enterprise in the Faroes, and all Faroese had to come there to trade legally. Tórshavn also housed a fort to guard the warehouse, the dean's church, the tiny Latin School, a few Danish officials, and a small population of landless paupers.

Modern Faroese history begins around 1830. It is largely the story of the growth of the export fishery, and of reaction to Danish hegemony.

In the years 1814–16 the Faroes had reached a low point in an already depressed history. Denmark lost Norway by the Treaty of Kiel in 1814, but retained Greenland, Iceland, and the Faroes. In 1816 the Løgting was dissolved and the remnants of the Faroes' political independence were stripped away. Although something of their peculiar status was recognized—the old Faroe-Norwegian law was kept in effect—the Faroes were henceforth to be governed as a Danish county (amt). This closer association with Denmark did not, however, have the results the Danish government must have anticipated.

Partly in response to internal demographic pressures, and partly because fish seemed likely to prove a more profitable export than wool, some efforts were made to improve the Faroes' lot, particularly during the period of liberal reforms in Denmark from 1830 to 1849. The Faroes' governors (Danish amtmænd) during these years were well-meaning career bureaucrats with no vested interest in the Faroe trade. A savings bank was established in 1832; several new villages were founded; the Monopoly opened three branch stores in the late 1830s and began to buy fish products; attempts were made, somewhat prematurely, to modernize the fishery; and the Faroese sent representatives to the Danish provincial (1834–50) and national (1850–) assemblies. In 1851/52, the Løgting was reconstituted as a consultative body along the lines of the Danish provincial assemblies, and, most important, the Monopoly was abolished as of 1 January 1856.

These reforms were aimed at spurring the Faroes to become a more prosperous part of Denmark. But if this was the goal, only half of it was realized; as they grew more prosperous, the Faroes grew away from Denmark. Prosperity came—slowly—with the growth of commercial fishing, which eventually supplanted the ancient export economy based on woolens. By the end of the century economic growth in turn fostered the development of a new sense of what it meant to be Faroese.

The Faroese fishing industry was at first a simple expansion of a long tradition of subsistence fishing from open boats. Fishing was part of an internal economy which also included fowling, whaling, sealing, and some agriculture and husbandry. Now population pressure, together with relaxed trade restrictions, triggered the fishery's development into a large-scale commercial enterprise.

The Faroese population had evidently remained constant around 4,000–4,500 at least since the beginning of the seventeenth century. By 1801 it had risen to above 5,000; it reached 11,220 by 1880 and 15,230 by 1901. As late as 1901, however, about 4,500 people, virtually the same number as in 1600, were supported by what the censuses call "agriculture." The additional population was at first sustained almost entirely from the sea. By 1921, however, the fishing industry could no longer absorb the increase. Secondary pursuits—light industry, trade, crafts—supported ever larger shares of the population, while "agriculture" dropped steadily. Today it sustains less than 3 percent of a total population of around 40,000, while just under a quarter is sustained directly by fishing. The rest is supported by transportation services (including cargo shipping), building and construction, commerce, light industry, administrative and liberal professions, and old age and disability pensions. Fishing remains the lifeblood of this newly diversified internal economy. It contributes directly about a third of the GNP, and fish and fish products account for about 98 percent of Faroese exports by value yearly. In some respects, then, the Faroese economy has not changed. It is a growing money economy, but it still depends on a monolithic export trade and is internally highly diversified. As always, Faroese fortunes depend on foreign trade.

Faroese society has changed a great deal, however. In the earliest "Viking" times, the old division of Scandinavian society into warrior lords, free farmers, and slaves was undoubtedly soon weakened in the Faroes by the fact that there was only a tiny territorial base for warlike ambitions. The Faroese was a peasant society, and there came to be two principal classes of Faroese farmers—tenants and freeholders. These are distinguished not by the manner of their farming, or even necessarily by the size of their holdings, which might be mixed freehold and tenant, but by types of land tenure.

All land in the Faroes is divided into infield (*bøur*) and outfield (*hagi*). These are separated by stone walls, but are not themselves much subdivided. The infield, in which the village is set, is used for winter grazing and in the summer for the land's meager crops—traditionally barley, now potatoes, and hay. The outfield provides summer grazing for sheep and a few cattle. Before the Reformation, tenant farmers worked lands owned by the church; since the king took over the extensive church lands, tenant farmers have been called "king's farmers" (*kongsbøndur*). They pay a small annual rent and pass on to their eldest sons the right to work the farms.[2] Since king's land is impartible, tenant farmers were traditionally rich men in the Faroes. So were the "priests," who had generous livings. Until 1865, rich farmers could require poor freeholders as well as their own hired hands to man their fishing boats. For all this, however, there was a certain precarious equality among Faroese, for, as Lucas Debes commented in 1673:

> the riches of the Inhabitants doth consist almost entirely in their Sheep, for those that have many of them, though few grow rich thereby, those means being very casual; for when there cometh a hard Winter and Sheep dye, they are all almost equally rich. [1676:133–34]

A few Faroese specialized as artisans—smithing on their own account, for example, or coopering for the Monopoly—but there was no indigenous artisan class to speak of until after the middle of the nineteenth century, let alone a commercial class, or even a truly urban center. Modernization and urbanization attended the rise of the commercial fishery. Fishing had already become more commercialized, but the first radical change in fishing techniques came towards 1880, when Faroese began to buy secondhand sloops and schooners. With these they fished not only locally, but also—and ultimately, almost solely—off Iceland and on other distant grounds, forced further from home as foreign fleets, principally British, scoured local waters with up-to-date, steam-driven trawlers. At the time the Faroes' three-mile fishing limit was virtually unpatrolled, and older folk still speak bitterly of "the trawler-times."

The next major change did not come until after the Second World War, despite some tentative beginnings in the depths of a depression that lasted from just after the First World War through the 1930s. A modern fleet of trawlers, long-liners, and other vessels was built up, both for deepwater work and for the inshore fishery, which grew up again after the establishment of a twelve-mile limit, drawn from straight baselines, in 1964. Many villages have since revived, as fishermen may now live by working nearby waters, selling their catch to local processing firms; but the more isolated and land-based villages are dwindling.

The abolition of the Monopoly and, a generation later, the rise of ship fishing, brought about the formation of an indigenous middle class and, particularly after 1880, the establishment of Tórshavn as the Faroes' intellectual as well as political and commercial capital. In 1880 Tórshavn was a town of fewer than a thousand people, 8.8 percent of the total population. But in the next decade it began for the first time to grow faster than the population as a whole. It now has over twelve thousand inhabitants, and about a third of the Faroese population lives there.

Along with this economic growth, an unintended result of Danish policy after 1830 was the creation of a small group of Faroese intellectuals educated in Copenhagen who, influenced by National Romanticism and the Slesvig-Holstein dispute of the late 1840s, and made uncomfortably aware by "real" Danes of their own differentness, set about reformulating Faroese culture explicitly. Far from disappearing, Faroese culture gained an official expression in a movement that was at once literary and political: literary in setting up (or writing down) Faroese language and folkways as something respectable in their own right; political in that it entailed reconsidering the fundamental point at issue in Faroese politics—how closely should the Faroes be tied to Denmark? After all, it appeared, the Faroese have a different culture. Shouldn't they have a political status to match?

The first chapter in modern Faroese separatism was written when a law for compulsory schooling, passed in 1845, was repealed in 1854 because of widespread Faroese protests. An achievement with more lasting consequences was V. U. Hammershaimb's publication, in 1846, of an orthography for Faroese. At first little was written in the language, but by 1890 Faroese literature and journalism, written by students in Copenhagen, was being brought home. A literary and political club, the Føringafelag ("Society of Faroese"), modeled after an earlier club of the same name in Copenhagen, was founded in Tórshavn in 1889, and early the next year its newspaper, *Føringatíðindi*, the first written in Faroese, began publication. In 1891 V. U. Hammershaimb republished his orthography, together with examples of both traditional and modern literature and a large Faroese-Danish glossary. The glossary was largely the work of the linguist Jakob Jakobsen, whose collection of legends and folktales appeared between 1898 and 1901.

With economic growth, with the vernacular reestablished as a written language, and with the beginnings of a local political tradition—the first two Faroese political parties, Self-Rule and Unionist, were founded in 1906—many Faroese now favored greater political autonomy. Though this was partially realized by a series of reforms in 1923, the Second World War brought a more decisive turn of events. As Germany occupied Denmark, the British occupied the Faroes. This brief separation from Denmark increased nationalist sentiment and a referendum was held in 1946. A slim plurality voted for complete independence. The referendum was annulled, but in 1948 a Home Rule Law gave the Faroes a new status.

The Faroes are no longer a Danish county. They are internally self-governing in some matters—taxation, customs regulations, economic affairs, etc. Other matters are controlled jointly by the Løgting and the Danish state, which is represented by a high commissioner (Danish *rigsombudsmand*, Faroese *ríkisumboðsmaður*); these affairs the Løgting may vote to take over at any time. Other matters, most notably currency and foreign affairs, are the exclusive province of the Danish state. The queen is the head of state. The Løgting is the Faroese legislature. Its members choose among themselves an executive committee called the Landsstýri, which is in effect the Faroese administration. Its foreman, who bears the ancient title of *løgmaður*, is in effect the prime minister. Danish must be taught thoroughly in the schools, but Faroese is the first language of instruction.

Faroese history is part of the general history of Scandinavia, and Faroese culture is one of modern Scandinavia's several kindred cultures.[3] The theme of this book is how and why Faroese culture has become distinctive, and remained so.

This matter of cultural differentiation and self-differentiation is central to Scandinavian studies. The nations of the North have, as

Einar Haugen has written, "a common cultural heritage which unites them and to some extent distinguishes them from other nations but does not make them identical" (1966:153). Indeed, like other Scandinavians, the Faroese are not absolutely distinct. Politically, for example, they do not form a state apart from Denmark, and linguistically their language is still close enough to Icelandic and some dialects of Norwegian to allow rudimentary conversation. Their distinctiveness is thus partly, as it were, a matter of accent—of different stresses and resonances.

The distinctiveness of Faroese culture is a problem akin to that of the distinctiveness of Scandinavia's many national, regional, and local cultures—and it has been a problem for the Faroese themselves. We approach it here in several complementary ways.

First, we examine the problem as it presents itself to the Faroese themselves, as a historical matter and in terms of a selective elaboration of the common cultural heritage of the North. Since the Viking Age, Faroese culture has developed a character of its own in response to the exigencies of life in natural and political-economic settings different from those of Iceland, say, or western Norway. We have tried to set Faroese cultural forms in their Faroese context.

Faroese culture has not grown up in isolation, however, but in contact with, for example, Bergen and Copenhagen. Second, then, like other students of Scandinavian societies, we are concerned with the points of contact between "our" people and the outside world. Within the Faroes in recent times, the locus of these contacts has been Tórshavn, where residents of the scattered villages meet each other, as well as the officials and institutions of the Danish state. Outside ties have also been concentrated in institutions with branches in the villages—the church, for example, and also, since the nineteenth century, the schools.

Our third line of approach is perhaps not so common in Scandinavian studies. We believe that a most important element of Scandinavian societies' common heritage is a habit of distinguishing official from everyday levels of thought and organization. As we shall point out in detail below, this distinction is crucial in many realms of Faroese life, from the structure of a folktale to the organization of a whale hunt, but it is paradigmatically important in language.

Finally, we follow a Scandinavian preoccupation in focusing our attention on language and language use. Language is not only the prime vehicle for cultural expression, but it also serves, perhaps here especially, as a symbol of the way of life it expresses; through elaboration it may become an official token of its speakers' everyday, common integrity.

Our studies here present a series of moments in the development of Faroese culture—a rather piecemeal approach, perhaps appropriate to the Faroes' still unsettled status.

We begin with an example from the more natural, most anciently rooted, and least official end of things—the adaptation of general Germanic and Scandinavian geographical conceptions to the Faroes' special environment and their elaboration into a wonderfully complicated system for knowing the land and its intersecting and surrounding waterways. Faroese idioms of orientation manifest an elaboration of basic continental ideas in the context of an island world. It is both a natural world of islands, fjords, hills, cliffs, and sounds and a human world of villages, parishes, and political districts. When you grow accustomed to it, the Faroes' human geography seems almost natural.

The following chapter turns from timelessness to the beginning of modern times. We focus on "Øskudólgur," a folktale about the Ashlad. Obviously akin to continental tales, "Øskudólgur" has, like the geographical concepts, taken on peculiarly local meanings from the context in which it was told. Moreover, the tale was gaining a new sort of context and a new sort of meaning at the time it was collected by Dr. Jakob Jakobsen in the late nineteenth century. As it was told, it discusses in a traditional form the strains put upon traditional Faroese society in the late nineteenth century. Jakobsen's act of writing it down and publishing it also suggests ways that the traditional culture might be reworked to provide a new but not discontinuous sense of Faroese identity. The traditional telling and the literary form mark the important distinction between everyday and official levels of culture.

The following chapter, perhaps the most central in the series, takes up the Faroese language, or rather the Faroese languages— both the everyday vernacular and the official written forms used in church, for trade and political debate, in schools, and (nowadays) over the radio. The elements of the structure of language use in the Faroes have changed from time to time; at the Reformation, Danish replaced Latin as the liturgical language, and has itself been replaced in the present century by Faroese. But the basic structure has remained intact; and, as the primary distinction today is between spoken Faroese and written Faroese, language use has acquired an explicitly political aspect. The written language establishes an officially unifying version of Faroese culture, and lends the Faroese a linguistically rooted sense of their nationhood.

The next chapter turns from language to action. It considers the famous Faroese *grindadráp*, or slaughter of pilot whales, as a collectively performed representation of how Faroese express their common concerns and discover their common identity.

The final chapter turns to Tórshavn, offering illustration by way of conclusion. It recounts a series of interviews conducted with people whose business it is to articulate the Faroes' modern sense of place in the world.

In writing these pieces we have kept in mind the image of the *dansiringur* — the "ring" of dancers singing ballads of wars and loves of heroic times. This kind of ballad dancing is not a native Faroese custom (almost nothing is); it is the last survival of a dancing style once common throughout Europe. Late medieval woodcuts and drawings show dancers forming a real circle in the open air, arms linked as the Faroese still link arms, moving round with a step that looks very much like the Faroese step. But the Faroese ring is only formally a circle; the Faroese dance indoors, in rooms almost too small to hold all the people, and the "ring" is a great convoluted affair, with loops and eddies and whorls, so that as you dance around you seem everywhere to be passing a line parallel to your own, instead of the open ground and the whole circle of the continental dance. The people pass close before you; individuals are brought face to face for a moment in the stream, to return again familiarly on another verse, or perhaps to disappear, if for some reason they drop out of the dance.

The *dansiringur* nearly represents, we feel, the Faroese adaptation of large forms to a land of closely known neighbors and landscapes, the complex inward turnings of Faroese culture, and its tortuous sense of wholeness.

2
A Sense of Place

Unless you knew that the Faroes were a
group of very small islands, you could
well believe that you had a continent
before you.

—J.-F. Jacobsen (1965:5)

The Faroes are not really a continent. But the land is bounded by
everything from stupendous sea cliffs to gentle sand beaches and is
deeply indented by narrow arms of the sea; it is broken by watery
passages whose tidal currents make navigation hazardous; it is composed of seventeen inhabited islands and innumerable smaller bits
of land; and its people live in dozens of towns and hamlets, each of
which has a distinctive dialect or subdialect. Because the Faroes are
geographically complicated, because until recently travel around
them has been slow and uncertain, and because they were for centuries peculiarly cut off from the rest of the world, the Faroese know
their tiny archipelago with a vocabulary so large and elaborate and
pervasive that the islands come to feel like a continent.

The most striking aspect of the Faroese sense of place is a large
collection of idioms of orientation. I was first impressed by this one
day early in my field work. I had gotten a job sorting fish for the
village filleting plant and asked the foreman where the haddock
should go. "NORTH, there," he said, and pointed to a pile of fish a

NORÐOYAR

VIÐOY
KUNOY
FUGLOY
KALSOY
VIÐAREIÐI
KIRKJA
HATTARVÍK

GJÓGV
EIÐI
FUNNÍNGUR
KUNOY
HVANNASUND
TJØRNUVÍK
OYNDARFJØRÐUR
VÍK
HÚSAR
SVÍNOY
SAKSUN
FUGLAFJØRÐUR
EYSTUROY
KLAKKSVÍK
HVALVÍK
LEIRVÍK
GØTA
BORÐOY
VESTMANNA
SELATRAÐ
STREYMOY
SKÁLI
LAMBA
KVIVIK
STRENDUR
VÁGAR
KOLLAFJØRÐUR
MYKINES
SØRVÁGUR
SANDÁVAGUR
KALDBAK
TOFTIR
NES
MIÐVÁGUR
TÓRSHAVN
62° N

KOLTUR
NÓLSOY

HESTUR
KIRKJUBØUR

SKOPUN

SANDOY
SANDUR
SKÁLAVÍK

HÚSAVÍK

SKÚVOY

STÓRA DÍMUN

SANDVÍK
LÍTLA DÍMUN
HVALBA

TVØROYRI

FAMJIN
SUÐUROY
HOV
VÁGUR
PORKERI

LOPRA

km   10   20   30   SUMBA
mi   10   20

7° 45' W

Figure 2. The Faroe Islands

14 ■ The Ring of Dancers

few yards away.[1] It struck me that if he had pointed farther away in the same direction, to an island across the FJORD, he would have said it lay "WEST." Learning to live in the village meant learning, among other things, dozens of such phrases, which varied with where one was standing, where one meant to go, and how one meant to get there. There did seem to be some system to it all; an immediately understandable phrase would be thought up for a new house, for a pile of fish which had not been there a few minutes ago and would be gone a few minutes hence, and for such immediate needs as gave rise to another of the first usages I noted, shouted from the roof of a house to a man with a ladder: "No, move it a little NORTH." Figure 3 illustrates some of the directions I could have traveled from the dock: NORTH to my pile of haddock, WEST to one island across the FJORD, IN to another island, and OVER to a third; NORTH to an island to the northeast, or NORTH to a headland to the west; "up" to a mountain behind me; "from-below" or, of course, HOME back to my house, OUT to the house next door to mine, and then HOME again to one neighboring village—or EAST (on the same road) to others. . . .

I quickly grew accustomed to all this and began to be able to orient myself in the native idiom. I began to realize, however, that, as surely as speaking with a village accent, the unthinking mastery of such usages establishes one's place in the Faroese world. Throughout the Faroes, the same terms are used according to the same general principles; but each district, village, neighborhood, and even household customarily uses them a little differently. People from other villages reassured me that they sometimes had as much trouble as I did in getting the hang of local usages, and when, on a trip round the islands a few years later, I began collecting idioms of orientation systematically, I quickly found that it was necessary to get them from "native speakers." Sometimes a woman who had lived for decades in her husband's village would be listening as eagerly as I was, and would put in from time to time, "Oh, is *that* how you say it; I never knew."

The idioms of orientation are thus complex and to some extent arbitrary. But they are not incoherent. It appears upon inspection that their coherence and complexity derive from several sorts of historical and linguistic circumstance. First, there is (or was) the naming of the land and the intersecting waterways which compose the Faroes. How did the Faroes' Norse settlers conceive of their new home? Second, there is (or was) the political and ecclesiastical division of the Faroes, often into districts coinciding with naturally

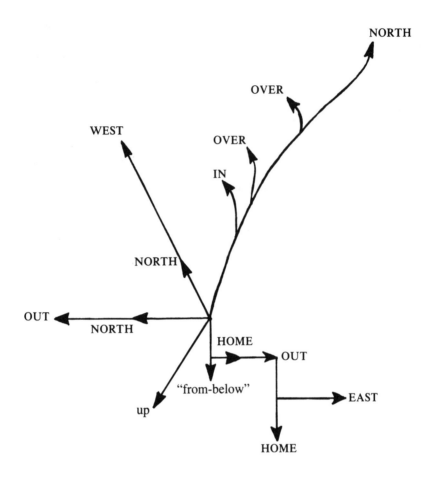

Figure 3. Some directions from a village dock

defined areas, like islands. Third, one finds overlaid on these a system of uncertain origin, but evidently common in Scandinavia, that uses compass terms to describe movement within sharply bounded areas. Just as Faroese as a whole have emphasized and elaborated elements of the cognitive and symbolic repertoire brought here by their ancestors, so each community continues to emphasize and elaborate elements of the Faroese system. The result is a certain arbitrariness—but one that, like the waterways by whose shores they live, unites Faroese with each other and with other Scandinavians, even as it distinguishes them. Historical and linguistic circumstance, therefore—the notions the Faroes' Norse settlers brought to a place more or less indescribable in continental terms, the founding of a new village, the establishment or disappearance of a church or a political boundary—is not just a factor accounting for flaws in a large, clean picture; it is the essence of knowing the Faroes as the Faroese have come to know them, with a picture of sometimes baroque elaboration on half-forgotten meanings, developed over centuries of close living in an isolated land.

Idioms of orientation typically take the form "NORTH to X." The first element is an adverb of place or direction (NORTH, SOUTH, IN, OVER, HOME, etc.), the second is a preposition, and the third is a place name or the name of a geographical feature. The prepositions vary with the name; the usual ones are *til* X, *frá* X, *í* X (to X, from X, in X), but some names require different combinations.[2] This essay takes up only the adverbial elements in idioms of orientation— a matter quite complicated enough.

As figure 3 suggests, the adverbial elements fall into several groups. First, IN, OUT, OVER, and ABOUT suggest movement with respect to bounded spaces: IN or OUT of a dwelling, a fenced field, or a FJORD; OVER a FJORD or a hill; ABOUT an island or a mountain. OVER indicates movement across a projecting barrier or above a given point, but the related senses of "across" and "through" hills or a FJORD dominate geographical idioms: "go OVER [the FJORD] to Kirkjubøur [from Skopun]," "go OVER [the ridge] to Tórshavn [from Kirkjubøur]." Idioms based on IN, OUT, OVER, and ABOUT derive their sense largely from conceptions of geographical features, particularly "island" (*oyggj*) and FJORD.

The second group comprises the points of the compass— NORTH, SOUTH, EAST, WEST—which suggest continuous travel in a direction defined by the sun or the stars. These terms are used idiomatically, however, to indicate movement toward a given area's northernmost, southernmost, easternmost, or westernmost points.

Third, HOME means to one's own house, of course, but it also means going toward the site of the district's original settlement or the parish church.

Finally, "up", "down", "from-below," and "from-above" clearly refer to vertical movement. Idioms of this group are for the most part quite transparent, and will not be treated here.[3] The other groups we shall take in order, beginning with the first, fundamental conceptions of island, FJORD, and other features of the Faroes' archipelagic geography.

Islands in the Stream

"OVER the FJORD" and "OVER the ridge"—these suggest, like many idioms of orientation, a certain equivalence of land and sea: a FJORD is a watery sort of ridge, or vice versa. The equivalence rests partly, of course, on the Faroes' settlement pattern; most villages are founded along the shore, between waterways and hills which must both be crossed by travelers. But it also derives from more ancient circumstances—the ways successive generations of Germanic settlers found to name new homelands along the Baltic and Atlantic coasts and out among the islands of Orkney, Shetland, Faroe, and Iceland. It is a vocabulary for describing plains and fenlands, patched and reseamed like an old slipcover to fit, finally, the new furniture of rockbound North Atlantic coasts and islands. This progressive mapping of inland terms onto seacoasts and seaways underlies two fundamental ideas expressed in idioms of orientation: (1) islands are lands bordering waterways, and (2) appearances to the contrary, waterways like FJORDS are not entirely open to the sea. Take, for example, the name of the Faroes' largest island, Streymoy.

Streym- (*streymur*) is cognate with English "stream." Both stem from Common Germanic **straumaz*, a watercourse or stream; *streymur*'s immediate ancestor, Old Norse *straumr*, accordingly meant a stream or current. In the Norse island colonies, Orkney, Shetland, Faroe, and Iceland, where the most spectacular "streams" are tidal currents along narrow arms of the sea, and whose settlers had more appropriate words available to name the inconsiderable inland watercourses, the sense of *straumr* was fitted to the action of the tides. *Streymur* means, in Faroese, a current, particularly a tidal current, and sometimes the tides themselves.

-oy means "island." It has a complicated and fascinating history. It stems ultimately from Indo-European **akua*, which gave both Latin *aqua* and Germanic **aȝwō*. **aȝwō* evidently meant water, perhaps particularly flowing water, and gave rise directly to such words, all meaning a stream, as Old Frisian *ā*, *ē*, Old Saxon and Old High German *aha*, Old English *ēa*, and Old Norse *á*—from the last of which Faroese *á* (stream, river, creek) is derived. Now, **aȝwō* also gave rise through an adjectival form to **aujō*, whose derivatives were used to describe land whose defining characteristic was water. The kind of land so defined evidently depended on the kind of landscape each wave of settlers discovered. Inland, **aujō* kept its old general meaning while rather haphazardly acquiring more specific ones. Old High German *ouwa* continued to mean

water or stream, but now also meant watery meadow, island, or peninsula—hence Modern German *Au*: river, brook, meadow, pasture. Along the coasts, *aujō* often developed into the first element of compound words naming pieces of land entirely surrounded by water: Old Frisian *eiland*, Middle Dutch and Middle Low German *eilant*, Old Norse *eyland*, and Old English *īegland*, *īgland*—hence Modern English "island."[4] Meanwhile, in the North, Old Norse *ey*, *eyja* kept well into the Viking Age the sense of a "flat stretch of fertile land along water," though the more usual sense was becoming peninsula or island (Jakobsen 1928). Thus Shetlandic Norn *ø generally meant an island, but, for example, Roe (from *rø-ø) may indicate either a true island (Muckle Roe, Little Roe) or a peninsula (Nort' Roe). Similarly, Orfase (from *ør-firis-ey) on South Yell is "a small isle which at ebb is connected with a mainland or large island by a reef submerged at flood-tide" (ibid.).

The Faroes' settlers brought with them, then, a lingering sense that an island is basically a stretch of land along a watercourse—a peninsular shore or one separated from the mainland by water. Etymologically, "Streymoy" represents "stream-water," elaborated to "(sea-)current-watery(-land)"—or "current-island" for short. But how, in this land of nothing but islands, are all these shores connected? And where now is the mainland?

To answer these questions, let us note another adaptation of continental habits of thought to archipelagic geography, an adaptation most fully realized in FJORD. FJORDS are the Faroes' principal waterways, and if islands are basically shores, then FJORDS are basically streams between shores. To this basic meaning Norse experience in western Norway and perhaps in the Orkneys and other Scottish islands added two more: FJORDS are distinct from the open sea, and they generally run east and west.

The etymology of FJORD begins with the Indo-European root *per*, to lead or pass over. In Latin, for example, this root eventually gave *portus*, "originally a mountain pass and a gate, a door, basically therefore a passage; hence a harbour" (*OED*). The cognate Germanic word was *ferþuz*, a ford or crossing place, from which Old Norse *fjǫrðr* derives.

The West Norwegian coast runs roughly north and south. It is mountainous and deeply pierced by long, branching arms of the sea, which open out around steep headlands and the countless islands rimming its seaward flank. The population is settled around the shores of these ocean inlets, beneath the inland heights and often far from the westward sea. In the West Norwegian experience, then, a *fjǫrðr* was a more or less steeply bounded, more or less inland waterway, across and around which travel was relatively easy, on the flatter stretches of whose shore villages were founded. By extension, and because *eyland* and *eyja* were becoming the labels for offshore shores—islands—*fjǫrðr* also became the name for the lands around a *fjǫrðr*. Thus Old Norse *fjǫrðr* and Modern Norwegian *fjord* mean both "a fjord, inlet (usually long and narrow)" and "the region bordering on a fjord" (Haugen 1965).

West Norwegian colonists fitted this double conception of a *fjǫrðr* to the geography of their North Atlantic island settlements. In the Shetlands, the sense of a relatively open area of water or land was greatly elaborated—a *fjord* became not only a firth or large bay, but also "an extensive fishing ground" and "a great stretch of arable land" (Jakobsen 1928). In Iceland, the latest colony but the one with the simplest coastline, *fjörður* has reverted to the primary meanings of Old Norse *fjǫrðr*—a long, deep bay, and the region bordering such a bay.

A couple of subtler modifications occurred in the Orkneys and the Faroes, the geographically more complicated colonies. The first modification derives from a West Norwegian *fjǫrðr*'s habit of running east and west, landlocked at one end and only partly open to the sea at the other. Now it might be open to the sea at both ends, a kind of oceanic stream distinct from the sea itself, like Pentland Firth between the Orkneys and the Scottish mainland. The fact that the Orkneys' and Faroes' most important "inland" waterways ran roughly east and west favored this new meaning. The second modification derives from the fact that a *fjǫrðr*'s defining characteristic, the shoreline, could now, on an archipelago, be an island lying north or south of the water. This was an anomaly from the West Norwegian point of view. So a cognitive compromise was worked out, whereby an island—*eyja*—was thought of as outlying, in that it lay away from the center of the "mainland" archipelago; but it was part of the "mainland" in that it lay on the opposite shore of a *fjǫrðr*.

Thus in the Faroes we find two kinds of FJORDS. One kind is very Norwegian: a long, narrow, more or less closed body of water running inland, named after some feature along its shore—a village, bay, cove, or high point. The other kind of FJORD is open to the sea at both ends. Such FJORDS run roughly east and west and are named for an island or settlement on the island-shore away from the archipelago's center, or "mainland," on Streymoy. The longest series of this kind of FJORD runs south from Streymoy; you cross Hestsfjørður to Hestur, then Skopunarfjørður to Skopun on Sandoy, then

Skúvoyarfjørður to Skúvoy, then Dímunarfjørður to Stóra Dímun, and finally Suðuroyarfjørður to Suðuroy. Thus a preliminary picture of the Faroes shows a group of islands centered on Streymoy, separated along their northern and southern coasts by waterways called FJORDS (see figure 4).

We must add two more details to this first, rough vision of the

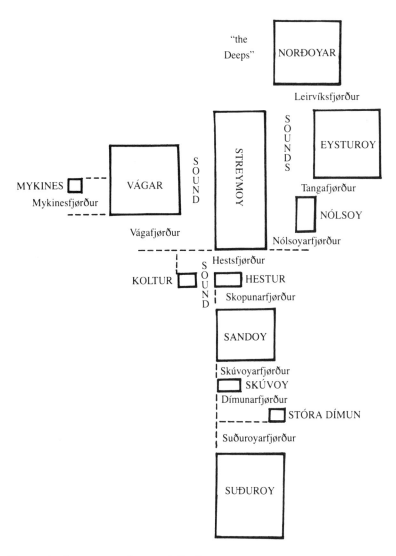

Figure 4. A conceptual map of the Faroes

Faroes. First, we must consider SOUNDS, the other main divider of the Faroes' scattered islands. And we must suggest something of the sense of closure between FJORDS and the open sea.

A SOUND is in some ways the opposite of a FJORD. It is a body of water running generally north and south, constricted in the middle but opening at both ends on wider stretches of water, typically a broad FJORD at one end and the open sea at the other.[5] Like FJORDS, however, SOUNDS are typically named after a constricting of otherwise prominent shore feature. SOUNDS are less important, in a way, than FJORDS. There are fewer of them, and for the most part they are too short, or their shores too precipitous, to allow settlement. The idioms of orientation I collected mostly describe travel from one village to another, and so do not include many involving SOUNDS. Generally, however, it seems that SOUNDS are treated very much like FJORDS in idioms of orientation.

FJORDS are not part of the open sea. Something of the sense of an Old Norse *fjǫrðr*'s closure appears in modern continental usages. In eastern Norway, a *fjord* is a long, narrow lake, and Swedish *fjärd* means an arm of the sea narrowed or constricted at its mouth. The same sense appears in, for example, the island-Norse derivatives of Old Norse *flói*. *Flói* seems originally to have meant a stretch of flooded ground. Hence it came to mean a large firth or the mouth of a firth, a wide bay or sea basin: for example, Scottish "flow," a morass or quicksand as well as the widening mouth of a bay (like Scapa Flow in the Orkneys); Shetlandic Norn *flo*, a bog, morass, or swampy place as well as "a wide mouth of a firth or widening of a bay, sea-basin" (Jakobsen 1928); Icelandic *flói*, both a bog and such wide sea reaches as Faxaflói and Húnaflói; and Faroese *flógvi*, the "mouth of a fjord between two islands, the continuation of a sound which broadens against the sea" (Jacobsen and Matras 1961). Many Faroese idioms of orientation likewise require us to conceive of "imaginary" boundaries between FJORDS and the open sea.

A Map of the Faroes

Let us hazard a map of the Faroes to represent roughly the picture we have developed so far (figure 4).

The Faroese live on islands separated and united by waterways.

The waterways are of two types: SOUNDS and FJORDS. The SOUNDS on our map run north and south between a FJORD at one end and the open sea at the other. There are two types of FJORDS. Some, not shown on the map, are in the Norwegian style, long and narrow and landlocked at one end. They run generally east and west, or at least their mouths open generally eastward or westward despite some inland twists and turns. The other FJORDS, which also run generally east and west, are actually, if not cognitively, open to the sea at both ends, and are named after an island or other shore feature on the coast away from Streymoy, the "mainland."

This map does a fair amount of violence to the actual geography of the archipelago. It lumps together the six Norðoyar (NORTH-islands) and places them simply north, instead of both east and north, of Eysturoy (EAST-island). It contains two FJORDS— Mykinesfjørður and Nólsoyarfjørður—which seem at first glance to run as much north and south as east and west. (A third such FJORD, Svínoyarfjørður, is in the Norðoyar and so not shown on this map.) It contains an almost shoreless FJORD, Vágafjørður. And the existence of boundaries between FJORDS and the open sea has not yet been documented. Its essential accuracy will show through, however, as we turn to consider a first series of idioms of orientation, those based on IN, OUT, OVER, and ABOUT.

In, Out, Over, and About

SOUNDS and FJORDS are uninhabited areas between shores and are similar in this respect to ranges of hills. You travel *directly* OVER them, just as you cross OVER hills: "OVER [the SOUND] to Vestmanna [from Oyragjógv]," "OVER [the FJORD] to Leirvík [from Klaksvík]," "OVER [the mountain] to Sandvík [from Hvalba]," and "OVER [the hills] to Skálavík [from Húsavík]" (see figure 5).

SOUNDS and FJORDS are also alike in that at at least one end they open out toward the sea. One may thus travel OUT or IN along their shores, on water or on land, toward the open sea or away from it. In this respect they resemble paths along their shores. In Sørvágur, for example, at the base of a long, narrow FJORD, one goes OUT along either shore toward Bøur on one side or the dock on the other, and IN either side toward the bottom of the FJORD (see figure 6). You would, of course, sail directly OVER to the dock.[6]

As in many idioms of orientation, it is one's route to an ulti-

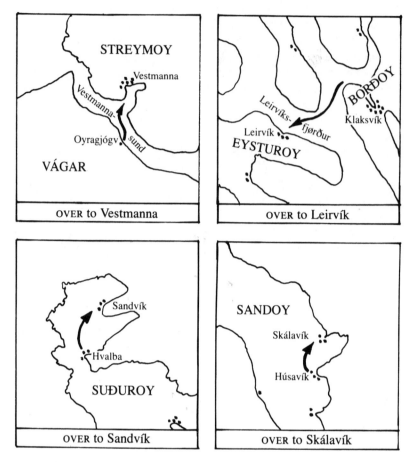

Figure 5. Four idioms based on OVER

mate destination which governs the choice of IN, OUT, or OVER. If, from a house on the road to Bøur, you intend to walk to the church, you would say "IN to the church" or "HOME to the church"; but if you intend to go on around to the dock you would say "OUT to the dock," picking up the term used in the center of the village, the waypoint from which you go on directly to the dock. Similarly, as "OUT to Mykines" is the appropriate expression in Sørvágur, where one embarks for Mykines, so people all over the Faroes say "OUT to Mykines."

"OUT to Mykines" presents another problem. Since OUT means basically along the shore toward the mouth of a FJORD or SOUND,

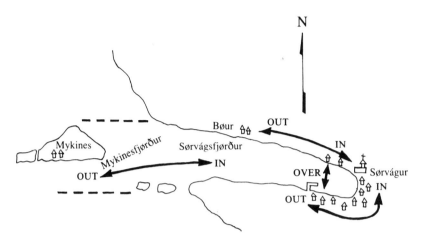

Figure 6. Sketch map of Sørvágsfjørður, showing uses of OVER, IN, *and* OUT

and since -*nes* means headland, it seems that Mykines is thought of as an extension of the mainland shore. This "imaginary" connection, indicated by dashed lines in figures 4 and 6, forms the boundaries between Mykinesfjørður and the open sea. Appearances to the contrary, therefore, Mykinesfjørður runs not north and south between Vágar and Mykines, but out westward, past the landing place for the village also named Mykines. One does not say "*OVER to Mykines," which would be the expected expression if Mykines were thought of as lying directly across Mykinesfjørður. Instead one speaks of going "OUT to Mykines" and of coming "IN" from it.

The notion that such essentially terrestrial boundaries may run between a FJORD and the sea is related to the common Norse sense of a *fjørðr's* closure, and to the basic idea that an island is a shore. Several other factors now lead us to suspect that drawing such "imaginary" lines on our conceptual map of the Faroes may prove crucial in understanding the Faroese sense of place and its corollary idioms of orientation.

First, boundaries in the sea are not really so imaginary—or anyway no more so than any boundary between topographical features. After all, a FJORD has to end somewhere.

Second, they help explain the several apparently anomalous FJORDS which, like Mykinesfjørður, seem at first glance to run north and south but are referred to as if they ran east and west. Thus, OUT and IN are used for travel to and from communities on Svínoy and Nólsoy; these islands actually are outlying and separated from the "mainland" by FJORDS named after them, but their FJORDS seem to run nearly north-south. Once we conceive of sea-boundaries running to these islands from their respective "mainlands," their FJORDS' orientation changes to east-west, and it becomes quite proper to speak of going "OUT to Nólsoy" and "OUT to Svínoy," or "IN" from them. The same sort of sleight-of-mind allows us to resolve the dilemma of Vágafjørður. No matter how complicated or apparently anomalous, every other FJORD in the Faroes at least runs between roughly parallel shores. But Vágafjørður has practically no shores at all. It opens on the sea to the south and west, into Vestmannasund to the northeast, and onto Hestsfjørður to the east. These difficulties may be largely resolved by drawing a single sea boundary on our map (figure 4), a line running westward from the southwestern tip of Streymoy. Vágafjørður now has three sides (one of them broken by Vestmannasund, and another bordering Hestsfjørður) and runs east and west, and is named after an appropriate shore feature, the bays (*vágar*) where the villages of Miðvágur and Sandavágur lie.

Finally, it appears that the reality of sea boundaries is rein-

Plate 2. Pausing on the way to the bird cliffs. The men are looking over the western end of Skopunarfjørður to Koltur, Vágar (on the left), and Streymoy (in the center). Compare figure 7. (Photograph: J. Wylie)

forced idiomatically in two ways. Most commonly, crossing them may entail shifting to idioms based on compass terms. The term used depends on the direction of crossing. Thus from Vágar you go "SOUTH" to the communities along the shores of Hestsfjørður—Koltur, Hestur, Kirkjubøur, and Velbastaður. By the same token, people from Skálavík, on the northeastern shore of Sandoy, say they sail "NORTH to Nólsoy"—that is, directly north across the southern sea-boundary of Nólsoyarfjørður (see figure 7).

Less commonly, ABOUT may be used to signify traveling within such boundaries, or crossing them as it were temporarily, while intending to remain, in the end, within the system of a given region. ABOUT is less common in idioms of orientation than in general expressions of time or space, in which it indicates actions occurring within a given period or a distinct area, or ones crossing from one such period or area to an essentially similar one.[7] The old Suðuroy expression "to go ABOUT the FJORD" meant to travel to Sandoy within and across Suðuroyarfjørður, Dímunarfjørður, and Skúvoyarfjørður. Similarly, the old Norðoyar idiom "ABOUT the mountain" meant to cross the mountain chain which formed the border between the Norðoyar's two political districts from "SOUTH of the mountain" to "NORTH of the mountain." ABOUT is often used as well with other words to stress the bounded nature of the area across which or around which one intends to travel. In Miðvágur, for example, one says "OUT ABOUT the lake" or "OVER ABOUT the lake" to mean going around to the far side of the lake near which the airport lies. The general expressions "ABOUT the stream" and "OVER ABOUT the stream," and "ABOUT the FJORD" and "OVER ABOUT the FJORD" mean across the stream or the FJORD, but express in the distinction between ABOUT and OVER ABOUT a not very translatable feeling about how formidable a barrier the stream (or FJORD) is, and how different its opposite banks are.

ABOUT may likewise be combined with compass terms. In Skopun, for example, one says that a boat sails directly OVER Skopunarfjørður to Kirkjubøur, and IN along Hestsfjørður to Hestur (see figure 7). These are clear examples of the IN-OUT-OVER system of FJORD idioms. But Skopuningar also say they sail WEST to Koltur and WEST ABOUT to Sandur. Here we have a crucial complication. Compass terms are used for travel on the open sea and for travel across FJORD-boundaries like the one at the western end of Skopunarfjørður. In these idioms, then, WEST indicates crossing this sea boundary, heading west on the customary route to Koltur or around by sea to Sandur, while in the latter idiom ABOUT means to

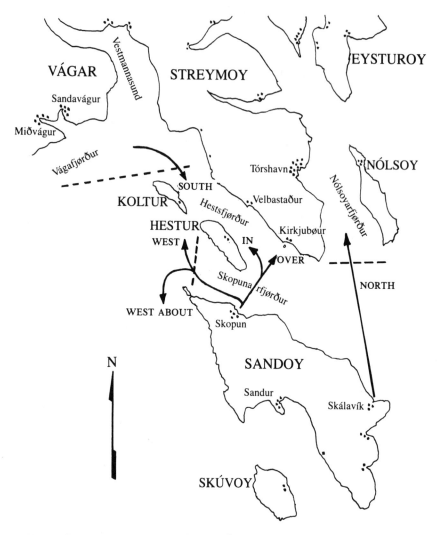

Figure 7. Some idioms from Hestsfjørður and Skopunarfjørður (compare plate 2)

skirt the boundary of the land itself, the shore. Thus, with its presuppositions and implications unraveled, "WEST ABOUT to Sandur" means here something like "the boat sails westward across the boundary separating Skopunarfjørður from the open sea, while keeping close to the shore on the way to the village of Sandur on the same island."

The Points of the Compass

The logic of applying compass terms not only to the open sea but also to sharply bounded areas is perhaps the most elegant aspect of the Faroese sense of place.

Imagine yourself on a featureless plain extending to the horizon, or—what amounts to the same thing—on the sea. You stand at the center of a geographical system toward whose ends you may travel, without ever reaching them, by reference to the sun or stars. The system may be represented by a circle with north, south, east, and west poles—that is, by the compass.

Now assume you find yourself on an island. The sea-horizon remains unchanged, unreachably far away, and you still navigate on the open waters, as the Faroese do and their Viking forebears did, by the sun and the stars and the points of the compass. But now, if you retain the notion of a horizon and apply it to the limited area of your island, you will find that the island also has north, south, east, and west poles, represented by its northernmost, southernmost, easternmost, and westernmost points (see figure 8). Ideally, the island is four-cornered, with the poles at the corners.

You and your fellow islanders live, however, like the Faroese, not in the center of the island, but along its shores. If you live at A and your cousin lives at B, you will travel WEST to visit him, and he will travel NORTH to visit you. NORTH and WEST no longer represent north and west by the compass, and, like any two compass points, may now be opposites. This peculiarity is more than made up for by the elegant result that, no matter how badly the road twists and turns from A to B, and so no matter what direction you happen to be facing at any given moment on your way to see your cousin, you still say you are "going WEST to B."

I do not know how this way of using the compass arose. It may, however, have been common in the North, since it informs not only the Faroese sense of place, but also the system described by Haugen (1957) for Iceland, whereby Iceland is thought of as having northernmost, southernmost, easternmost, and westernmost areas, and travel in the *ultimate* direction of one of them is called, whatever happens to be your *immediate* direction of travel, "north," "south," "east," or "west." The Faroese system is logically the same, but considerably more complicated in practice. The Faroes, thought of as one big island, have their north pole in the Norðoyar (NORTH-islands), their south pole on Suðuroy (SOUTH-island), their west pole on Vágar, and their rather weak east pole on Eysturoy (EAST-

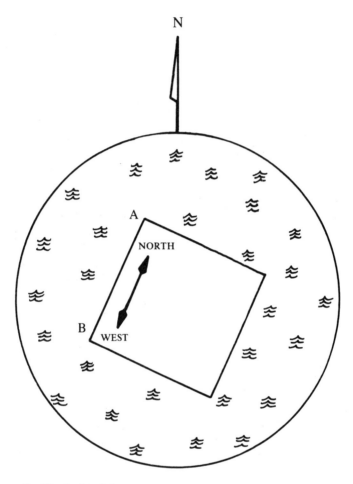

Figure 8. The logic of the compass

island). Thus one speaks of going "NORTH to the Norðoyar" and being "NORTH" there, of going "SOUTH to Suðuroy" and being "SOUTH" there, and of going "WEST to Vágar" and being "WEST" there. (Among the compass terms, incidentally, NORTH is primary, followed closely by SOUTH and then at some distance by EAST and WEST. NORTH is often chosen over EAST or WEST in cases where either might be possible. The "NORTH" tip of Sandoy is also its westernmost point; the Norðoyar were divided into NORTHERN and SOUTHERN districts, which are now thought of as NORTHERN and

WESTERN; there is no *Vesturoy, and Eysturoy itself is cast as a rather doubtful east pole.)

The reader will already have discovered the main flaws and complications in this unnaturally clean picture of the Faroes. First, the Faroes are not one big island, though they may sometimes be thought of as if they were. The Faroes are made up of many little islands, each with its own poles, and it may even happen that parts of an island have poles of their own. Second, the Faroes are not four-cornered, so that a westernmost point, say, may also be a northernmost point. Most spectacularly, the Norðoyar (NORTH-islands) actually lie north *and* east of Eysturoy (EAST-island). The solution to the first problem is in practice fairly simple; you just have to know, from the context or the place name element in the idiom, what region, island, or island group you are talking about. The solution to the second rests partly on an apparent primacy of NORTH over the other compass terms, but in some cases (particularly that of the Norðoyar, to which we must return) it involves considerable cognitive hanky-panky.

Three Rules and Three Implications

We have now worked out two rules for constructing Faroese idioms of orientation. We may summarize them quickly and add a third.

The first is realized in IN, OUT, OVER, and ABOUT. It fits to an archipelagic geography the essentially continental notion that settlements are founded along the shores (islands) of waterways (FJORDS, SOUNDS). Ashore or on the water, one travels IN or OUT along a waterway, and directly OVER it or OVER a range of hills. One travels ABOUT the contours of sea or land. In short, IN, OUT, OVER, and the less common ABOUT carry the traveler around and across the Faroes' shores and waterways.

The second is realized in NORTH, SOUTH, EAST, and WEST. It fits the notion of infinite horizons to the very finite horizons of groups of islands, single islands, and areas within islands. It is used in three related ways: (1) for travel on the open sea; (2) for travel across boundaries between inland waterways and the open sea; and (3) for travel to, or toward, an area's "poles." In short, NORTH, SOUTH, EAST, and WEST carry the traveler to, and through, the ends of the island system.[8]

The third is a kind of wild card, realized only in HOME. An original settlement and/or the site of the parish church is referred to as HOME. An old example is the Tórshavn idiom "HOME to Kirkjubøur"; Kirkjubøur was until the Reformation the site of Tórshavn's church. A recently formed example is the Sandvík idiom "HOME to Hvalba"; Sandvík was founded from Hvalba in the early nineteenth century. With one exception—people everywhere in the Faroes say "HOME to Sandur," though outside Sandoy they generally use the idiom half-humorously, sometimes assuming a Sandur accent—HOME is used only within areas of parish size or smaller. It is a common base for idioms, but its usage is restricted; people from one area seldom know its usage in another.

We have devoted our efforts so far to working out these rules by considering a few idioms of orientation and a few of the fundamental geographical concepts the Faroes' settlers brought with them. Presently we must consider a couple of representative sets of idioms in detail and see how they work out in practice. Before plunging into the confusion of practical life, however, let us test the waters by noting some implications of our argument so far.

It is clear, in the first place, that Faroese idioms of orientation express not only a living system for describing how to get around the Faroes, but also the way this system has developed, with the continual elaboration of old ideas to fit new circumstances. It embodies two sorts of histories. One, a branch of the linguistic history of the Germanic peoples, and particularly of the Norsemen who colonized the North Atlantic rim from Scotland to Vinland, provides a kind of general conceptual grammar generating not only idioms of orientation, but also such occasional phrases as "Put the haddock NORTH, there." The other is more local and circumstantial, reflecting the establishment of customary habits of thought in particular areas of the Faroes, and reflected in the generation and perpetuation of each area's idioms: "HOME to Hvalba" from Sandvík, "HOME to Kirkjubøur" from Tórshavn.

Second, it is clear that a crucial element in the development of the whole system has been the establishment of distinct areas of reference, ranging in size from the Faroes as a whole, down through island groups such as the Norðoyar, to islands, parishes, villages, and to some extent even single households—not to mention FJORDS, which have boundaries of their own. Moreover, any point in any of these areas may serve at any given moment as the center of the whole system. This eccentricity is reinforced by the fact that the Faroese are shore dwellers, so that the Faroes as a whole have, as it were, many centers along their edges. This prompts two questions.

How, in practice, does one construct idioms for travel from one area to another—and particularly for travel between distant areas? If every point in the Faroes had its own idioms for reaching every other point, the repertoire of idioms would be impossibly large. We must also ask if, in theory, the Faroes do not have a kind of latent central point.

Idioms for travel from one area to another show two tendencies. One is to consider one's destination as a waypoint on a trip to one of the Faroes' poles. To go from Tórshavn to Skopun, for example, is to go "SOUTH to Skopun," because Skopun lies along the way to the Faroes' south pole on Suðuroy (see below, p. 40). The second tendency is to adopt the idioms of the place where one enters the area in which one's destination lies. Thus, as Mykines is part of Vágar county and the Sørvágsfjørður area, people everywhere in the Faroes adopt the Sørvágsfjørður and hence the Vágar usage, and say "OUT to Mykines." Probably the Skopun expression "OVER to Tórshavn" is another example of this kind of thing, since the traditional route to Tórshavn entered the Tórshavn area, South Streymoy, at Kirkjubøur, where the expression is "OVER [the ridge] to Tórshavn." This tendency sometimes has the same verbal result as the first, since individual islands and island systems have their own poles as well. To go from Tórshavn to the northern villages of Eysturoy, for example, is to go "NORTH"—that is, not only towards the Faroes' north pole in the Norðoyar, but also, perhaps more decisively, having entered the Eysturoy system, to move NORTH within it. As this example suggests, idioms of orientation may often have several explanations, based on the several overlapping conceptions of the land and waterways.

This emphasis on waypoints is at least partly conscious. A man from Vágar offered one of the few explanations anyone was able to give me for the choice of terms in constructing idioms when I asked him how people from Sørvágur say "to go to Oyragjógv." Oyragjógv is the landing place for the ferry to Vestmanna (see figure 9 and p. 135, below). He had just told me that people from Miðvágur and Sandavágur say "NORTH to Oyragjógv"—perhaps, I guessed, because the new road between Sandavágur and Oyragjógv follows for a way the old path "NORTH to Slættanes." The Miðvágur usage "NORTH to Oyragjógv" thus probably represents an adoption of the Sandavágur usage, since "NORTH" in Miðvágur itself indicates travel beginning westward out of town, "NORTH to Vatnsoyrar" near the airport, and that way around "NORTH to Slættanes." (From Slættanes, incidentally, one goes "HOME" to both Miðvágur and

N

Slættanes

Vestmanna

STREYMOY

Víkar

Bøur VÁGAR

Oyragjógv

Vatnsoyrar

Sørvágur

Sandavágur

Miðvágur

Figure 9. Vágar, showing some uses of NORTH

Sandavágur.) Well, this man said, the old path from Sørvágur to Oyragjógv used to lie directly over the mountains—maybe they used to say "OVER to Oyragjógv." But now the road has been built, and they say "NORTH to Oyragjógv," he said, because you go "OVER the other villages" (*yvir hinar bygdar*). In other words, now that people reach Oyragjógv from Sørvágur by driving OVER the villages of Miðvágur and Sandavágur, they have adopted these villages' idioms.

Together with the inherent logic of using compass terms, this emphasis on waypoints has the important consequence of establishing Tórshavn as the formal center of the Faroes. Returning to our diagram of the single, four-cornered island in the middle of the sea, a trip WEST from A to B may represent in fact, as it certainly implies formally, first going to the center of the island and then going WEST from there. Now Tórshavn is fairly close to the geographical center of the archipelago, the point where the arms of the Faroese compass cross. It is accordingly the point of reference for the polar island names Suðuroy, Eysturoy, and the Norðoyar; and its area, South Streymoy, serves as the "mainland" for outwardly reaching FJORD names. Originally Tórshavn was the Faroes' political center, and thus was founded, like the meeting places of other Norse parliaments, in a central, but uninhabited place. Its commercial importance dates partly from the days of the trade monopolies and partly from the second half of the nineteenth century. The Faroes' religious center was established at Kirkjubøur with the coming of Christianity, and was moved to Tórshavn only after the Reformation; hence the idiom "HOME to Kirkjubøur [from Tórshavn]." Historically, as this idiom indicates, Tórshavn is only the formal center of a geographical system adapted in everyday practice to life around the system's very edges. The universally used idioms "WEST to Vágar," "SOUTH to Suðuroy," and "NORTH to the Norðoyar" indicate *both* traveling (in practice) edgewise to the Faroes' west, south, and north poles, *and* traveling (in theory) first to the center of the archipelago in Tórshavn and then to the poles. The latter is logically primary, though a traveler from Vágar SOUTH to Suðuroy, say, need not actually pass by way of Tórshavn at all.[9]

Finally, it is clear that the rules for constructing idioms of orientation leave room for a fair amount of free play in the system as a whole. They define areas rather differently, and the areas they define—islands, shores, parishes, "poles," political and ecclesiastical districts, and so forth—often overlap and may always be described in several complementary ways. Moreover, the actual lay of the land is naturally far more complicated than the rules for describing it. Predictably, therefore, while customary usages in any given settlement, or area, are reasonably coherent, they may differ considerably between settlements, even when the same travels and geographical features are being described. One example of this is a set (or sets) of idioms from the communities around Hestsfjørður (see figure 10). From the point of view of someone in Kirkjubøur or Velbastaður, Hestur is an outlying island in rather the same sense that Mykines is an outlying island—an outer shore of a FJORD named after it. So from Velbastaður and Kirkjubøur you go "OUT to Hestur." By the same token, you go IN along the shore from Kirkjubøur to Velbastaður. And, since these villages lie across the ridge from Tórshavn, you go "OVER to Tórshavn" from Velbastaður and Kirkjubøur. But from the point of view of someone living on Hestur, Velbastaður and Kirkjubøur lie directly OVER the FJORD. That is, from the Hestur point of view, Hestur is not an outlying island, but simply the opposite shore of Hestsfjørður. Thus people from Hestur travel "OVER to Kirkjubøur."

In other words, the FJORD is conventionally described differently depending on where you are looking at it from. Both "*IN to Kirkjubøur" and "OVER to Kirkjubøur" are possible idioms looking

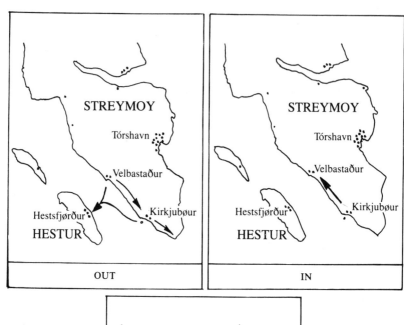

Figure 10. Some uses of OUT, IN, *and* OVER *on South Streymoy and* Hestsfjørður

at a "real" map; so are "OUT to Hestur" and "*OVER to Hestur." But by using the same rules rather differently, people in different places have constructed rather different cognitive maps on the same geographical foundations. The differences, however, are not completely arbitrary; they are consistent with usages within Hestur on the one hand and South Streymoy on the other. Given the general South Streymoy usage "OVER to Tórshavn," for example, "OUT to Hestur" is less ambiguous than "*OVER to Hestur" would be.

The amount of play in the system of orientation, and the consistency of regional and subregional sets of idioms, must engage our attention as we turn to consider in detail the idioms of Sandoy and the Norðoyar.

Two Sets of Idioms

The Norðoyar:
History, HOME, and a Skewed Compass

As their name indicates, the Norðoyar are the northernmost islands in the Faroes. But these six islands are also in fact the Faroes' easternmost group. This peculiar state of affairs has skewed the idiomatic compass orientation of the group as a whole well around to the east, while within regions of the Norðoyar NORTH is sometimes skewed around in the opposite direction, toward the northwest.[10] The regions are politically as well as naturally defined (see figure 11).

The Norðoyar have long formed a political district whose parliament met once a year at "a depression on the way over the mountains on Borðoy, above the village of Árnafjørður. Here there stands a stone which is called *Tingsteinur* [parliament-stone]." The district was divided "by Nature," as Dr. Matras says, into two parts along the high spine of Borðoy from Múli at the island's northern tip down past Árnafjørður. These subdistricts were called "NORTH of the mountain"—actually more east than north—and "SOUTH of the mountain"—actually more west than south. To go from one to the other was "to go ABOUT the mountain" (cf. p. 27 above).[11]

This remarkable skewing of the compass helps explain the name "Kalsoyarfjørður." Kalsoyarfjørður is a problematic FJORD for two reasons: its actual orientation is very close to north-south, suggesting that it might more properly have been called a SOUND; and unlike every other FJORD, it is named after an island nearer Strey-

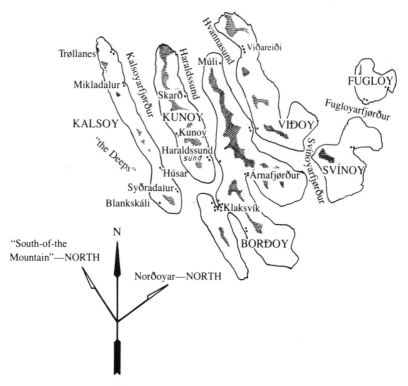

Figure 11. The Norðoyar, showing land over 500 meters, and names mentioned in the text.

moy.[12] These anomalies may be resolved if we consider Kalsoy to be first and foremost a part of the Norðoyar rather than directly a part of the Faroes as a whole. Thus Kalsoyarfjørður is named with respect to the Norðoyar, according to whose skewed compass it runs nearly east-west, as a FJORD should. On the other hand, the almost parallel body of water called Haraldssund is a SOUND not only because like other SOUNDS it is clearly constricted in the middle and runs nearly north-south, but also because its once-uninhabited shores are the ridges running NORTH-SOUTH (and OUT-IN) along Kunoy and Borðoy. In other words, Haraldssund is named with respect to the subdistrict "SOUTH of the mountain," while Kalsoyarfjørður is named with respect to the whole district of the Norðoyar.

Kalsoy's more direct association with the Norðoyar than with the rest of the Faroes is reinforced by the name of the more or less open body of water between it and Eysturoy, "the Deeps." The water is indeed deep here, but "the Deeps" is a singular expression for a body of water—it usually indicates an upland depression. The problem is, of course, that while in fact Eysturoy lies west of Kalsoy, conceptually it lies far away to the south and east, being named EAST-island for its orientation to Streymoy. "The Deeps" solves the problem by being in effect a "hole" in the sea rather than the FJORD or SOUND it might otherwise have been.[13]

Kalsoy and Kunoy have remarkable series of idioms based on HOME. On Kunoy, HOME

> means in place-names "in proximity to (in greater proximity than other places of the same type) an original starting-point, for example the village, the oldest hamlet, the oldest farmstead inside a hamlet, etc." Even more commonly used in place-names is the adverb of direction HOME, which means "in the direction of the original starting-point." This word is of great value, for it can tell us, for example, about various villages' mutual relations (ages). When, thus, it is said on Kallsoy to go HOME to Húsar from all the other villages, we know from this that Húsar is the oldest village on the island. Similarly, when one says, both in Haraldssund and Skarð to go HOME to Kunoy, it indicates that the two settlements are from Kunoy, or, more correctly: Haraldssund is the one, since in Skarð one also says go HOME to Haraldssund, which shows that Skarð can be taken to be a settlement from Haraldssund—but the village í Kunoy is the oldest on the island of Kunoy. [Matras 1933:140]

Matras argues, in short, that the village of Haraldssund was settled from the village of Kunoy, and the village of Skarð was settled in turn from Haraldssund.

Kalsoy has a similar series of idioms. The oldest village, as Dr. Matras points out, is Húsar, toward which all roads lead HOME. From Húsar were settled, to the south, the now abandoned hamlet of Blankskáli and from there, about a hundred and fifty years ago, the hamlet of Syðradalur (ibid.:19). Meanwhile, to the north, Húsar spawned Mikladalur, and Mikladalur spawned the tiny hamlet of Trøllanes. Among these three northern settlements—Húsar, Mikladalur, and Trøllanes—the opposite of HOME is NORTH—NORTH within the island, now, of course, not NORTH within the Norðoyar. In Húsar, for example, one says "NORTH to Trøllanes," while in Trøllanes one says "HOME to Húsar." In fact, one says "NORTH to Trøllanes" from just about everywhere in the Faroes, because Trøllanes is in the Norðoyar, and because one enters the Kalsoy system of which it is a part at Húsar, and thereby picks up the Húsar term.

The Kunoy and Kalsoy usages shift somewhat as one moves toward the center of the Norðoyar. People from both islands go "IN to Klaksvík"—that is, into the FJORD and then the bay at whose head Klaksvík lies. Klaksvík is a big, new, booming town, the economic and political center of the Norðoyar and the headquarters of the Faroese deepwater fishery. This exalted status is very recent. Klaksvík (which used to be called NORTH-in-the-Bay to distinguish it from SOUTH-in-the-Bay [Vágur on Suðuroy] and WEST-in-the-Bays [Vágar]) was once no more than the landing place for people from the Kalsoyarfjørður communities on their way to the Norðoyar parliament. People in Klaksvík still say, however, letting the old insignificance of the site show through, "HOME to Kunoy."

These series of idioms provide, therefore, a miniature short-hand history of the settlement of the Norðoyar's villages, and a schematic account of the sometimes problematic relationship between the several parts of the Norðoyar and between the Norðoyar and the rest of the Faroes.

Sandoy's Chinese Boxes

As the similarity between a "real" map and a conceptual map of the Faroes indicates, Sandoy's relationship to the rest of the Faroes is quite straightforward. On an all-Faroese scale, one speaks every-where on Sandoy of going "WEST to Vágar," "SOUTH to Suðuroy," and "NORTH to the Norðoyar." Similarly, from most places in the Faroes one goes "SOUTH to Sandoy," because the island is on the way to the Faroes' south pole in Suðuroy. This "SOUTH" is rein-forced by the fact that most travel to Sandoy by sea must cross going south the "imaginary" boundaries of Vágafjørður or Nólsoyarfjørður (see figure 7 above). The idioms of orientation within Sandoy are less simple.

As we have seen, a small area's NORTH need not coincide with an island's NORTH, any more than either coincides with the Faroes' NORTH—let alone compass north. Sandoy has several such systems nested inside one another. It has a strong north pole, a residual south pole, an eastern area in which a stronger south pole is recognized, and (because the island's westernmost point is also its northernmost) no west pole (see figure 12). The village of Sandur, where the district's sheriff and minister live, is considered HOME. Everywhere on the island one speaks of going "HOME to Sandur." The island's north pole is in its northwestern corner, the area including the village of Skopun. Accordingly one speaks everywhere on the island of going "NORTH to Skopun," and the people of Skopun speak of walking

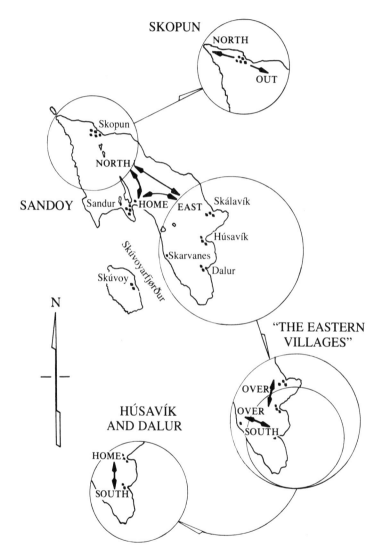

Figure 12. Some subsystems on Sandoy

along a road more or less west out of the village toward the end of the island as going "NORTH."

Inside Skopun the pull of the island's north pole is very strong, so that one hears expressions like "NORTH to uncle"—meaning something like "across the street in the direction of the northernmost point of Sandoy to my uncle's house." Some other directions in Skopun are indicated in figure 12.

Sandoy's residual south pole appears in only a very few place names and idioms; an outfield near Skopun is divided into NORTH-ERN and SOUTHERN halves, for example. But in general on this part of the island, centered as it is "HOME in Sandur," HOME means south-ward. (Skopun is a new village, settled partly from Sandur.) The people of Skarvanes say "SOUTH to Dalur." Dalur is indeed the southernmost village on the island, and a strong south pole within the subsystem of the "Eastern Villages" of Skálavík, Húsavík, and Dalur. Although Skarvanes is not one of these villages, it is part of Húsavík parish, and the expression "SOUTH to Dalur" probably represents picking up the Húsavík expression, since Dalur is likewise within Húsavík parish. The perhaps more predictable expression "*OVER to Dalur" would be unclear, since in Skarvanes OVER indicates directly OVER the FJORD to Skúvoy.

Sandoy has an eastern area rather than a specific east pole, the three "Eastern Villages." You go EAST to them from Sandur and Skopun. The Eastern Villages have only a south pole; NORTH has already been preempted three times—on an all-Faroese scale, for travel toward the Norðoyar; by the Skálavík idiom "NORTH to Tórshavn"; and on the Sandoy scale, by "NORTH to Skopun." "NORTH" preempts "*WEST" for travel within the island, and "*EAST" would of course be meaningless. So you speak in Húsavík of going "OVER to Skálavík," and in Skálavík you go back "OVER to Húsavík."

As this "OVER" suggests, the Eastern Villages are divided in two parts, not only by a range of hills but also politically and ecclesiastically. One is the village of Skálavík. The other is the villages of Húsavík and Dalur. Dalur is the south pole of the latter, as well as of the Eastern Villages as a whole. You say "SOUTH to Dalur [from Skálavík]" because this is the general usage in the Eastern Villages and because, in particular, it is the usage in Húsavík, the point at which you enter the Húsavík-Dalur subsystem and pick up the Húsavík term. Accordingly, you say "OVER to Skálavík [from Dalur]," picking up the Húsavík term as you enter Skálavík's own system.

A stream divides Húsavík itself into two parts, called "HOME of the stream" and "SOUTH of the stream."

Finally, in Dalur you say "HOME to Húsavík"—a usage with several explanations. Húsavík used to be the church village for Dalur (and may, before the Black Death, have had a chapel) and is the administrative center of the township; it is also, less decisively perhaps, a waypoint on one route HOME to Sandur.

Meanwhile, OVER in Skálavík, few of whose idioms I know, the names of outfields suggest that it also has a "HOME"—but opposed to NORTH on the one hand and to IN on the other. The "HOME-most outfield" lies closest to the village; past it, toward Skopun, is the "NORTH-most outfield." Past it in another direction, along the present road to Sandur ("HOME to Sandur" on an all-Sandoy scale) lies the "IN-most outfield"—IN, that is, toward the head of the valley, and perhaps also nearest IN toward the head of Skúvoyarfjørður.

These, then, are some of the systems nested inside Sandoy. Sandoy itself is inside the Faroes; Sandoy alone has its north pole around Skopun and a less distinct east pole in the Eastern Villages; the Eastern Villages are divided into two areas OVER the hills from one another. Each of these areas is oriented in terms of, among other things, a HOME and a compass point—NORTH in Skopun and Skálavík, and SOUTH in Húsavík-Dalur. Of course there are other systems nested into Sandoy. There is the system of Sandur itself, and the FJORD system from Sandur OUT to Skarvanes on one shore and Skúvoy on the other; and then there is Skúvoy's system, where NORTH is the opposite of OUT.

But perhaps enough has been said to give the reader a feel for how elaborately packed with these systems the Faroes are.

Conclusion

We have considered three sets of Faroese idioms of orientation, the rules underlying their construction, and a couple of regional systems of usage. As Jørgen-Frantz Jacobsen muses in the passage heading this chapter, "you could well believe that you had a continent before you."

The notion that the Faroes are a sort of continent is less fanciful than Jacobsen implies. In elaborating a basically continental repertoire of geographical concepts, the Faroese have contrived a large world in a small place, retaining and elaborating a large and complicated geographical vision, rather than discarding its least appropriate bits and pieces or reworking them into a single system covering the Faroes as a whole. The complications of the system as it is used today derive not only from fitting large ideas to small spaces, but also from the not-quite-compatible natures of the several principles underlying it. The compass point system envisages the lie of the land differently from the FJORDS-and-islands system realized in IN/OUT/OVER/(ABOUT), and the HOME system is overlaid on both.

Faroese idioms of orientation thus express a peculiarly conservative sense of place. It is conservative in being inseparable, upon analysis, from its Germanic and West Scandinavian base; in recalling in fixed expressions such historical circumstances as the division of the land into political and ecclesiastical districts and the settlement of one village from another; and in its intimate detailing of the local landscape.

Yet its conservativeness does not represent a moribund way of looking at things, and its complexity does not render it incoherent. Its coherence derives from a popular adherence to a grammar for describing the world that not only defines areas of reference within its system, with each area fitted to the next and with less comprehensive ones nested inside more comprehensive ones, but also defines the context within which each idiom is used. It was perfectly clear, in context, to which of several NORTHs I was supposed to take the haddock. Within the bounds set by the land itself, its divisions and subdivisions, and the way these are idiomatically perpetuated, the Faroese vision of the Faroes is open to further change and elaboration. The idioms of orientation themselves are derived from an old genius in adapting former ideas to new circumstances; existing ideas may still be adapted to current circumstances, and as new idioms become fixed, the sense of place gains a lively new elaboration. The song goes on, while a new dancer steps into the eddying ring.

It is worth stressing again, finally, how pervasive these idioms are. Curious though they may seem to an outsider, they come naturally to Faroese. As you move a ladder (borrowed from someone OUT by the stream) a little NORTH, your child is boarding a bus to go HOME to school. Your wife has already set out "from-above" to the dock, to work trimming haddock unloaded from a boat which had been WEST to fish. On Sunday she went OVER to Tórshavn to visit her cousin—the one who married SOUTH to Suðuroy—OUT at the new hospital. They talked about another cousin from OUT on Mykines. Soon you must go NORTH to Klaksvík to join your trawler, first going IN to Strendur to do an errand for your skipper (who hails from WEST on Vágar). . . .

Details change, but the sense of place remains a way of coming to terms with change. With the social world as inseparable from the landscape as it is from the past, knowing one's place in the Faroese world seems quite as natural as speaking the language.

3

Øskudólgur, Social Change, and the Meaning of Faroese Folklore

*Gomlu sagnir okkara eru stuttligar og spennandi
bæði fyri ung og gomul—og tær fara altíð at hava
stóran siðsøguligan áhuga, tí tær siga okkum frá
føroyskum livihátti og hugsunarhátti í gomlum
døgum.*

*Our old legends are entertaining and exciting for
both young and old—and they will always be of
great cultural-historical interest, for they tell us of
the Faroese way of life and thought in bygone times.*

—*Blurb for Jakobsen (1974)*

Føringatíðindi, the first Faroese newspaper written in Faroese, reported in its issue of 6 October 1898: "Dr. Jákup Jákupson is now collecting stories on Vágar, which is the only island in the Faroes he has not visited for this purpose. When he returns to Denmark, all that he has collected is going to the printers." Dr. Jakobsen's collection of legends (*sagnir*) and folktales (*ævintýr*), with a learned commentary in Danish, was duly published, and when its first volume reached the Faroes' bookstore in the spring, *Føringatíðindi* commented, "The stories are so pithy and engaging, that they bear proud witness to the spiritual life of the old Faroese, and at the same time demonstrate the skill and love for the mother tongue which we have long since learned to know in our eminent compatriot Dr. Jakobsen."[1]

Jakobsen, fearful lest Faroese language and folklore fade away, as had the Shetlandic Norse language, Norn, about which he had written his doctoral dissertation, set out on field trips around the islands in 1892–93 and in 1898 to preserve the Faroes' folkloric

Plate 3. Jakob Jakobsen (1864–1918), philologist and folklorist. (Fróðskaparsetur Føroya)

heritage in written form. In doing so he provided both contemporary and future generations of Faroese with an extensive representation of traditional Faroese culture. The tales are not timeless, however. They illustrate and reflect upon the Faroes' difficult passage, around the time when Jakobsen collected them, from old-fashioned times to modern ones; and from a culture whose bearers could understand their world in, for example, story and song, to one in which this function of folk literature was taken over by newspapers and by such self-consciously cultural performances as a reading of "some of the tales he has written," given by Jakobsen in Tórshavn in November 1898 (*Føringatíðindi*, 17 November 1898). The tales not only map out the strains placed upon the traditional Faroese way of life by the economic and demographic growth following the establishment of free trade in 1856 and the rise of the deepwater commercial fishery after about 1880, but also suggest how Faroese found a way to rework their old culture and build up a new consciousness of what it means to be Faroese.

This is nowhere clearer than in the Øskudólgur ("Ashlad") tales—according to Jakobsen, "greatly favored and widespread" among his informants (1898–1901:xli). Here is a version of one of these tales.

Øskudòlgur

Once there was a man who had three sons. The youngest was a contemptible wretch whom nobody valued at all, and who always lay poking in the ashes; but the other two were like most men, and did all the work.

For several nights in a row, grain was stolen from their father's loft. So one day the father says to his eldest son that it would be a good idea for him to sit up that night to find out who the thief was. The son thinks this no great matter, and sits down to stay awake; but the night is no more than half gone when he falls asleep. Never had so much grain been stolen as on that morning. The father now asks the middle boy to sit up the next night. Yes, he says, he'll be sure to know how to stay awake and not fall asleep. He stays awake until on toward dawn, and then falls asleep. Just as much grain was gone that morning as before. Then the youngest, Øskudólgur ["Ashlad"], asks his father to let him sit up that night. His brothers make fun of him: he was thinking of staying up, when he wasn't good for anything except scraping in the ashes. But the father says, "It can't be any worse than it is—he'll fall asleep, and you two slept."

Øskudólgur got set to stay awake. The first part of the night he was a bit drowsy, but he tried to fight against it. When it got on toward dawn he was more awake. At dawn, he heard a loud racket. A great big bird came, and at once Øskudólgur got his hands around its neck. Now he was going to kill it. But the bird begged him so

Plate 4. An old-fashioned hearth. In this picture of a fairly prosperous home, taken in 1898, the man is standing next to the window of the parlor (*glasstova*). (From Daniel Bruun, *Gammel Bygningsskik paa Færøerne* [Kristiania (Oslo): Grøndahl & Søns, 1907], p. 128)

piteously not to kill it. Oh yes, said Øskudólgur, because it had stolen grain from his father. It wouldn't do that any more, said the bird. He would do it anyway, said Øskudólgur. But then the bird said that he would get the largest feather from its wing, and when he held it up in the air, he would get whatever he wished for. Øskudólgur took the feather and let the bird go. That morning, none of the grain was gone, nor was there any gone the mornings after; but the other brothers were furiously angry at Øskudólgur because of this.

Now it should be related that a king had made his daughter a glass castle on top of a steep mountain. Then he let it be known that whoever could ride all the way up would receive his daughter for his wife. Many high-born and wealthy men came to try their luck, but they only got a very little way up the mountain, no more than a few steps above the ground—then their horses couldn't do any more. A lot of people were present to watch, and among them were both of Øskudólgur's brothers; Øskudólgur wasn't allowed to go with them. It was not for him to try such things, they said: he could sit at home and poke in the ashes with his feather the way he always did.

When the brothers had gone, Øskudólgur left, stuck the feather up in the air and wished for a green horse and blue clothes. They were there in an instant. He put on the new clothes and mounted the horse. Then he went to where the crowd of suitors were trying their luck, rode halfway up the mountain, but wheeled around, went back down, and disappeared immediately.

In the evening, when the brothers came home, Øskudólgur was sitting by the fire in his rags. They told him that they had seen something that day he hadn't seen, worthless creature: a man had been there to try his luck; he got halfway up—no one had gotten so far before—he had a green horse and a blue outfit. "I saw that too," said Øskudólgur. "Where did you see that?" they asked. "I stood up on father's drying shed." "You filthy thing! You won't have that to stand on for long," and then they tore the drying shed down.

The next day, when the brothers had gone, Øskudólgur went out with the feather again, stuck it up in the air and wished for white clothes and a red horse. Then he rode into the crowd, went right up to the edge of the flat mountaintop, then down again, and disappeared as he had come.

In the evening the brothers came home and said to Øskudólgur, who was sitting by the fire in his rags, that he had seen little of what they had seen that day—he who was always poking in the ashes. What did they see, then, asked Øskudólgur. They said there had been a stranger there to try his luck, exceptionally elegant, dressed in white on a red horse. They expected him for sure to be able to get up the mountain the first day. "I saw that too," said Øskudólgur. "Where were you then?" "I stood up on father's stone shed." "You filthy thing! You won't have that to stand on for long," and then they knocked the stone shed down.

On the third day, when the brothers had set out, Øskudólgur again went out with the feather, and wished for a white horse and red clothes. This time he got all the way up and went into the room to the princess. She looked him over from top to bottom, and then tied a golden ring in his hair, the better to recognize him again. Then he rode down again, went home and put on the rags, and sat down again to poke in the ashes.

In the evening the brothers came home, made fun of Øskudólgur and said to him that they had seen something that day that he hadn't seen—he who was always lying around, poking in the ashes. "What was it?" They said that they were sure that the king would hold a wedding feast soon; a strange man had made it up to the princess that day. He was exceptionally elegant and dressed up, clothed in red on a white horse. "I saw that too," said Øskudólgur. "You filthy thing! Where did you see that?" "Up on our hay shed." But then they swore he wouldn't have that to stand on any more, that Øskudólgur, and so they knocked the hay shed down.

Now it remained to look for the man who had been with the princess. They searched both well and long, but no man could be found. Then the king called a great assembly, and all the men in the place were ordered to assemble. When all the people had come, the princess looked at them carefully, but she recognized none of them, and didn't find the ring in anyone's hair. The king asked if there wasn't some man left. No, he was answered, no one was left. Then someone said that Øskudólgur hadn't come yet; but the brothers made fun of this, laughed and asked the king not to bother sending for him—who never did anything but poke in the ashes. But the king said that he could come too, since everyone else had assembled; it was his right.

So Øskudólgur was summoned. He put on the red clothing, took his white horse and came riding into the castle. The brothers didn't want to recognize him, but the princess knew him immediately and found the ring in his hair. So the wedding was held, and then the brothers were about to explode with anger. When the king died, Øskudólgur was chosen king after him and ruled the kingdom both long and well, although the brothers always tried to cause trouble for him.

This tale does not seem completely strange. It is of the widespread type called "The Princess on the Glass Mountain" by Aarne and Thompson (1964), and is closely related to other Scandinavian tales about the Ashlad; Jakobsen notes similar tales from all over Scandinavia (1898–1901:522), and American readers will recognize its affinity to "Cinderella."[2] But the mere fact of a tale's being of a widespread type does not tell us much about why it should have been popular in, for example, the Faroe Islands in the 1890s, nor—which amounts to the same thing—what meaning it bore for its tellers and listeners. Even if a Faroese had told a tale identical to a Norwegian one, it would still have had a peculiarly Faroese import in its new setting. It is the specifically Faroese meaning of "Øskudólgur" that we propose to investigate here. We would also like to know about its relationship to the rest of Jakobsen's collection, and about the relationship between the folktale (ævintýr) genre and the other main genres of Faroese folk literature—legends (*sagnir*) and satiric and heroic ballads (*tættir, kvæðir*)—at a time when the traditional culture of which they were a part was passing away.

This chapter, then, seeks to answer three main questions: (1) What did "Øskudólgur" mean in its late nineteenth-century Faroese context, and why were it and its multiforms so popular? (2) What light does an analysis of "Øskudólgur" shed on the rest of the collection? And (3) what do the answers to these two questions add to a general understanding of the role of Faroese folk literature at the time?

We can answer these questions by trying to put the tale in its social, cultural, and historical context, and attempting to tease out as we go along the structure of its most salient concerns. This structure may be abstractly stated (Margolin 1970); the comment that Øskudólgur's brothers were "like most men, and did all the work," for example, suggests that Øskudólgur's sex is ambiguously marked. But its immediate relevance derives from its fit with the pattern of everyday concerns in village life, as these informed the norms and expectations of the teller and his audience. What *was* "all the work" Øskudólgur's brothers did? What is unmanly about messing about in the ashes? It appears that the tale as a whole, seen in the light of the local implications of its specific features, provides a commentary on contemporary everyday life. It is a kind of folk editorial, whose gist may be stated in a preliminary way as follows: What is our place in the world, now that our economy is less and less dependent on the land?

Øskudòlgur and the Talking Bird: "Most Men" and the Traditional Village Setting

The Faroese way of life remained essentially unchanged from the early seventeenth century until well into the nineteenth, based on a remarkably mixed economy. All year round, weather permitting, men fished from open boats on banks around the islands. In the spring and summer they harvested the cliffs for birds, eggs, and feathers, and at unpredictable intervals they would drop whatever they might be doing to drive and slaughter passing pods of caaing or pilot whales (see chapter 5). They also grew a few crops—mostly hay and barley—and kept sheep. The produce of the sea, the bird cliffs, and the fields was largely used for home consumption. Sheep provided the wool and woolens that were the Faroes' main exports, and with which the necessary additional supplies of timber, grain, and other foodstuffs and building materials could be bought.

The units of economic activity were the farm (*garður*) and, to some extent, the village or hamlet. The village consisted of clustered houses near a landing place, surrounded by infields (*bøur*), where crops were raised in the summer and where sheep were let in to graze during the rest of the year. The infield was (and is) surrounded by a stone wall; beyond the wall lies the outfield (*hagi*), which, although it might contain small enclosed areas under cultivation (*træðir*) was primarily grazing land for sheep and a few milk cows. The *garður* (farm) was not, then, a consolidated area of land about the farmhouse, but consisted of scattered plots in the infields and outfields. The farmstead itself, and its main outbuildings, stood with others in the village.

There are two types of land tenure. A freehold farmer (*óðalsbóndi*) owns lands outright, but as these are forever being divided by inheritance, they tend to be small and scattered. A tenant farmer or "king's farmer" (*kongsbóndi*) holds a lease from the king, to whom he pays (or paid) a modest yearly rent. The leasehold is inherited by male primogeniture.

The farm—freehold, king's, or of mixed type—was to some extent a family enterprise, but the household often also included male and female laborers who might, of course, be related to the farmer or his wife. In 1843, for example, Jóhan Hendrik Matras, Jakobsen's informant some fifty years later for this version of "Øskudólgur," had come from Viðareiði on Viðoy to Kirkja on Fugloy, to work on the modestly prosperous farm of his older half-sister Elsebeth, who had married there in 1826. Her husband had recently been killed in a fall on the bird cliffs. "It is recorded that Jóhan Hendrik's pay as a hired hand was 3 *dálar* and 2 *skinn* a year, which must have been a great deal at that time; but this was a quite good house, which suddenly lay man-less." In 1858 Jóhan Hendrik married Elsebeth's daughter, Malene. In 1870, the household included Jóhan Hendrik himself, then 47 years old; Malene, 41; their three young children; Elsebeth, 70; a widowed relative, 63, whose mother had once lived in the house and "lived from her own lands," which were presumably worked by Jóhan Hendrik; and a 28-year-old maidservant from Fuglafjørður (J. S. Hansen 1971:72).

Jóhan Hendrik's having married the farmer's daughter and taken over the farm lends a certain psychological immediacy to his Øskudólgur; but the indispensable, aspiring hired hand was a common figure in fact as well as in folktale and legend in the Faroes. It had long been law that in order to get married a man and woman had to have rights over a certain amount of land, freehold or king's. The latest (1777) version of the law "forbade everyone to marry unless they had half a *mørk* of land, freehold or leasehold, or could earn a living as blacksmiths or carpenters, and in any case both boys and girls had to have served a farmer for at least four years and to have received a good recommendation from him" (J. S. Hansen 1966:115). (There were, in addition, stiff penalties against bearing or fathering children out of wedlock.) This law was repealed in 1846, by which time population pressure and the earnings even landless men might earn by fishing were making it a dead letter—an early token of economic and demographic changes that were to become more pronounced later in the century.

With this information in mind, we may tackle the opening sentence of Jóhan Hendrik's "Øskudólgur": "Once there was a man who had three sons." First, "once" (*eina ferð*) is not always the opening phrase of Faroese folktales. Its use here stresses the fact that the tale will concern old-fashioned society. Second, it is a necessary inference—so obvious, particularly in the context of "once," that for a Faroese audience it could go without saying—that the man has a farm, since he has children. It also goes without saying that he is, or has been, married. Third, it quickly becomes clear that the tale's central concern will be with men, their work, and their place in society: "The youngest was a contemptible wretch whom nobody valued at all, and who always lay poking in the ashes; but the other two were like most men, and did all the work." What work did they do?

Men's work was remarkably varied; it included fishing, whaling, harvesting the bird cliffs, managing sheep, cutting hay, digging peat, reaping barley, and more. All these pursuits share two characteristics: men generally work out of doors, almost always during the day and almost always with other men; and their work is markedly different from women's. Men rowed out to fish in crews of up to thirteen, and took part in even larger groups in two or three major sheep drives a year. This entailed chasing the half-wild sheep through the steep, rugged terrain of the outfields on the slopes and mountains around the village. Dogs were used to some extent, but the men's cooperative effort was essential. Men might sometimes go fowling alone or in pairs, but large crews were needed to haul the stout line on which one man was lowered to the bird cliffs. Many of these activities involved using others' equipment—one man's boat, another's line—and each crew had its skipper or foreman. One

Plate 5. Returning from a sheep drive. The village is at left. (Photograph: J. Wylie)

man, for example, was chosen to be "shepherd" (*seyðamaður*) for each section of outfield, to which several farmers might have rights. But this ascendancy was temporary, foremen changing with the task at hand. Since men exchanged labor, each man's standing derived from his ability to carry out strenuous cooperative pursuits.

Men and adolescent boys might sometimes work inside, for example when the weather was particularly bad, repairing tools or carding and spinning the wool that the women then wove and knitted. They might also be out at night, for example holding a restive pod of whales until it was light enough to drive them ashore. But these were clearly exceptional occasions, and indoor or night work was an adjunct of daytime tasks outside the house and outside the village. Even when men and women worked together, the division of labor was marked: men dug peat and women stacked it; men carried it home, and women used it for cooking; men reaped barley, but women watched over it as it dried over peat fires.

For women, the house was the center of daily life. It is true that in the summer, groups of women would make two milking trips a day to the outfield where cows were put to graze; but this was clearly subordinate to their inside tasks. Usually they would knit on their way along a main path to the pasture. This almost never involved climbing away from the path into rugged terrain, and men would be called upon to do the milking in bad weather, or whenever the cows strayed into steep areas. Otherwise, women knitted and sewed at home, minded the younger children, prepared meals, and visited each other to gossip and knit. Women generally went to bed later than men, staying up to bank the fire for the morning meal and to do other final household chores. Come morning, the first person up was a woman, rising to prepare breakfast. The open fireplace was located in the center of the house and was a place of constant female activity. Even today, men do not do women's work. Wylie tells the following story:

> Boys and men are pretty incompetent around the house, and though the womenfolk serve them meals and snacks, for example, and pick up after them, they do so without any sense of deference. My own inclination to lend a hand with the dishes, and my ability to cook for myself when my hosts went on vacation for a couple of weeks made me an awkward kind of anomaly. "You're almost a woman yourself (*Tú ert næstan konufólk sjálvur*)," a woman told me once. [1974:35]

The drastic sexual division of labor and its locational and temporal connotations suggest why Øskudólgur is such a "contemptible wretch." His poking all day in the ashes involves him in the women's domain. Although he is not by nature female and actually does no women's work, his failure to perform specifically male tasks in male places at male times marks him as not being really male either.

Øskudólgur's ambiguity is confirmed and elaborated in the first incident of the tale, whose logic we are now in a position to follow. As proper men, the elder brothers cannot stay awake all night watching over the grain. Øskudólgur is able to do so (with difficulty—women did not often stay up all night either)—and is ready when the giant bird appears. Now the tale suggests an implication of his sexual ambiguity. If Øskudólgur does not conform to the male sex role (or, for that matter, to the female one), is he really completely human? He puts his hands round the bird's neck, prepared to kill it. This is the way one normally kills small birds on the bird cliffs; but this is the house, and the bird is clearly no ordinary fowl. Of monstrous size, and with a preference for domestic food, it is as ambiguous a beast as Øskudólgur is a person. Not surprisingly, especially in view of Øskudólgur's threat to kill it like other birds, it talks. The ambiguous boy and the ambiguous beast strike a bargain.

Øskudólgur has already shown that he is abnormal. Now,

though he deals somewhat strangely with the bird, he reveals that he is after all human, and has (in this respect "like other men") the best interests of the community at heart. He says he will kill the bird because it has been stealing grain. The bird, by contrast, demonstrates that even though it is able to function to some extent humanly, on human ground, its basic identity is animal. But just as Øskudólgur is a different sort of human, the bird is a different sort of animal. As the price of escape, it gives Øskudólgur a magic feather, and the feather, being supernatural, lends Øskudólgur superhuman powers.

Human and animal are distinguished, then, but at the cost of making Øskudólgur's future more problematic than ever, suggesting that a realm exists where he may succeed while "other men" cannot. Equipped with the magic feather, he is even less like his brothers than before. Though they don't know about the feather, they resent their "worthless" brother's effortless success.

Øskudólgur and the King's Challenge: A Special Man and the Artificial Setting of Village Life

The first episode of "Øskudólgur" ends with its hero still ambiguously male in the context of everyday village life. By way of exploring the additional ambiguity of his being human nonetheless, the tale now moves from the village proper to the setting of a contest sponsored by "a king." In doing so, it shifts the context according to which its audience would attribute meaning to it from the everyday round of village life to one informed by, first, the body of oral literature (consisting of several genres in addition to the folktales), and, second, the realm of kings and nobility—that is, the realm of the king in Copenhagen and his agents, as far as they were known in the Faroes. This context, at once literary and political, was in a sense of course part of the universe of Faroese village culture, as the story-king's evidently having built his daughter's castle nearby suggests. It was, however, a part of that universe defined by contrast with the culture of everyday life. It represents an aspect of the whole of Faroese culture which was becoming increasingly problematic in the late nineteenth century.

The rich store of medieval ballads (kvæðir) provided Faroese with almost innumerable descriptions of the behavior of kings and princes in their courts, as well as of sports and heroic games. The resulting image of nobility is consistent with the king's contest in "Øskudólgur," but almost completely incompatible with behavior appropriate to village men. As we have seen, two of the prime characteristics of the village were cooperation and reciprocity, especially among men. Many tasks required the concerted effort of several men, the one aided being obliged to help the others in return. While individual energy and initiative were valued, they were always seen within the general frame of the community. This differs markedly from the ballad-picture of an individual hero sailing over the sea, waging battles in order to win a fair lady or a crown, and from the kind of situation now presented in "Øskudólgur." The fabled "high-born and wealthy men" do not do the kind of work Faroese men did, nor are they bound to cooperate or to exchange services. Rather, their inherent control of economic resources enables them to hire other people to work for them. A king is the most extreme type of noble, since he is able to order other people—even nobles—to do things, without even paying. Noblemen (and kings) are thus questionable men from the Faroese village standpoint, never cooperating, never working, living in castles where they always have authority over everyone else.

The king's situation in the tale reverses many elements of the village situation. That a man should make or have someone else make (presumably the king did not build it with his own hands) a house for his daughter, let alone a castle of glass, was unheard of. To put this castle on top of a mountain would be equally queer. That this should have been done as part of a contest for his daughter's hand is odder still. Parents took no active part in their children's matches, and a girl did not marry against her wishes. If a house was to be built for the young couple, it was the groom who built it, aided by other village men. The wedding took place only after the house was built. The house would be in the village, not on a mountain top, where only sheep and sheep herders ventured. Nor would the house be of glass—a material not only far less practical than the sod, field-stone, and timber with which real houses were built, but also, even for windows, a late and expensive import characterizing the Danish-influenced parlor (*glasstova*, literally "glass-room"). Traditionally, few houses had such rooms; Jóhan Hendrik Matras's wife's grandfather is said to have had only "half a *glasstova*" (J. S. Hansen 1971:71).

Faroese experience of actual royalty was indirect but pervasive. The king in Copenhagen stood at the head of the Faroes' ecclesiastical, political-judicial, and, until 1856, commercial systems.

He appointed the merchants of the royal trade monopoly (1709–1856), the bailiff (*fúti*), and the governor (*amtmaður*, 1821–1948); his bishops appointed the dean (*próstur*), who was head of the Faroese church. One way or another, then, all Faroese officialdom, from its lowest, native-born members like the sheriffs (*sýslumenn*) to its foreign potentates like the bailiff and the *amtmaður*, were officers of the crown.[3] The crown was an integral part of Faroese life. In fact in the aftermath of the Reformation the crown had become, from the Faroese point of view, the protector of village ways: "Ideally, the King was supposed to watch over the Faroes' precarious cultural distinctiveness by preserving the local economy and serving as the final giver and arbiter of law" (Wylie 1978:35). But by the middle of the nineteenth century the crown's perception of its business in the Faroes had begun to differ radically from the Faroese perception:

> By the time the Faroes had dwindled to a Danish *amt*, there was little left which appeared distinctively Faroese in Danish eyes, except a quaint "dialect" and a backwards economy. It was expected that with the removal of the commercial middlemen [by the establishment of free trade in 1856] the former would disappear and the latter would revive.
> From the Faroese point of view, however, it was precisely this dialect and this backwards economy—this way of describing and working the land and the sea—which constituted what Danish agents were supposed to preserve. They were the aspects of Faroese culture which the Reformation had left most untouched: indeed, the Reformation had preserved them. Moreover, the Monopoly's importance was as much cultural as economic, for because of it "the islands had truly been preserved as a relic of the middle ages since four hundred years ago—a society which lived its own narrow life, unattended by the outside world and without paying attention to it. This also came to set its mark on the character of the people" [Joensen, Mortensen, and Petersen 1955:75]. In short, commercially unmediated relations with the Danish state proved culturally dangerous, for they brought to light a fundamental difference between the Faroese and Danish views of the Faroes. [Ibid.: 37–38]

Traditionally, therefore, Faroese culture was a two-tiered affair. It consisted not only of village ways, but also of nominally foreign—Danish—ways. The latter level, which we are here calling "royal" in honor of its embodiment in the king, was in many respects the antithesis of the former, but served to distinguish it and protect it. But by the end of the nineteenth century, the royal level of Faroese culture had failed, as a matter of policy and as a result of economic change, to preserve the integrity of village culture. The *whole* of Faroese culture, village-*cum*-king, thus threatened to come apart at the seams. "Øskudólgur" illustrates this crisis of identity, and suggests its resolution.

The king builds his daughter a castle and sets appropriately royal rules of a contest for her hand. "High-born and wealthy" men come to try to win the princess. They fail; their horses cannot climb the mountain. Their problem is that they are not royal enough. They are the high-born counterparts of Øskudólgur's brothers—noble in their lack of cooperativeness and in having horses in the first place, but otherwise like them in lacking independent initiative and in being insufficiently free of natural limitations.[4] They are noble enough to respond actively to the king's challenge, whereas the brothers merely come to watch the contest; but they are as dependent on their all-too-ordinary horses as the brothers are on their own strength in doing "all the work."

"A lot of people"—the whole village, as it were—have turned out to watch the contest. Øskudólgur, however, is not a proper villager, and has been told by his brothers to "sit at home and poke in the ashes with his feather the way he always did." So he takes the feather and wishes for a special horse and special clothes. In this he is acting like a king, exercising effortless power to procure objects useless in the village. Without any trouble he rides halfway up the mountain, wheels about, and is at home again when his brothers return with the news. When they find he has seen the event, they tear down in a rage the shed (*hjallur*) he claims to have seen it from.

Why are they so self-destructively angry? And why did Øskudólgur make it only halfway up the mountain?

Øskudólgur has acted like a king, but his source of power is different from the king's. Effortless power is in the nature of kingship, but a king's power is not, like Øskudólgur's, derived from nature—even from such a mysteriously supernatural creature as a talking bird. Kingship is after all a human institution. Thus Øskudólgur's problem with his first ride is rather like the nobles'—his horse is not right, being as green as the pastures where theirs graze.

By a similar logic, Øskudólgur's claim to have seen the day's events is metaphorically very close to the truth. A *hjallur* is a shed in which meat and fish are hung to wind-dry; they thus nearly become a cultural item, food, by a natural process. ("Nearly," because they must still sometimes be cooked, and in any case served with other items, to make a proper meal.) A *hjallur*'s contents, then, are halfway to being food, just as Øskudólgur was halfway up the mountain. In tearing down their *hjallur*, his brothers in effect deny his supernatural expertise in the king's superhuman contest. Øskudólgur is himself beyond interference from their realm of everyday life, but he still threatens its integrity. No longer of the village world, he is not yet part of the royal one.

Øskudólgur repeats his ride the next day. This time he has white clothing and a red horse, and he rides "right up to the edge" of the mountaintop. His colors are now those of the Danish flag, but he still does not have it quite right—royal uniforms are red. His brothers angrily tear down the "stone shed" (*gróthús*)—most likely a shed for storing peat, or a winter barn for livestock. The following day Øskudólgur rides up the mountain again. This time he is once more tricked out in red and white, but his clothing is now red, and his horse is white. He reaches the princess, and his brothers destroy the hay shed, completing a process of destroying outbuildings that has moved from one used for the produce of the sea and of the outfields to one used for the crops of the infield. Presumably the farmhouse itself will be next—but this dire eventuality is forestalled by Øskudólgur's forthcoming removal from the domestic scene.

We have seen that Øskudólgur's initial problem was one of ambiguous masculinity. This ambiguity was marked primarily by his preference for the female domain of the hearth, and by his difference from his brothers. It was also partly a matter of his age. Unlike his father, he is unmarried, and is in addition obviously unfit to take over the farm. A real man is married; unmarried men are called *gamlir dreingir* ("old boys") in Faroese, while a husband is a *maður* ("man") or *húsbóndi* (literally, "house-farmer"). Thus one aspect, at least, of Øskudólgur's problem is resolved when he finds a wife.[5] But another, fundamental consequence of his ambiguity remains, for his sexual ambiguity has called the cultural integrity of the village into question. This aspect of his problem, and the village's, is resolved now by his being removed from the village to the royal level of society, where he can employ his extraordinary power for the common good.

Having ridden as far as the princess, Øskudólgur returns to his ash-poking. A search must be undertaken to locate the successful suitor. His ambiguous masculinity is reemphasized; he does not come when the king summons "all the men in the place." The princess does not find her suitor among them, and "the king asked if there wasn't some man left." Someone remembers Øskudólgur, but his brothers laugh; he never does anything but poke in the ashes. He is hardly a man. The king holds judiciously, however, that Øskudólgur should come; it is his right.[6] He dons his fine clothes and mounts his white steed, and is at once recognized by the princess. They are married, and when her father dies Øskudólgur is chosen king; he "ruled the kingdom both long and well." Thus, just as his sexual ambiguity is resolved by marriage, the critical cultural ambiguity it implies is also resolved by his establishment on the royal level of culture, preserving the integrity of the village from which he is, by the same token, estranged.[7]

The tale ends humorously, with the brothers continuing to make trouble. (This element is not found in other variants, the sort of detail, probably, that would vary with each teller's style.) There is a good chuckle, at least, in the phrase "the brothers were about to explode with anger." Faroese are amused by things which *almost* happen, and someone's "almost" dying of exhaustion, bafflement, or rage is a stock ending for funny stories.

As village life returns to normal, the brothers no longer pull down their sheds, but dwindle to the sort of grumblers one finds in any village—prime candidates, indeed, for a satirical ballad (*táttur*).

"Øskudólgur" and Changing Times: Folk Literature and Its Transformations

The tale we have examined is formally the simplest of the Øskudólgur stories. All of them, however, involve the same process—removing a disturbing, ambiguous figure from the level of everyday village life; his adventures with supernatural beings and in outlandish exploits; and, except in a few cases where he sails off "to another land," his eventual integration into the royal level of society, where his abnormal power becomes socially beneficent.

The picture of Faroese culture reflected in the tale is essentially accurate. It has two realms: the village realm, or level, of the first part of the tale, characterized by (among other things) cooperation and reciprocity among men and by well-differentiated sex roles; and the antithetical royal level of the second part of the tale. The levels are geographically as well as socially distinct. In the village, the women's domain was the household, while men worked mostly out of doors. Royalty, on the other hand, was outside the village. Its real agents and agencies were present in Tórshavn, while its ideal heroic character and its ideal function as guardian of village life were recalled in folktales and ballads, and in petitions to the real king, who oversaw indirectly the Faroes' church, trade, and law. Ideally, the whole system was a quantum arrangement; if an individual did not belong on one level, he had to belong on the other. He might fish or herd sheep, *or* collect the tithe; slaughter whales *or* divide them up; pay taxes *or* collect them; speak Faroese *or* speak Danish. The integrity of Faroese culture depended on keeping these levels distinct—in practical political terms, on remaining loyal to the crown while preserving the norms of domestic life and traditional pursuits. The danger, in literary terms, was that someone like Øskudólgur might exist between these levels; domestic anomaly thus threatened the whole system. Nor was this danger purely literary. Faroese acquiesced to official Danish hegemony, but for that reason resisted changes that struck literally too close to home. In the nineteenth century, well-meaning educational reformers, and those with such pet projects as introducing plows to the Faroes, met stubborn resistance; they must often have echoed Lucas Debes's exasperated comment, that Faroese were "so minded in general that they will not change their ways" (1676:257).

In real life there were no boys quite so ambiguous as Øskudólgur, and no men who would tear down sheds because their kid brother wished for a green horse; but at the time this tale was told there were no easy conceptual solutions, either. For a basic structural problem existed in Faroese society—how to socialize local males who have great economic power outside the traditional system of land-based rights and reciprocal obligations. We return to a traditional village at the end of the tale—but the old way of life in real villages was passing.

As commercial fishing increased in importance during the nineteenth century, the traditional division between full, married adults supported from the land, and marginal, single adults, largely employed by the former group as farmhands and serving women, began to break down. Fishing offered an alternative to the traditional system of acquiring economic control over one's life and so establishing one's identity as a full, married adult. The old system had guarded by law against uneconomical marriage, but it was threatened once a satisfactory living could be made from the sea. Even landless men might make enough money as commercial fishermen to set up house on their own.[8] Young women might do the same, as they often worked processing the catch in their home villages or in the new centers of the commercial export fishery.

Nor were fishing and farming the only alternatives. The Faroese population tripled between 1801 and 1901, and Faroese society developed an urban center in Tórshavn and an indigenous middle class—exactly the sort of place and sort of class that do not exist in "Øskudólgur's" model of village and court. Moreover, there was now also a small but vital literary intelligentsia, whose pursuits were hardly more manly from the traditional point of view than Øskudólgur's poking in the ashes, but who were nevertheless clearly important in the establishment and preservation of Faroese culture.

The issue of *Føringatíðindi* that announced Jakobsen's field trip to Vágar illustrates how times were changing. On the one hand it reports—as it might have been reported orally for centuries—that the weather has been very damp all fall. In the western parts of the Faroes only about half the hay has been gotten in, and the peat is not ready: "People are going to be short of both hay and peat this winter." In other local news, *Føringatíðindi* reports, "The [inshore] fishing has recently been nothing to speak of, because it has hardly been possible to get to sea."

But there is a modern kind of news as well: the fishing ships are almost all home, but their catches have been uneven, and the weather has been bad. Several ships are selling their catch in Shetland, where the price is good; others have sold theirs in Iceland. *Føringatíðindi* reminds skippers sailing abroad that they must get health certificates. Sixty-one ships worked the Iceland grounds that year, with a total crew of 816—figures that later increased greatly, due partly to the depredations of English trawlers on local grounds.[9] *Føringatíðindi* comments: "Still, as earlier this year, many English trawlers are about the Faroes. During the day they trawl outside the [three-mile] limit, but as soon as night comes they lie under the land. It is seen from this that if we do not get a ship to guard the land, it will be impossible to keep the trawlers out or to take them for breaking the law." Foreign trawlers continued to be a sore point for years, and even today Faroese complain that the Danish navy does not patrol local waters well enough.

This is a small example of the many critical political questions raised by the Faroes' new relations with Denmark and the world beyond. But *Føringatíðindi* also bears witness to the liveliness of self-consciously cultural interests. The Faroese Book Club has chosen its officers, and hopes to put out its first book by Christmas. Dr. Jakobsen is collecting folklore on Vágar. Some young Faroese in Copenhagen are planning to put out a collection of "the Faroese poems which have been composed recently." There will, the editors hope, soon be a continuation of the Bible stories. . . .

We are now in a position to answer our first two questions about "Øskudólgur": Why was it so popular, and what did it mean to its audience? And what light does an analysis of this particular tale shed on the rest of the collection?

We have no direct evidence as to what "Øskudólgur's" village audience thought the tale "meant." It is clear, however, that the tale treats a social and cultural problem that touched them closely—how to maintain the integrity of Faroese life at a time when the traditional economy based on the land was being overtaken by one based on seafaring. Though couched in the conventional, seemingly oblique idiom of the folktale, its import actually appears quite direct and detailed when we are aware, as its audience must have been, of the implications of the tale's settings, times, and characters— especially Øskudólgur's failure to act like most other men, who "did all the work." The tale's meaning for us, and in a less explicit way for its village audience, lies in its statement of a crisis of Faroese identity. The fact that the Øskudólgur tales were "greatly favored and wide-spread," as Jakobsen put it, is a measure of the depth of this crisis.

We may also say with hindsight that, despite its ultimate return to a traditional village setting, "Øskudólgur" suggests the solution Faroese found to their crisis: the creation of, as it were, a class of Øskudólgurs to assume, as the crown's oversight died away, the role of defining Faroese culture from above—folklorists, poets, journal- ists, bibliophiles, teachers, historians, shippers, politicians, bank- ers, artists, and a Faroe-born priesthood. "Øskudólgur" as written down by Jakobsen thus gained a second, more literary sort of mean- ing. It and the collection of which it is a part became a symbol of the fading traditional culture upon which a modern sense of Faroese- ness was built. As Føringatíðindi said in greeting the first volume of stories, "they bear proud witness to the spiritual life of the old Faroese."

"Øskudólgur" was intrinsically well fitted for discussing the problems presented by the untraditional pursuits now available to the generations grown up since the abolition of the Monopoly and the establishment of deepwater fishing.[10] It was not the only vehicle, however. Turning to the whole collection, one immediately has the impression that a large repertoire has been selectively elaborated to treat this and closely related problems; thirty-one of the remaining eighty tales deal with boys' unconventional success, for example.[11] All in all, depending on how you reckon it, at least 70 percent of the tales deal directly with Øskudólgur's problem. They assume various points of view and take up different aspects of the problem, but they stress many of the same points. It is interesting, for example, that the largest number of tales have male central figures. Establishing an adequate reputation as an adult male was not easy even in traditional terms, and the possibility of entering upon such new, untraditional pursuits as scholarship and journalism made it even less so (cf. Wylie 1974:303–5). The Faroes' new home-grown (but often foreign-educated) "royalty" was almost entirely male. Thus, although Øskudólgur's problem was critical for all Faroese, it was especially pressing for men.

Although only eighteen tales have central figures who may be considered Øskudólgur's female counterparts, these form the second largest category of tales. One, the Cinderella-tale "Crow's Daughter and Man's Daughter" ("Krákudóttir og Kalsdóttir," tale no. 19 in Jakobsen's collection), was about as popular as "Øskudólgur" (Jakobsen 1898–1901:xli). These tales about girls are of various types and often quite complex, but as a rule their heroines' predicaments and achievements are notably less fantastical than Øskudólgur's. Given the strong sexual role differentiation in Faroese society, the far more assured and central status of women, and the fact that the modernization of Faroese life touched men more immediately, girls' circumstances were culturally less deeply problematic than boys', and could thus be treated more conventionally. "Øskudólgur" is motivated by its hero's being unlike most other men, who "did all the work," and it ends with Øskudólgur removed from the domestic scene. His female counterparts are very much like hardworking real girls; they may leave home, but their tales end with their making a proper home of their own, preferably, but not necessarily, married to a prince. In cultural terms, the plots complement "Øskudólgur's"; a woman at home and an Øskudólgur on the throne are the twin foundations of Faroese culture.

The girls in these stories generally find themselves in anomalous initial situations, not, like Øskudólgur, through some fault of their own, but because they have been sent away from home, or because anomalous figures have invaded it—uncaring stepmothers, for example. More spectacularly, in "The Girl in the Giant's Cave" ("Gentan í Risahellinum," tale no. 4 in Jakobsen's collection), a robber band attacks the priest's house where the heroine is working. She seizes a sword and kills all but one of the robbers; these girls are not demure and passive maidens. In most tales, girls work for someone else, generally a giant. Giants are not a bad lot, on the whole. In fact they are a good deal like ordinary men; they spend the day on mysterious business out of doors, and get out of sorts in the evening if they find the housekeeping or the spinning has been poorly done. (Cosseted stepsisters make notoriously bad house-keepers.) Giants are not ungrateful, and they reward good work generously—in "Crow's Daughter and Man's Daughter" with a grubby-looking box in which the girl later finds the wonderful clothes and golden shoes with which she wins a prince, and in "The Girl in the Giant's Cave" by bequeathing her nine wishes and the key to a room "where she can see everything that goes on outside." But while giants are rather sympathetically portrayed, girls do not relish working for them; in "The Giant's Stump" ("Risans Klóta," tale no. 2) the girl goes so far as to trick the giant, who has fallen in love with her, into killing himself in the fire. In this tale, as in several others, the girl simply returns home with the giant's gold. Sometimes she turns his farmstead over to her father. Otherwise her adventures continue until she marries a prince.

From the girls' point of view, the problem is not that they should have to work for a living, or that they should have to work for someone else for a while. Nor do they find themselves disposed, like Øskudólgur, to occupy themselves with peculiar tasks; they do not herd sheep or go fishing, but do such appropriately female work as spinning and keeping house. Their problem is twofold. First, and most important, they are not mistresses of their own homes; and second, they are not mistresses of their own homes because they are not married, and giants are simply not suitable husbands—except in "Beauty and the Beast" ("Vakurleikin og Beistið," tale no. 48), where it turns out that the beast, a troll, is really a bewitched prince. In presenting this problem, the girls' tales touch closely on real life.

Real-life girls did not marry princes. But it was usual for them, as it was for boys, to work away from home for a time. They sometimes worked as servants for priests or well-to-do farmers, but after the rise of the commercial fishery they also found jobs processing fish in the centers of the new industry. This sometimes led to marriage away from their home villages. Traditionally, however, women married away from home far more often than men, and in those days of difficult transportation they might never return to the village where they were born. The pattern of female migration at marriage persists today. In one modern village, 90 percent of the married male population is village-born, compared with only 44 percent of the female population. About 90 percent of the unmarried population of both sexes is village-born (Wylie 1974:241).

All this means several things so far as the girls' folktales are concerned. First, real girls' work away from home was often of a very traditional sort; there is nothing untoward about the heroine of "The Girl in the Giant's Cave" who is working for a priest. Second, even if their work was not traditional (and in the tales it always is), it could be treated as something temporary, leading to a reaffirmation of traditional values; the girl would find a husband, or else she would come back home with her earnings. Finally, her leaving the village, temporarily or at marriage, was no more unusual in the tales than in real life. Moreover, a woman's work is pretty much the same anywhere, and a woman is at home wherever she makes her home. Story-girls found the way from cottage to palace a bit roundabout, perhaps, since there were giants they had to work for, but more human on the whole than Øskudólgur's route. Even a giant or a wicked stepmother is far more human than a talking bird, and keeping house for a giant is more immediately understandable than brandishing a feather and riding up to a glass castle.

In short, the real social problems posed in the late nineteenth century by increased mobility and the availability of new kinds of jobs for women could be comprehended quite conventionally in folktales about girls. The problems faced by Øskudólgur and by real boys were more acute and proved more difficult to deal with, since their solution involved reformulating Faroese culture. Øskudólgur is insufficiently a man, and must leave the village. A woman with a home of her own is sufficiently a woman; but whether cottage or palace, it must be *her* home. Indeed, one wonders how life turned out at Øskudólgur's palace. In a sense, "Øskudólgur's" nearest complement is "The Beautiful and Clever Queen" ("Hin Vakra og Vituga Drottningin," tale no. 32), in which we discover what lived-happily-ever-after means from a woman's point of view. Cleverly overcoming the tests and conditions of the king who marries her, the heroine establishes not only her position in the household, but also her "right to give counsel, at her discretion, in all affairs of state." [12]

These observations suggest the answer to our final question: How may we understand the role of Faroese folklore generally during this period?

There were four main genres of Faroese folk literature: the folktales proper (*ævintýr*), like "Øskudólgur"; the local legends (*sagnir*), which form the first part of Jakobsen's collection; the heroic ballads (*kvæðir*), which form an extensive corpus dating largely from the Middle Ages; and the satirical ballads (*tættir*). *Tættir* are often considered a minor genre of the heroic ballads, since they are sung to the same kind of melody and danced to in the same way.

But they continued to be composed well into the twentieth century, and their subject matter is different; *tættir* concern individuals in the village whose behavior departs significantly and presumably consistently from the norm.[13]

Each genre had a normative function. Folktales, as our analysis has shown, illustrated the limits of village life by fantastical departures from the village and its ways. What would happen if a boy lay poking in the ashes all the time? Legends codified the past, sometimes quite realistically, and sometimes with the help of *huldufólk*, a gray, elvish people of the outfields whose society shadows that of the village. *Tættir* obviously provided object lessons for the village, and their effect was heightened by forcing the subject to take part in the first performance of the composition ridiculing him.

The heroic ballads, which represent a tradition that has been lost for centuries in the rest of western Europe, mostly concern the exploits of heroes of the dim but often historic past, such as the Germanic Sigurd (*Sjúrðarkvæði*), the Frankish Charlemagne and Roland (*Rólantskvæði*), the Viking Olaf Tryggvasson (*Ormurin Langi*), and the Faroese Sigmundur (*Sigmundskvæði*). The heroic ballads provided and controlled exposure to kinds of behavior inappropriate to everyday village life, and in this respect they complement the folktales. At the same time they served to maintain the concept of membership in a wider culture, that of western Scandinavia. From the Reformation onward, this membership had been indirect, and in opposition to Danish dominance. Performing the heroic ballads expressed a village-based solidarity, in contrast to the outside, "royal" level of society of which they sang; with the development of an internally defined, distinctly Faroese culture, to whose definition their collection contributed greatly, they continue to function as symbols of generalized Faroese solidarity, as well as of membership in the wider Scandinavian world.

Each genre had a customary time and place for its performance. The folktales and legends were told by adults for an audience of both adults and children at informal gatherings, for example in the evenings or when the weather was too vile for outdoor work. The heroic and satirical ballads were (and still are) sung and danced to on special occasions—wedding feasts, holidays, during the night following a whale slaughter, and so forth. No age, sex, or residence distinctions are made among the dancers, who may keep at it all night, or even, as at a traditional wedding feast, for three nights running. Many of the heroic ballads are over a hundred stanzas long. The energetic but vicarious exposure to the strikingly individualistic and disruptive matter of the heroic ballads' plots probably provided an outlet for potentially destructive individual frustrations among the dancers (see chapter 5).

By the end of the nineteenth century, however, the traditional legends and folktales collected by Jakobsen were ceasing to be the common heritage they had been before the ascendancy of deepwater commercial fishing. Although *Føringatíðindi* was able to report, evidently rather defensively, that "the best information [given by Dr. Jakobsen on the occasion of his reading some of the tales he had "written"] was, according to him, that people in the Faroes first and foremost knew the land's old legends, the land's customs, and the land's language,"[14] the folktales and legends were soon to disappear completely from oral tradition. Today they are little known outside classes in Faroese language and literature, or by people who have read them in Jakobsen's version. For one thing, the occasions for telling them have faded away. Already in the late nineteenth century, many men spent months fishing far from home, and as the importance of wool production dwindled, so did gatherings to card, spin, knit, and weave.

Balladry has lasted longer as a living tradition. Its occasions, being ceremonial, persisted, and although virtually all of the satirical ballads have disappeared, a limited number of heroic ones are still danced to on special, primarily public occasions. Traditional dancing has become a kind of recreation in several more conservative villages, and in Tórshavn, Klaksvík, and other modern towns, where ballad clubs have been formed.

Yet it would not be quite correct to say that folk literature has disappeared entirely. That is, although its genres have mostly disappeared in their old forms, their functions have been taken over by professional works and institutions whose productions still provide popular entertainment and greatly enliven the Faroe scene. The first and probably still the most important medium for transmitting the modern equivalents of the folktales is journalism, both written and (nowadays) broadcast over the radio. We have already suggested the "editorial" function of the traditional folktales, and, opening at random the modern facsimile edition of *Føringatíðindi*, one finds several anecdotes that might just as well be called folktales: a nine-and-a-half-year-old Norwegian girl saves four people from drowning; a Glasgow doctor bequeathes all his money to his two sisters, but asks one of them to give his wife five *krónur* as thanks for having gone away and left him in peace; three little children die in Denmark when, their mother having gone out milking and their father being away at work, they play in the fire and succumb to the smoke; and somewhere a man takes his youngest child off to another parish and has it baptized—and its mother knows "least of all what name the child would get" (Føringatíðindi, 4 October 1894). Such outlandish anecdotes still find space in Faroese newspapers, along with items of local news and editorials expatiating on local developments and the current state of Faroe-Danish relations. (In a sense, almost all the news is political, since the newspapers are party organs.)

Legends persist in a similarly restricted way in the anecdotes that Faroese love to tell about contemporary eccentric characters, and in recollections of important local events. For the most part, however, they have been superseded by such written genres as "village histories" (bygdarsøgur) and in the simplified versions of Faroese history presented in school textbooks. The satirical ballads have similarly been transformed into the extraordinarily vital and popular genre of political parody. The topical and personal aspects of the tættir are now expressed in verses sung to modern tunes by radio entertainers, and in cartoons put out in the newspapers or in special cartoon-books published at Ólavsøka, the national holiday.

The heroic ballads have retained their form, although no new ones have been composed since the late eighteenth and early nineteenth centuries. Some are remembered, still, and danced to. Their modern transformation has thus been of a rather different order from that of the other genres—different, but in a way suggesting the most important role of traditional Faroese folklore today.

The essential point is that the ballads survive primarily in written form. As they are collected and studied by specialists, instead of being danced to while they are sung by whole village populations, they still recall the heroic past through which Faroese are linked with other Norse peoples; but now they also articulate and celebrate a custom which has died out along with much else in traditional village culture. Yet as Faroese society has modernized, and has in many respects come more and more to resemble others in western Europe, its members find tokens of their collective distinctiveness in the traditional past. The ballads are one such token. They have thus become symbols of Faroese culture as well as expressions of it, self-conscious articulations of what it is that makes Faroese culture distinctive and respectable, timeless and enduring, in still-changing times. The same is true of the other genres of traditional folk literature: their written forms symbolize a modern culture in which they are themselves obsolete. It is an outcome appropriate to the people who once found "Øskudólgur" fascinating. As young men today resemble Øskudólgur or remote ballad heroes more than they do their own fathers and grandfathers, they have found their overseeing "royalty" in books of lore about affairs outside the run of everyday life. The official symbolization of the past has allowed Faroese culture to modernize without radical discontinuity.

Folk literature does not provide the only symbols of Faroese identity. Perhaps the most important is the language itself, whose uses have of course included reducing folk literature to writing. We turn in the next chapter to the Faroese language, the way it was itself made into a written language, and the implications of this development. Chapter 5 then considers the *grindadráp*, or slaughter of pilot whales. The *grindadráp* is one of the most notable events in which ballad-dancing has remained a living custom; it is also an event which has become appreciated in the literature as something archetypically Faroese.

4
Language Roles and Culture Contact: The Linguistic Development of the Faroe Islands

If my hypothesis is correct, the primary function of
writing, as a means of communication, is to
facilitate the enslavement of other human beings.
The use of writing for disinterested ends, and with a
view to satisfactions of the mind in the fields either
of science or the arts, is a secondary result of its
invention—and may even be no more than a way of
dissimulating its primary function.

—Claude Lévi-Strauss (1968:292)

Collecting folktales in the 1880s was part of the process whereby
Faroese was transformed from a spoken "peasant" dialect to a written, "national" standard. At first, this redefinition of language use
was not expressly political; but as it also involved reevaluating the
position of Danish—and hence Denmark—in Faroese society, it
symbolized and engendered the political awakening that led to Faroese home rule in 1948.

The Faroese had long been bilingual. By the end of the sixteenth century, the Faroese dialect of West Scandinavian was developing, mainly phonologically, into a distinct language, which was
in turn internally diversified into a number of dialects of its own.
Since the Reformation, however, Danish was the Faroes' only written language—the language of trade, church, and state. In the nineteenth century those who wished to give Faroese a standard written
form found they faced two problems: overcoming the language's
internal dialect diversity, and demonstrating its ennobling affinity to
the old West Scandinavian base. These problems were solved—not

without difficulty and debate—by establishing an etymological orthography for Faroese. This elegant solution not only overcame the problem of dialects and fitted Faroese to become a respectable modern language, but also elaborated an ancient distinction between ritual and everyday varieties of language that was older in the Faroes than the political hegemony of Denmark and the linguistic hegemony of Danish.

Since the Faroes' Norse settlement in the ninth century, there was a clear distinction between the language variety used for ritual purposes and that used in nonritual situations. What changed was the languages that filled these roles, and the definition of ritual and nonritual situations. We propose, in this chapter, to map out the fundamental structural continuity of language use in the Faroes, and to note the main changes and complications of detail. By following this linguistic development, it is possible to determine the precise points of contact between outside culture and outside social forms, and indigenous Faroese categories. This in turn traces out the islands' metamorphosis from an independent Norse settlement, to a minor appendage of Denmark, to a political entity in its own right.

850–1000

Any account of the first centuries of Norse settlement in the Faroes must be partly conjectural. But the better-documented case of Iceland probably provides a close parallel that, together with sketchy Faroese evidence, allows us to work out a rough but reasonable idea of how things developed in the Faroes.

When Scandinavian settlers arrived in the Faroes in the first part of the ninth century, they were able to some extent to occupy farms left by the retreating Irish monks. Other suitable farm sites were probably claimed by householders, so that the first settlements were individual farms worked by a man and his sons, together with their thralls and possibly with other relations. But with land so scarce (the total area of the Faroes is only about fourteen hundred square kilometers, and only about 6 percent of this is cultivated), these farms must have developed early on into hamlets reminiscent of those reported in historic times. Land tenure was the basic requirement for economic viability, but associated rights to birds, eggs, and whales were also important, while fishing was the mainstay of the internal subsistence economy.

The settled areas are scattered around the shores of the islands; many are accessible only by boat, and some not at all in rough weather. But modern evidence and the Icelandic "Saga of the Faroe Islanders" suggest that there was frequent contact between the men of adjacent hamlets who might come together when out fishing, when on trading trips, or when a man was courting a woman in another settlement. Politically, moreover, the Faroes were soon divided into districts with local assemblies where free men came together, perhaps several times a year, to settle minor conflicts and discuss legal issues, in the tradition of western Norway (cf. Matras 1932). A most important institution was a central assembly that met on neutral, sacred ground; here all the free men of the islands were entitled to gather once a year to settle more serious cases and discuss issues of importance for all the islands.

The Faroes' central assembly place was the Tinganes, a rocky spit of land between the two harbors of Tórshavn. It was significant as a ritual center where the social order was validated and reinforced. Alongside and interconnected with this political and legal institution, which came to be called the Løgting, was the office of *goði*. The *goði*, or priest-chieftain, is best known from medieval Icelandic literature. In Iceland the *goði* held a well-defined office as priest of a shrine to one of the Scandinavian gods and functioned as a middleman between humans and gods. He was also the most important political figure, with the responsibility of representing men in his district at the Alþing, as Iceland's great assembly was called. From among the priest-chieftains, or other men well-versed in traditional law, was chosen the *løgsøgumaðr*, or law-speaker, whose role was to recite a section of the laws at every meeting of the Alþing. While it is difficult to postulate this complete system for the Faroes in the absence of more direct evidence, it is reasonable to assume that there was some such division of the location of political and religious ritual in the Faroes. And Tórshavn's role as the central assembly place is historically indisputable.

This cultural and social background forms the basis for the division of language roles in early medieval times in the Faroes. From 850 to 1000 primary social language registers consisted of ritual and nonritual varieties. The ritual level of Old Norse (or more precisely Old West Scandinavian) consisted of political and religious varieties, of which the political variety was only spoken, while the religious variety was primarily spoken but had a secondary written (Runic) component. The nonritual level was logically a residual category, consisting of everyday speech in the closely related dialects. The tradition of writing using Runic characters, a secondary development of ritual speech connected with religious practices, was apparently marginal in the Faroes. Only two runestones have been found there (Matras 1968).

1100–1530

The Faroes' status as an autonomous society bound to Norway presumably through trade ties alone did not last for long. By 1035 the islands were "held" by a local leader for King Magnus the Good of Norway. The precise significance of this allegiance is not clear. The situation was evidently rather fluid at first, and probably did not transform the position of the assemblies within the islands until later (cf. Wylie 1978). The introduction of Christianity had more profound effects.

By 1080 at the latest, the Faroes were a separate bishopric under the archbishop in Norway. The seat of the Faroe bishopric was in Kirkjubøur ("church-infield"), some miles away from the Løgting's assembly place in Tórshavn, across a high barren ridge on the land of one of the largest farms in the Faroes. This was quite consistent with the earlier (and Icelandic) practice of locating shrines on the land of powerful farmers, who filled the office of goði. Also consistent with earlier practice was the political involvement of the bishop in local affairs. In these respects, the structure of Faroese society was retained, so that the new religion was rather a redefinition of cultural material than a drastic change in the relation of categories.

The church brought with it a rather elaborate set of language varieties. Primary was the use of Latin as the vehicle of the holy word; secondary to this was the spoken ritual of religious services. In addition to the use of Latin was the well-established use of the vernacular in written form for paraphrases of the scriptures and for explanations of religious doctrine; this presumably had a secondary spoken form as well, used for reading aloud from the formal texts. Finally, the use of writing in connection with a ritual variety of the vernacular was extended quite early to the secular political-legal tradition and used for setting the laws down in a permanent form— in the Faroes, at the end of the thirteenth century (cf. Haugen 1968). The written laws helped formalize the Faroes' status as a Norwegian dependency or crown colony.

These changes combined with the older system to result in the pattern of language use prevailing in the Faroes until the Reformation. From 1100 to 1530, language registers consisted of ritual and nonritual varieties. The ritual level consisted of a Christian and a non-Christian or political variety. The Christian variety consisted of a primary Latin form and a secondary, vernacular one; both forms were primarily written, with secondary spoken components. The political variety, also primarily written, used only the West Scandinavian vernacular. The nonritual language, Faroese, was used for all other purposes.

The high degree of literacy implied by this system was undoubtedly not characteristic of the population as a whole, but, consistent with the ritual/nonritual distinction, was probably limited mostly to the priesthood. There was a church school connected to the bishop's residence at Kirkjubøur, where Faroese boys were trained for religious roles. The vernacular writing tradition taught there was presumably that of Bergen. At that time, however, the dialect difference between Bergen and the Faroes was probably small, so that the priests were literate in a West Scandinavian dialect closely related to their own.

1550–1900

The second major transformation of the system of language use in the Faroes resulted from the introduction of Danish Lutheranism and administration to the Faroes. By the sixteenth century, the place of written Norwegian had already been greatly weakened. In 1299 the Norwegian royal chancery was moved from Bergen to Oslo, diminishing the influence of the Bergen writing tradition (Haugen 1976). From 1387 especially, Queen Margaret of Denmark decided to promote Danish as the written language of administration; in its increasingly dependent position, the Norwegian government came to rely more and more on Danish norms, as Danish scribes and officials were appointed to posts in Norway. In addition, Bergen became the seat of the Hanseatic League in the North Atlantic, and Middle Low German became the official business language there. All of this indicated a weakening of the position of Norwegian in general in written usage, but especially of the Bergen writing tradition; this was presumably reflected in Faroese usage, since the Faroes continued to be ruled from Bergen.

By 1500, written Norwegian had completely disappeared as an

official language. Therefore, when the Reformation swept the Danish kingdom in the early and mid-1500s, there was no question of translating the scriptures into anything except Danish. A Danish New Testament was published in 1529, and the whole Bible appeared in 1550. The full effect of this linguistic reformation accompanying the ecclesiastical one was not felt at once in the Faroes. The priesthood did not become predominantly Danish until well into the next century, and old Norwegian law as it applied to the Faroes was not translated immediately (cf. Wylie 1978). Nevertheless, the Reformation did replace the elaborate linguistic apparatus of the Catholic church with the much simpler Danish Lutheran practice of using a ritual, primarily written variety of Danish for all religious purposes. Thus the linguistic tie with Norway, which had probably been weakening as written Norwegian was displaced, was now formally and finally cut.

Lutheran ministers were not the only Danes who came to the Faroes in this period; the merchants who oversaw the Faroe trade were Danes, and the government administration was now also in the hands of Danes (or at least Danish speakers—some were of German or Norwegian background).

These changes were the more drastic in that they collapsed the previous distinction between social and religious centers. The cathedral at Kirkjubøur was closed down, and Tórshavn was made the Faroes' religious center. From a Danish point of view, the Faroes now apparently resembled the familiar Danish model of a coastal market town with adjacent villages and hamlets. This was obviously a model the Faroese did not share, but the imposition of Danish control and dominance forced a change in the Faroese model nonetheless. While Tórshavn was still a center of social ritual, it was now also a religious center. Socially, it was the center of Danish bureaucracy and trade as well as of an attenuated version of the ancient tradition of political assembly; religiously, it harbored a new religion with strong connotations of Danish culture.

Linguistically, now, formal or "high" Danish became the appropriate "high" language variety, with a subdivision into religious and bureaucratic varieties. Thus, a new pattern developed. From the Danish point of view the Faroese were simply a peculiar type of Danish peasant, speaking some "dialect" among themselves but able to converse in Danish at least in the "market town" that doubled as their political and religious center. From the Faroese point of view, their special, ritual language had to change to meet the new conditions. Danish became in effect a special kind of Faroese. Thus, although the Faroese did not consider themselves Danes, their symbolic expressions of group identity were destroyed or absorbed into a different system, leaving only the diffuse characteristics of daily life in the villages.

From 1550 until around 1900, then, language roles consisted of a Danish and a non-Danish variety. The Danish variety was characteristic of religious ritual and bureaucratic affairs. Both religious and bureaucratic varieties were primarily written, with secondary spoken components. The non-Danish variety was Faroese, only spoken in phonetically distinct island and village dialects.

It becomes possible in this period to document in detail the linguistic development of the Faroes. Some insights are available, for example, concerning the manner in which Faroese learned spoken Danish, and the nature of the Danish they learned. The episcopal school at Kirkjubøur had closed down in 1538, and a Danish Lutheran school opened in Tórshavn in 1547. This school still taught Latin as a major subject, but Danish was of central importance. What is more, boys who had been educated at this school but who did not become ministers evidently returned to their villages and there taught other men to read (Lützen 1958). With the increased emphasis on reading Danish in church, it appears likely that the norm for reading aloud was that of the Danish clergy, spread to the villagers through church services and by local students from the "Latin School" in Tórshavn. By the early 1600s, most men could probably read, and some could write as well. From then through the 1850s, literacy training took place in the household, undoubtedly based on the norms learned in the sixteenth century; it was this standard for reading aloud that then formed the basis of the sound system of Danish as spoken by Faroese (Faroese *gøtudanskt*, "street Danish"). This by now peculiarly Faroese brand of Danish is only just beginning to be replaced by more standard (or more modern) Danish pronunciation.

Meanwhile, Faroese itself was developing a character of its own. By 1600 understanding of the old form of the language, as recorded on documents from before the Reformation, "had begun to fade among Faroese" (Zachariasen 1961:320). This old form of Faroese was not too different from the Icelandic of the time. Indeed, as late as 1616, a visiting Icelander sold one Icelandic book to a Faroese and gave him another, reporting: "He read them easily, for there was no great difference between their tongue and ours, and it was the same in many ways with their customs." Only now, the Icelander went on, "Danish manners have come in there, both in churches and outside it, with common Danish speech" (Blöndal 1908:121; the translation here follows Phillpotts 1923:143). In fact the influence of Danish on Faroese proved small. Danish was adopted wholesale in the church and for official business, but otherwise Faroese developed independently. This independence was not so surprising as it may seem. Faroese remained the language of everyday life and of economic pursuits confirmed and promoted by the Reformation (Wylie 1978:22). Faroese was not seriously threatened until the late nineteenth century, when the *loosening* of Danish control promoted a new economic order.

Two developments in Faroese must be noted: its divergence from other West Scandinavian tongues, and its internal dialect diversification.[1] Both developments were largely phonological, although the first was also marked by a certain morphological conservatism. Faroese thus retained four noun cases (nominative, accusative, dative, and genitive) as well as a complete set of case inflections for adjectives. Phonologically, the formerly long vowels were diphthongized here as elsewhere in Scandinavia, but the Faroese set of diphthongs was locally characteristic. Most curiously, perhaps, for someone familiar with Icelandic, ð was generally reduced to silence in Faroese, or to the glide consonants [j, v, w]—but it is occasionally also pronounced [g]. It never has the original (and Icelandic) value of *th* as in English o*th*er. Similarly, *g* may be voiced, voiceless, or silent, or become one of the glides, or have the values [ɟ, k, d].

Within the Faroes, dialect distinctions are almost completely phonetic, but they were reportedly enough to make communication difficult between speakers from the extreme north and south. Each village has its own characteristic speech (Faroese *bygdarmál*), but there are two main dialects, the southern dialect from south of Skopunarfjørður and the northern dialect from north of Skopunarfjørður. Each may be subdivided, the southern one into Sandoy and Suðuroy forms, and the northern one—which has more marked further subdivisions—into forms embracing South Streymoy, Vágar, Nólsoy, Hestur, and Koltur on the one hand, and North Streymoy, Eysturoy, and the Norðoyar on the other.[2]

The Faroes' last links to Norway were severed by around 1620. "There was a sort of stability about Faroese life for at least two hundred years—an artifical stability, a bleak, bitter and often hungry one, which perpetuated the Faroes' peculiar status as a cultural enclave and an economic and political dependency. Royal policy and the interests of the trade monopoly institutionalized a constrained version of the old way of life" (Wylie 1978:21–22). It was in this economic and social context that formal education began in the islands, and met considerable resistance.

In 1739 an ordinance was passed in Denmark requiring all children to be literate in Danish, as well as instructed in Lutheran doctrine, before being confirmed into the church. The ordinance was retracted in the Faroes in 1741, due to lack of financial support; no one would pay for the instruction. In 1814, a law establishing public elementary education had been passed in Denmark, and when the Faroes became a province of Denmark in 1816, the question of its applicability to the Faroes arose. In the following decades, some schools were built in the villages, where committees of local men decided how long a traveling teacher should stay and how many hours school should last. In 1845, a provisional ordinance requiring compulsory public elementary education went into effect in the Faroes. It met extremely strong resistance, and was finally retracted in 1854.

The point at issue here was obviously the delineation of Danish influence in local affairs. Faroese control over education was real, though not explicit, and the Danish incursion into the home was resisted. From the Danish point of view, the Faroese, being formally Danish, were strangely resistant to being treated like "other Danes." From the Faroese point of view, formal Danishness was a way of preserving a real Faroeseness. As a series of editorials in *Føringatíðindi* pointed out near the end of the century, by which time this point of view was better refined and articulated,

> It is said, that our language-struggle has dug a deep ditch between Faroese and Danes in the Faroes, and this is rightly held to be a mistake; for a discord between people in one country is, as everyone knows, damaging. . . . Danes and Faroese are so closely bound to one another, that one party does not fare well when the other fares badly. [*Føringatíðindi*, 7 November 1895]

> Faroese are renowned men of intelligence—they have kept what our relatives in neighboring countries have forgotten. The kitchen was the school, where the old ones recalled the fatherland's history and whatever else they believed to be useful and needful. [*Føringatíðindi*, 21 November 1895]

It is worth pointing out that educational reform was resisted, whereas the inclusion of the Faroes as a Danish province in 1816 was not. To teach Danish for everyday purposes at home was a radical threat; but the Faroes' political incorporation into Denmark only realized formally a trend that had begun with the Reformation. The Løgting had lost any real power generations before its abolition in 1816. That the Faroes should be a Danish county did not, on the face of things, seriously affect Faroese culture.

In the 1830s, however, the liberalization of the Danish state combined with favorable economic conditions on the continent to foster the beginning of commercial fishing in the Faroes, and to strengthen the Faroes' intellectual ties with Copenhagen. In Denmark's liberal political atmosphere from the 1830s on into the 1850s, a National Romantic movement emerged that emphasized language and oral tradition as a people's distinguishing characteristics. After the growth of German nationalism led to civil war in Slesvig-Holstein in 1848, Danish liberals were able to end the period of absolute monarchy in Denmark and to gain administrative powers for Parliament. The liberal constitution of 1849 included the Faroes as an integral part of Denmark. Although this inclusion proceeded without consultation with the Faroese people, there was no public outcry; again, it was a confirmation of the prevailing situation. But now the closer association with Denmark, together with economic growth and the rising spirit of liberalism and nationalism, instigated a century-long transition period during which the culture of the Faroes was redefined. The central issue was language roles. A Faroese national movement was gradually formed, based on the redefinition of Faroese as the language of the Faroese people, with a concomitant redefinition of Danish as an external language.

Modern Times

In 1844, a meeting of Danish officials was held in Denmark to discuss the problem of elementary education in the Faroes. Its report, recommending the adoption of the ordinance of 1845 mentioned above, expressed the common view that Faroese was a debased, mixed dialect of Danish and Icelandic. This attitude was immediately attacked by the Faroese theology student V. U. Hammershaimb in a newspaper article giving the Faroese point of view with a historical-linguistic justification. At the same time, Svend Grundtvig, a Danish folklorist interested in Faroese oral tradition, published a small book entitled *Danish in the Faroes: An Analogue to German in Slesvig*.[3] Grundtvig discussed the schooling issue and argued the distinctiveness of Faroese as a language in its own right, but his book must have made uncomfortable reading for Danish liberals (and nationalists), particularly in its more polemical passages:

> It is not . . . merely for the sake of the Faroese, but also for our own, that this matter lays claim to all enlightened, upright, honorable Danish attention; not for the Faroese, but for our own sake, that we should beware lest we profane the righteous fight we are carrying on to erect in Slesvig a rampart against German's invasion, and to obtain for our southernmost compatriots the permission and opportunity to retain their mother tongue and nationality uncorrupted—to profane this fight against foreign assault and unrighteousness, while against the North itself to make ourselves guilty of the same offense, *there* to play the role of "Schleswig-Holsteiner," by endeavoring to extirpate a people and a nationality that we have neglected all too long.

National Romanticism lent the Faroese an ideology for articulating their cultural differentness. It did not, for the moment, give them much more. The main problem, both practical and ideological, was that Faroese was not a written language. Thus, while Faroese villagers thwarted the new regulation through passive resistance, Faroese students in Copenhagen discussed the means of creating a Faroese written language.

The background of this movement was older than the immediate pressure of the schooling ordinance, and was tied to the development of scholarly interest in comparative linguistics and oral tradition; but only at this point did it become a matter of general Faroese intellectual concern. The main practical problem was how to reconcile the dialect differences of Faroese. Earlier modern attempts to write Faroese had used more or less phonetic systems, and thus tended to favor one dialect over another.

In the late eighteenth century, the Faroese student J. C. Svabo had collected ballads and written a Faroese-Danish-Latin dictionary as a way of preserving historically interesting material which he considered bound for extinction. He developed an orthography based on the phonetics of his own dialect of Faroese for this purpose. Although Svabo's material was not published until this century, his example was instrumental in interesting others in writing the language. In 1815, the Faroese minister J. H. Schrøter applied to the Danish Bible Society for permission to translate the New Testament. Tentative permission was granted, contingent on a satisfactory translation of the Gospel of Matthew. His orthography was essentially Svabo's, though with a different dialect base and some modifications. Significantly, the book met with a good deal of opposition from the Faroese when it appeared in 1823, as being "too everyday" in tone for the holy scriptures. No further translations were made at the time.

In 1845, upon receiving an invitation to attend in Copenhagen the founding meeting of a society to further a Faroese written language, the Danish linguist N. M. Petersen responded with an article pointing out that there was in fact no Faroese written language, only a semiphonetic orthography based on spoken dialects. "The written language," he maintained, "is what is harmonic in dialects, related back to the language's simple, noble, original form. When it is torn away from that, it ceases to be what it should be: the common and most noble expression of a whole people's thoughts" (cited in Trap 1968:173). This objection touched off a series of debates as to the direction to follow. For some time there had been a writing system to rival Svabo's, to a certain extent modeled on Icelandic; Jákup Nolsøe, the resident manager of the Monopoly, and a poet, was said to have read Icelandic sagas aloud in Faroese, and in about 1830 wrote an unpublished Faroese grammar. His son Napoleon Nolsøe, the Faroes' first native doctor and a collector of ballads, was a champion of the alternative orthography. He was no linguist, however, and Schrøter's revised version of Svabo's system was more adequate.

The idea of returning to some earlier stage of the language to escape the dialect problem was being discussed, especially since this method had been adopted for written Icelandic; there, the difficulty was not dialect diversity, but (as was also true in the Faroes) the creation of a sufficiently "respectable" norm. Therefore, when the philologist C. C. Rafn received some magic formulas collected in the Faroes and written using Schrøter's orthography, he felt that he could not print them in that form. Probably on Petersen's advice, he sent the manuscript to an Icelandic student who reworked it into a more Icelandic form. Although this was checked by Petersen and Hammershaimb, the published version was essentially the work of the Icelander Jón Sigurðsson. Hammershaimb then followed the direction indicated by this experience, and published in 1846 the basis for the orthography which is in virtually all respects that of today.

The following verses from the beginning of the Faroese ballad with the most ancient pedigree, *Sjúrðarkvæði* (the ballad of Sigurd the dragon-slayer), in Schrøter's and Hammershaimb's versions illustrate the basic difference between their orthographies:

Schrøter (1951–53 [1819]):1)	Hammershaimb (1851:3–4)
Siure Qveaje	Sjúrðar Kvæði

1 Villija tear nu Luja aa   1 Viljið tàr nú lýða á,
  meene Ee man qvöa   meðan eg mann kvøða
  Um Tajr ruiku Konganar   um teir ríku kongarnar,
  sum Ee vill nu umröa.   sum eg vil nú umrøða.

4 Thaa vear hear so migijil   5 Tá vàr hàr so mikil
  Rujdamanna [sic] Gongd   ríka manna gongd,
  Oufriur giæk aa   ófriður gekk á
  Kongijins Land.   hin ríka kongins lond.

7 Ruja Tajr uj Bardajun   8 Ríða teir í bardàgar,
  Loudu hear sujt Luiv   làta hàr sítt lív,
  Etterlivur Hiördis   eftir livir Hjördis,
  Sigmunda Vuiv   Sigmundar vív.

Literal translation: 1 Will you now lend an ear while I shall sing of the rich kings whom I shall now discuss. 4 (5) Then there was such a great coming and going of rich men, dissension came over (the rich) king's land (lands). 7 (8) They ride in (into) battles, give up their lives there, H. survives, Sigmund's wife.

Schrøter's version is more or less phonetic; Hammershaimb's differs from the modern standard only in the spelling *mann* for modern *man* (1, line 2), and in using the grave accent to mark diphthongized *a*, where the modern spelling is either *a* or *æ* (i.e., *tàr, vàr, hàr* for modern *tær, var, har*).

Note that Schrøter's version at once gives a fairly good idea of how the Faroese language sounds, particularly if the reader is familiar with Danish orthographic conventions. Hammershaimb's, on the other hand, immediately recalls Icelandic, but often gives little or no idea how different from Icelandic Faroese sounds. In Icelandic, for example, the second word in the title would also be written *kvæði*, pronounced [kvaıðı]; the Faroese pronunciation is [kvɛajı], reflecting the different diphthongization of Faroese vowels, and the reduction of ð to (in this case) a glide. Sometimes the difference between Faroese and Icelandic is more marked in the writing; thus the second word in the first verse, *tær* (Hammershaimb's early *tàr*), would be *þér* in Icelandic.

What Hammershaimb's orthography aimed at was not, in fact, so much a similarity to Icelandic, as a dissimilarity to Danish and, most important, an ennobling reflection of the language of the sagas.[4] It promised at the same time a way of circumventing the dialect problem; each villager could pronounce the written word according to the norms of his or her *bygdarmál*. The arguments in favor of Hammershaimb's system were set out most clearly and forcefully in the first issue of *Føringatíðindi*, in an editorial that deserves to be quoted at length. The editor begins almost apologetically, hoping that what is printed in the paper will be interesting enough that "in a land where few have learned to read and fewer still to write the mother tongue," readers will trouble to "spell their way through the unfamiliar runes." *Føringatíðindi* will try, he says, to follow the writing system Hammershaimb and Grundtvig found best.

> We do not want the Faroese language more than other languages to stand in the place where it was from ancient times, though it must not be forgotten that the language has now fallen into neglect. People do not now, as they did before, exert themselves to speak properly. Words are said differently without thinking of their basis. A writing system in which each sound has its mark and little stress is laid on what meaning is in the words would undoubtedly help to drive home all signs of the decline Faroese have now found themselves in for several hundred years. Nor must it be forgotten, that the *bygdarmál* have come so far from one another that it is necessary to get an estate (a writing system) to fit them all into. For each *bygdarmál* would rightly demand its own sound-writing. The Føringafelag's goal is not to tear apart, but instead to bind together; thus the society's paper must try to make the *bygdarmál* equal together, and this may soonest and best be arranged by joining them through the roots from which they have sprung. Many people say that what has been written in *Dimmalætting* [another newspaper, which occasionally printed items in Faroese] and in the Føringafelag's writings is Icelandic—although it is a good distance from Icelandic, if it does resemble it—and why shouldn't it resemble it? . . . There are so many sounds in the Faroese language, that one is not much helped by the letters which are used in Danish writing. These new letters must appear unfamiliar to those who have not learnt to read anything but Danish. But it will be possible for those who are interested in doing so to read this writing, and pronounce it, each after his own *bygdarmál*. It will quickly be learned that a must often be pronounced as $\overline{ea}$, that in the north æ is pronounced just like a—south on Suðuroy like e; that á is pronounced something like $\overline{oa}$; that i and y are pronounced alike; that í and ý are pronounced uj; that ó is pronounced like $\overline{ou}$ and ú like yv, ei like aj, that g and k have special sounds before e, i and ey. . . .
> Good men have said, as it is said in the verse, that the

FØRINGATÍÐINDI.

Nr. 1. | Januar 1890. | 1. Árg.

FÖRINGATÍÐINDI kemur út fyrsta Tórsdagin í hvörjum mánaði og kostar 1 krónu um árið.

FÖRINGATÍÐINDI vil fremja tað, ið Föringafelag stevnur at, sum er: at verja Förja mál og Förja siðir; royna at vekja og styrkja samanhald millum Föringar og fáa teir at verða fríir í sinni og skinni.

FÖRINGATÍÐINDI vil framföra mangt og hvat, sum kan verða til gagn fyri okkara vinnuvegir á sjógvi og landi.

FÖRINGATÍÐINDI vil, stutt og greitt, siga nýgjastu tíðindi úr Förjum og öðrum londum.

FÖRINGATÍÐINDI vil frambera av vísum, skjemtisögum og ymsum öðrum, ið skrivast á Föroyskum máli, so mikið, sum rúmast kann.

Tá, ið nevndin fyri Föringafelag tók sær fyri at utgeva· eitt blað í Föroyskum máli, var tað ikke frítt, at hon stúrdi fyri tí, at blaðið vildi fáa óv nógv ímóti sær. I einum landi, hvar í fá hava lært at læsa og enn færri at skriva moðurmálið, er tað litið væntandi, at eitt blað sum Föringatíðindi skal kunna blíva ein vælkomin gestur í hyönsmans húsi. Tað, sum í tí stendur, krevur at vera valgt við umhugsan, so at folk kann hava hug at stava seg ígjögnum tær ókunnugu rúnirnar. Hann, sum er biðin til at vera stýrari fyri blaðnum, heldur seg ikki at vera föran at gera tað so væl, sum tað átti at gerast; men hevur tó tikið sær tað uppá, hopandi at teir, sum nakað evna, vilja hjálpa honum og at fólk ikki vil finnast óv illa at tí, ið rangt kann vera.

Í hesum árinum, sum nú er farið, hevur nógv verið orðað í «Dimmalætting» um, hvussi Föroyska málið rættast skal skrivast ella stavast. Her skal ikki sigast mikið um, hvat ið kann förast framm frá ymsum síðum til styrk fyri hendan ella handan

mátan. Heri blaðnum verður enn so leingi roynt at fylgja tí stavingalag, Provst Hammershaimb og Professor Svend Grundtvig hildu vera tað besta. Vit vilja ikki. at Förjamál heldri enn onnur mál skal standa í stað, sum tað var av úrölds tíð. tó má ikki gloymast, at málið nú er komið í órökt. Fólk hava ikki nú sum fyrr lagt seg eftir at hava grein í sínum máli. Orðini sigast ólíkliga utan at hugsa um grundina í teimum. Eitt. stavingalag, hvar í hvört ljóð hevur sitt merki og lítið dent verður lagt uppá, hvat höpi er í orðinum, vildi ivaleyst hjálpt til at sláa fast öll merkir av tí niðurgangi. Föringar nú í fleiri hundra ár hava verið staddir í. Heldri ikke má glovmast. at bygdamálini eru komin so langt frá hvörjum öðrum, at nevð er at fáa ein húna (eitt stavingalag) til at höska uppi á teimum öllum. Tí kravdi við röttum hvörjum byrdamáli sína ljóðskrift. Föringafelags endamál er ikki at slíta sundur. men heldri at knýta saman; tí má felagsblaðið royna at javna bygdamálini saman, og tað mann helst og best fáast í lag, við at beina tey ígjögnum ta rót, sum tev eru útsprungin av. Mangur sigur, at hettar, sum skrivað hevur verið í «Dimmalætting» og í Föringafelags skriftum er Íslenskt; — tað er tó væl langt frá Íslenskum, um tað enn er líkt tí; — og hví skuldi tað ikki líkst tí? Hann er ikki svínum líkur, ið sínum er líkur. Tað éru so mong ljóð í tí Föroyska málinum, at man ikki hjálpist væl við teimum bókstavum, sum brúkast í Danskari skrift. Hesir nýggju bókstavirnir mugu falla teimum ókunnigur fyri, sum ikki hava lært at lesa annað enn Danskt. Tó vil tað vera gjörlist fyri tey, sum hava hug til tað, at lesa hesa skriftina og uttala hana, hvör eftir sínum bygdamáli. Tað vil skjött lærast at a ofta má úttalast sum ea, at æ norðan fjörð úttalast líka sum a — suðuri á Suðuroynni sum e; at á úttalast naka ð sum oa; at i og y úttalast líka: at í og ý úttalast uj; at ó úttalast sum ou og ú sum yv, ei sum aj, at g og k hava

---

Plate 6. The first issue of *Føringatíðindi*.

Faroese language these days "is good for nothing but farmer's bawling." If what is said is true, then it would be hard to do anything about it. Still, there is good counsel against all bad counsel. If we cannot fly up amidst "the great and intelligent," let us hold ourselves lower, where we believe it is high enough.—Let it be called farmer's bawling.—The name of farmer has not been a dog's name in the Faroes. [*Føringatíðindi*, January 1890]

The orthography proposed by Hammershaimb thus took as its basis a linguistic form that both resolved internal differences among Faroese, and implied Faroese membership in the traditions of western Scandinavia. In his own words,

> I chose the etymological writing system because it seemed to me to offer the greatest advantage to the language, that it should have some future before it: not only that communications in Faroese might be easier for foreigners to read and more comely in appearance, but also that Faroese people might thereby come closer to the closely related languages, Icelandic and Danish, and find it easier to take advantage of what is common among them instead of isolating themselves by letting their variously distorted pronunciation be given expression in the written language. [1891:lv].

This association with already written languages acted as a validation of Faroese culture within Scandinavia, so that the development of the orthography was itself an important element in transforming Faroese from a "low" language variety characterized by local dialect variation to a "high" variety characterized by unity within the Faroes, and by similarity outside the Faroes to such a closely related language as Icelandic. It also validated Faroese culture through the Romantic idealization of the Germanic heritage as seen in the Icelandic heroic lays and sagas, and made the rich store of Faroese ballads even more significant.

Again, the position of Tórshavn is symptomatic of the Faroese situation. From a Danish or general European viewpoint, it would be logical to assume that a written language would be based on an urban dialect, since the conditions in which a written language would have to function would be those of a cultural, administrative, and market center. But Tórshavn was hardly a city in 1850—its population was only 841—and its connotations were almost all Danish. The problem was to find a means of counteracting Danish influence. The first choice was the diffuse resources of the Faroese villages, but when they proved unsuitable, another solution was found that explicitly united the villages and by the same token implicitly denied the existence of Danish Tórshavn, or reduced it to the status of one village among many. It was not until the 1880s that Tórshavn began to grow faster than the Faroese population as a whole (Wylie 1974:97ff.); and it was evidently not until then that Faroese thought of Tórshavn as a real city. As a correspondent wrote in *Føringatíðindi* in November 1890, "Now . . . Tórshavn has become a great, 'fine' place, which is lit up at night with more than a hundred petroleum lamps and has many other glories and fine things. . . ." (He went on to complain that the city had no public toilets for "villagers who come to the place"; one assumes that this small problem of urbanization was taken care of in due course.)

Significantly, then, "the center of conscious Faroese ideological and cultural life was, one could say, Copenhagen, where Faroese [students] had become acquainted with radical-cultural and national movements" (Djupedal 1964:171). In 1881 a Faroese Society was founded in Copenhagen to consider not only the advancement of the Faroese language, but also political and social issues. In 1889 a similar society, the Føringafelag, was founded in the Faroes, to promote and "honor" the Faroese language and Faroese customs, and to help unite Faroese for progress and their common good. From 1890 through 1901 the Føringafelag published its own newspaper, *Føringatíðindi*, in Faroese. Editorially *Føringatíðindi* took the sometimes awkward position that promoting Faroese interests did not entail separatism.

An indication of the symbolic meaning of written Faroese can be seen in the conflict that arose in the mid-1890s when Jakob Jakobsen, the Faroese folklorist, a student of philology and a key figure in the movement, suggested revising Hammershaimb's orthography to bring it more in line with the spoken language—particularly that of South Streymoy—so that children could learn it more easily. The controversy that resulted ended in a temporary compromise of minor scope, and the dissolution of the Føringafelag in the Faroes.[5] We would suggest that Jakobsen's reform implied a return to the view of Faroese as primarily a spoken language characterized by a development away from the old West Scandinavian form. At best it was premature, since the place of written Faroese was anything but assured in relation to written Danish, and the South Streymoy dialect was not felt to be a desirable standard.

Meanwhile, changes had gradually been made in the nature of formal education. The repeal of the compulsory education ordinance had been followed, surprisingly enough on the surface, by a widespread interest in elementary education in the villages. This led in 1869 to a suggestion by the Løgting, which had been revived as a consultative assembly in 1852, that Faroese teachers be trained through tutoring by teachers from the Danish high school (*realskole*) in Tórshavn, which had been established in 1854. The Danish governor denied this request on the grounds that training local teachers would be dangerously separatist, and rejected Hammershaimb's argument that the language difference would make Danish teachers unsuitable. But everyone else, including the school board for the Faroes, agreed, and in 1870 a teachers college was established. Faroese first became a subject there in 1907, indicating that the issue was control over primary education through determination of the classroom environment, not of the curriculum per se. Only Danish and traditional Danish subjects were taught, but Faroese could be used as the language of instruction.

From 1872, Faroese townships (Danish *kommuner*) were made responsible for the elementary education of all children over seven years old; in the Faroes, this new regulation reinforced the old pattern of local control. In 1899, the Faroese Folk High School was founded by two Faroese teachers active in the language movement; it was inspired by the Danish Folk High School movement begun by N. F. S. Grundtvig in the first half of the century. Beginning in the 1870s, a number of Faroese students had been encouraged to attend these schools, where traditional Danish culture was emphasized. The relevance to the Faroese situation was obvious. Significantly, the Faroese Folk High School was founded in a small village on an island far from Tórshavn, where it remained until it was moved to Tórshavn in 1909. The language of instruction at the Folk High School was Faroese, and a Faroese curriculum was gradually developed.

After 1900, the language issue became absorbed in broader social and cultural controversies as Faroese found themselves in increasing disagreement as to the islands' future relationship with Denmark. The ability to disagree openly about such matters without seriously threatening the coherence of Faroese society is a measure of the success of the language movement. In principle, if not in detail, the movement for a recognized and universally usable Faroese language had triumphed by the time the Faroes' first political parties were formed in 1906.

From the turn of the century on, the growth of written Faroese was very even, characterized by the regular appearance of school books and the expansion of the language into roles and places formerly filled by Danish. This process was marked in all areas by constant pressure increasing to positive opposition only when met with official resistance. Thus in 1912 a law was passed making Danish the mandatory language of instruction for older pupils; the resignation of one teacher, increasingly casual violation of the law, and mounting public protest led to Danish concession of the point in 1938. Faroese was approved for use in church services in 1903; in 1939, with the translation of the rituals and hymnal, authority was given for its general use in the church. Similarly, with regard to the use of Faroese in law courts, Faroese could by 1924 be used in legal documents, with translations to be provided only if demanded.

The Faroese were separated from Denmark during World War II. While the British occupied the islands and insured that supplies were available, their interference with local administration was minimal. This meant in effect Faroese home rule, which, along with the end of the worst part of an economic depression that had begun in the 1920s, greatly furthered the cause of Faroese nationalism. In fact, the war marks the end of the transition period in the formation of Faroese society. Even before, such primary institutions for the promotion of written Faroese as the Folk High School had served their functions and passed out of the center of Faroese political activity, now focused on different shades of nationalism and on economic issues.

Essentially, with the linguistic retaking of Tórshavn through the agency of an internally motivated written language, the Faroese not only redefined their language, but also forced the redefinition of their entire system of language use. The linguistic situation in turn corresponds to the present social and cultural identity of the Faroes since the Home Rule Act of 1948. As of 1980, language roles consist of an internal variety (Faroese) and external varieties. The internal variety consists of a restricted "high" form and a general "low" form. The "high" form consists of a religious and a bureaucratic variety, both of which are primarily written, with a secondary spoken component, whereas the "low" form is primarily spoken, with a secondary written component. The external variety may be Danish, other Scandinavian languages, English, German, etc.

This situation is evident in the developments of the transition period; as a result of the redefinition of Faroese as the internal language of the Faroes, Danish has correspondingly been redefined as an external language. However, observations of the situation in 1970–71 and the summer of 1974 indicate that a number of residual ambiguities remain.

Older people, who were educated before the war, still tend to regard Danish as a "high" language variety; they may be uncomfortable with the idea of using Faroese as such, and are often unwilling to address any Dane in Faroese. A number of Danes live in the Faroes, and their place in the system is rather complicated. The ambiguity arises from the logical contradiction of people who should be external to the society acting as if they were internal to it. For instance, a Danish man who has settled permanently in the Faroes and married a Faroese woman is often addressed in Faroese by his friends and relatives; but he always answers in Danish. The situation regarding Danish wives of Faroese men who have settled permanently in the Faroes is quite different. In the two cases I know of, the wife uses only Faroese unless talking to another Dane, suggesting that whatever her nationality the traditional role of the woman as the central, integrating figure in the family is still of basic importance.

In formal education, while Faroese textbooks for the elementary grades are available in all subjects, the importance of foreign (overwhelmingly Danish) texts increases in the upper grades, until they become the large majority of books used in, for example, the Teachers College. The fact that the language of instruction is everywhere Faroese, however, appears to be the relevant factor; with the role of Faroese secure, Danish no longer poses a direct threat. This is evident also in the fact that Danish is not the only language used in external situations such as reading foreign books or talking with foreigners. Although it is still the most commonly used foreign language, there is a tendency to regard it as a variant of "pan-Scandinavian"—a view reinforced by the local, *gøtudanskt* pronunciation's being more like Norwegian or Swedish than modern Danish. English and German are becoming more common as the number of high school graduates increases, and may soon approach the level of occurrence characteristic of the continental Scandinavian countries.

There is still some ambiguity with regard to norms for the "high" variety of Faroese, especially in bureaucratic and educational use. Conscious concern has focused mainly on the relative importance of loanwords for nonnative concepts and objects, as opposed to the creation of new Faroese forms. The issue is frequently discussed, and such institutions as the Faroese Academy (Fróðskaparsetur Føroya) and Radio Faroes (Útvarp Føroya) often disagree on particular usages. But a general compromise appears to be in effect, whereby many older loanwords and foreign names of new objects are borrowed, in Faroese phonemic shape. There is quite a bit of resistance to translating literature from Danish wherever such an undertaking would require the use of many new Faroese words or even loanwords to interpret concepts or experiences from another cultural setting. That is, such books are considered external to the society, and should not properly be translated from the primary external language, Danish; "Everyone can read them anyway," people say. Translations of books about situations reminiscent of the Faroes are not so strongly objected to, since they do not disturb the role of Faroese as the language of internal solidarity.

It is evident that the development of language role systems in the Faroes is closely tied to the interaction of indigenous and foreign assumptions about the implications of overt social behavior, including language use. Danish involvement in the Faroes was a continuation of Norwegian administration of a dependency; differences arose from the conversion to Lutheranism and specific Danish assumptions about the nature of a "provincial" area. The Faroese economic base, settlement pattern, houses, social structure, and political organization were all similar to those of Danish peasants, and almost identical to conditions in western Norway. In the same way, the physical appearance of the people themselves was familiar, and their language could be recognized as some sort of Scandinavian "dialect," however "debased." These similarities led Danes to assume that Faroese people's underlying values and motivations were the same as those of the people of rural Denmark, including self-identification as Danes. Thus the Faroese problem in trying to define some kind of sociocultural boundary that would not totally disrupt the native culture was to convince the Danes that they, the Faroese, were not merely Danish peasants.

We have seen that one of the most disturbing results of Danish dominance in the Faroes was the transformation of Tórshavn from a central assembly place where a conceptually autonomous Faroese society was validated to a Danish economic and administrative center where the Faroes' subordinate position within the Danish kingdom was emphasized. One of the most significant symbolic results of the Faroese language movement was thus the reestablishment of Tórshavn as the Faroese center of the Faroes. Tórshavn is still in some respects a mediating, ambiguous place, where outside forms and behavior are adapted and absorbed into local life; but instead of proceeding through the agency of Danes and standard Danish, this dynamic process is now channeled through Faroese people and the newly established standard Faroese language. In a way, the Faroese have countered direct Danish influence by adopting a Danish misconception—the view of Tórshavn as a "provincial" capital. At the same time, however, the National Romantic movement restored Tórshavn's ancient structural identity, however much the modern city differs in content from the old uninhabited meeting place, by forcing Danish officials to recognize its significance as the *Faroese* capital.

To much the same effect, the problem of reconciling the conflicting categories of "Faroese" and "outside" has been largely eliminated by recasting the situation in terms of a single "high" form of language within the country, and multiple forms outside it. Within the Faroes, Faroese has replaced Danish, and outside the Faroes, Danish has been replaced by many tongues. Within the Faroes, then, the old variation of *bygdarmál* has been supplemented by an overlapping categorization in terms of different levels of Faroese: "modern" and "old-fashioned," "high" and "low," written and spoken.

Such a redefinition and elaboration of conceptual structures is a very basic component of Faroese culture. We have seen its importance in understanding idioms of orientation (chapter 2), "Ashlad" tales (chapter 3), and now the development of language roles. It has offered the Faroese a way of reformulating tokens of their shared identity in changing times—of adapting without radical cultural discontinuity to profound changes in social structure and in the Faroes' relationship with the outside world. To all intents and purposes, the Faroes' identity is now national; although they are still tied to Denmark by law, the Faroes are conceptually a separate nation already.

We have been concerned so far with expressions of Faroese identity in language. The following chapter turns to the formation of identity in action, in the slaughter of pilot whales. This slaughter, called the *grindadráp*, has long provided an occasion for Faroese to work out the order of their lives.

5
Grindadráp

Ja, grindadrápið er ein góð, gomul
føroysk ítrótt. . . . Men tað er ikki til
stuttleika, at vit drepa grind.

Yes, the *grindadráp* is a good, old
Faroese sport. . . . But it's not for fun
that we kill a *grind*.

—A panelist on the V-4 radio program,
Útvarp Føroya, 4 April 1972

A *grind* is a school of *grindahvalir*—blackfish in New England, and
elsewhere in the English-speaking world pilot whales, pothead
whales, or caaing whales. Biologists know the species as *Globioce-*
phala melaena (Traill). A *grindadráp* is the slaughter of a *grind*.

The *grindadráp* has five stages. A *grind* is a sighted and the
hunters set out (*grindaboð*); it is chased (*grindarakstur*); it is
slaughtered (the *grindadráp* itself, properly speaking); the participants and others dance all night while the sheriff decides the apportionment (*grindadansur*); and in the morning the whales are divided
up, carved in pieces, and taken home (*grindabýti*).

"*Grindaboð!*" is surely the most exciting word in Faroese. It means,
literally, *grind* announcement. *Grindir*, ranging in size from a few
dozen to over a thousand whales, may appear about the Faroes at
any time, though they usually come in late summer. If fishermen
sight a *grind* they raise something—a sweater, perhaps—on a has-
tily rigged mast to tell other boats and people ashore that a *grind* has

come. The raising of the makeshift flag also constitutes a claim to the largest whale in the school. Traditionally, if the sighting was from land, or when a boat's *grindaboð* was seen from land, the news was passed by burning bonfires or spreading out sheets in prearranged patterns or places to show where the *grind* was. Runners set out for villages where such signals could not be seen. Nowadays most boats have radios, and the news goes out by radio and telephone. Men rush to their boats to take part in the hunt and to receive a share of meat and blubber. Jørgen-Frantz Jacobsen exaggerates only slightly when he says that "a psychosis of haste grips the population" (1970: 58), breaking the measured calm of everyday village life.

For all the excitement, the chase and the ensuing slaughter are quite deliberate affairs. The chase (*grindarakstur*) is supervised by a *grind* foreman, one of four elected in each town or district that has a sandy-beached bay suitable for driving the whales ashore. The hunters are called *rakstrarmenn* ("pursuit men") or *grindamenn*, which implies that a man is especially "strong" at the hunting. The idea of the chase is to herd the *grind* into the bay by forming a half-circle of boats behind it. The men slowly drive the *grind* by throwing stones or weights attached to lines into the water. It is tricky work. A *grind* may find the currents in its favor in long fjords open to the sea at both ends; it may sound, or outflank its hunters; it may split into smaller schools; and in the end it may find the surf more frightening than the weights splashing between it and the open sea. The chase may go on for several days, day and night. It is important not to panic the whales; they may sometimes be held, restive but docile, some distance from the shore, until each crew is ready for the final drive, or until the tides and currents are right. The *grind* foreman's boat flies the Faroese flag.

The critical moment comes when the whales are very close to shore. Then the *grind* foreman spears a chosen whale in the back, behind the fin, in the hope that it will panic toward the shore and, in beaching itself, lead the rest to the slaughter. Often, however, the speared whale swims off bleeding through the crowd, which mills about desperately, but keeps clear of the shore. More spearing is usually needed before the whales will strand themselves in the shallows. It is said as a matter of observation that the whales will not leave the bloodied area of water—another reason why the spearing must be done as close to shore as possible.

As individual whales run aground, men leap from the boats and wade out chest-deep from shore with *grindaknívar*, special knives

Plate 7. Scene at a *grindadráp*, Húsavík, 11 October 1971. This *grind* was very small, and only about thirty-five whales were taken. The men at right are hauling a stranded whale ashore; the man at left is about to kill a whale that has already been hauled in. (Photograph: J. Wylie)

with sturdy blades perhaps ten inches or a foot long. With these they slit the whales behind the head, severing the spinal cord, or so weakening it that the whale's thrashing snaps its neck. A practised man makes quick work of the killing; two strokes should do it—a deep cut a hand-span behind the blowhole, followed by a pithing stab. It is dangerous work because of the bad footing and the flailing flukes.

Men wade out from shore with *sóknaronglar*, which resemble monstrous fishhooks without a barb, attached to a rope. They plunge a *sóknarongul* into a dead or dying whale, and long lines of men haul the bodies up beyond the reach of the waves. It is illegal simply to stand on shore and watch the action—not that it's any problem, for even tourists (and anthropologists) tend to forget about photography in the excitement, and lend a hand on the lines.

A small *grind* dies in a matter of minutes. It may be several hours before the last member of a large one is killed, since the *grind* must be slaughtered in waves. The sleek black carcasses clutter the shallows. One by one they are hauled up past the high tide mark.

It is hard to describe the mood of the *grindadráp*. It is inevitably rather wild, but there is no mayhem and no one runs berserk. Faroese look down on irresponsible behavior in this as well as in other activities—partly, here, because overeager spearing might spoil the whole hunt, and false heroics would endanger everyone amid the knives and flukes. The killing itself is quick and as merciful as possible.[1] There is an eager, somewhat grim resolution about it all, and a pride in doing the job well, without the casualness of gutting fish or the private determination of slaughtering sheep. For all the gore and the deep smell of whale blood, despite scruples against killing so indiscriminately creatures who die, close up, so humanly, one feels it a fundamentally human experience. It is a communal hunt, which ends rightly when fresh-killed carcasses line the sand, each with a neat red gash gaping behind the head. The hunting ends fitly with a great, unbossed, intricately coordinated extertion. You feel worked up, like having a meal of fresh meat, like dancing and maybe drinking all night.

The local sheriff takes charge of the dead *grind*. He first designates the food whale (*matarhvalur*), which is portioned out among the households of the village where the slaughter took place so that everyone may have a meal of fresh meat and blubber. The rest of the whales may not be touched until morning, except that anyone may cut out the kidneys or liver, which must be eaten at once lest they spoil. The carcasses must be opened up anyway, since unless they are bled and cooled the meat "burns" and is not good eating. The blubber (*spik*) is spoiled only if the whale has been speared too much.

The *grindadráp* presently becomes a social occasion; kinsmen and old friends from different villages get together, and younger folk may court. There is a good deal of visiting around, and anyone is welcome in any house for a meal of fresh *grind*, to rest or to dry his clothes, and to exchange gossip. Some of the men begin to drink a great deal, and one is told that in the old days they used to engage in contests of strength, a kind of wrestling match in which a pair of men tried to throw each other by grabbing and tugging at one another's sleeves and shoulders. Such rivalry between men from different villages and competing boats may have been an expected feature of the occasion, but it was not institutionalized like the meal of fresh meat served to all comers in each house.

The sheriff and chosen measuring men (*metingarmenn*) are meanwhile numbering each whale and estimating its weight. The sheriff appoints a guard to watch over the carcasses on the beach all night, while he works out how the apportionment will go in the morning.

The dancing (*grindadansur*) begins in the evening. At the village dancehall—or, before villages had dancehalls, in a house rented for the occasion—men and women link arms to form a long, twisting circle. Anyone may join the circle at any point. They dance with a rhythmically shuffling, kicking step to the singing of the ballads. There is no instrumental accompaniment. A *skipari* (leader) sings the verses of a ballad, while the rest of the dancers join in on the verses (if they know them) and on the refrain. When one ballad ends, the ring keeps moving round for a few moments until a new *skipari* starts up a new one. The oldest ballads recount heroic exploits and romances of Charlemagne, Norse heroes, the Niebelungen cycle, and of local figures like Tróndur í Gøtu and Sigmundur, as a result of whose legendary struggles, or so the story goes, the Faroese were all converted to Christianity and brought under the Norwegian crown in about the year 1000. A few of the more recent ballads are in Danish, including the *grindavísa* composed by Governor Pløyen in the early nineteenth century, which is often sung at *grindadansir*. Today people also do "English dancing"—any nontraditional style—to an accordion or record player.

The mood is high; the turning circle fills the room; the floor resounds to the beat as the dancers, backs straight and heads turned, "tread the measure underfoot," two steps forward and one, with a slight kick, back. Most of the dancers are men, since the hunters are all men and women do not traditionally leave their villages for the *grindadráp* or the dance. The dance is a celebration, of course, but it also has practical aspects. It keeps spirits high while damping everyday rivalries, the aggressive excitement left over from the hunt, and alcoholic passions—drunks are not much appreciated; their singing is garbled, and their staggering disrupts the line. Nor is the "English dancing" much appreciated, especially if there are many fewer women than men, who then cannot all find partners and must line the walls of the dancehall until a ballad starts up again. I saw this happen once at a dance after a *grindadráp* in Miðvágur; the evening was occasionally unpleasant, and fighting almost broke out during some "English dancing." The man on whose boat I'd gone to Miðvágur told me later that there isn't much point to the "English dancing." The whole purpose of it, he complained, seems to be just to hug a girl. You don't get the right feeling—he could express it only by working his arms as if he were ballad dancing—release, perhaps, or uplift.

The dance goes on all night.

Come morning, the division of the catch (*grindabýti*) is the sheriff's responsibility. Its rules are rather complicated—we'll come back to them later—but the general idea is that each crew of hunters gets a share; the rest is portioned out to people who played special roles in the hunt and, if the *grind* was large enough, to each household in specially defined *grind* districts. Some is sold as well. The procedure is simple, however. The sheriff, having heard all claims and reckoned out who shall receive each whale, passes out a slip of paper to each person (or representative of each group of persons, for instance the skipper of a participating boat) entitled to receive a share, marked with the number of his whale. The cutting up is businesslike, calm, and thorough. Clusters of tired men hunch over each whale, flensing the white blubber and carving the red meat, still steaming in the cool morning air. Pieces of meat are laid on strips of blubber placed skin side down on the sand. Another cluster of men surrounds the sheriff and takes part in the auction, which proceeds in muttered undertones. One by one the men load up their boats, or trucks, and go home. Nowadays whole whales may be loaded onto trucks or large boats to be divided up at home. The *grind* will be eaten fresh-boiled with pieces of blubber (*spik*) and potatoes, or salted down, or hung out to dry for future meals.

How may we understand the *grindadráp*? Some observers, foreigners for the most part, have found it a throwback to Viking ferocity:

> Now your patient, childlike peace loving Faeroese becomes a veritable monster. . . . Seeing the whale slaughter—the utter abandonment to the lust of killing and the swilling of blood— it is impossible to believe that 27,000 of these people live such law abiding lives that most villages have neither policeman nor magistrate and that murder has never been known on the islands. A whale killing is the only thing which will persuade the Faeroese to raise their hands on Sundays. [Norgate 1943:5]

The Faroese writer Jørgen-Frantz Jacobsen, writing in Danish, likewise says:

> It is strange that the Faroese, who do not know war or murder, love the *grindadráp*. They simply cannot resist this drama. It must be a kind of atavism. The Viking spirit awakens suddenly to life again. . . . [1970:60]

And when Anne Morrow Lindbergh and her husband passed

through the Faroes in 1933, reconnoitering possible trans-Atlantic air routes, their host on Suðuroy told them about the *grindadráp*: "And all the sea is blood!" (1974:99).

On the other hand, dramatic accounts of the *grindadráp* are often told wryly to foreigners, partly by way of suggesting that there *is*, after all, something dramatic about these placid and reasonable folk, and partly because it is amusing to see how appalling foreigners may find the slaughter. The story is told—I have heard variants from both Miðvágur and Sandur—about a British officer who came down to the beach just after a *grindadráp* during the war. He was horrified, and finally managed to ask, "My God! How many were killed?" It had been a very large *grind*, and the man he'd asked said, "About a thousand." "Men?" the poor Britisher gasped.

The point is, from the Faroese point of view, exciting as the actual slaughter may be, it is an eminently practical business; and as for the blood—well, how would you kill whales without shedding a lot of it? None of the *grindamenn* I have talked to say that they take any particular joy in the killing; it is hard, dangerous work, and even rather distasteful, something to be done as expeditiously as possible in unavoidably difficult circumstances, a time when you must at all costs keep your wits about you.

For us, the point is that the slaughter itself is not the whole of the *grindadráp*. It is the central episode in a series of events triggered by the appearance of a *grind*, which, taken as a whole, make the *grindadráp* more than mere butchery, more than a purely commercial enterprise or a "Viking" atavism. The appearance of a *grind* calls forth behavior with analogues and ramifications in nearly every realm of Faroese life, so that the *grindadráp* as a whole becomes, as Williamson puts it, "an integral part of Faeroese nationhood . . . , one of the most significant factors in the curious identity of [Faroese] life" (1970:96). Our task must be, then, to put the *grindadráp* in context, tracing some of its more important associations to other, more mundane customs and pursuits. The *grindadráp* has no more meaning alone than the slaughter has without the dance. The exaltation of the hunt does not derive just from a break with everyday affairs, but also from the concentrated reenactment of less exceptional pastimes and pursuits. It is, in short, a "cultural text," in which the Faroese "forms and discovers his temperament and his society's temper at the same time" (Geertz 1972:28).

So much said, we must note two things. First, although the actual dealing of death is upon reflection less interesting than the events which lead up to it and then lead one back to everyday life, it is not altogether clear why the slaughter should, in effect, pose questions whose answers must be acted out so elaborately. What is so special about whales, and about killing a school of them? The answer seems to lie not so much with the nature of whales as with the nature of a *grind*. *Grindir* show up unpredictably, and a successful hunt provides vast amounts of food. Thus, if a *grind* is to be taken at all, men must act quickly and in concert; and the distribution of the spoils requires elaborate consideration in order to be equitable. A *grindadráp* thus involves, at heart, the recreation of Faroese norms of collective enterprise.

Second, this recreation involves associations with so many other aspects of local life that we can hardly hope to deal with all of them here. They include the following: historically and ecologically, the fact that a successful *grindadráp* meant "keeping the worst want away from the door for the 4–5000 people who were then in the Faroes" (J. S. Hansen 1966:152); in terms of diet, the fact that whales' bodies offer two of the three main elements in a meal, animal protein and fat (Wylie 1974); geographically, the exploitation of both land and sea, and the definition of special *grind* districts; economically, the combination of traditional techniques for fishing and sheep herding; ritually, the celebratory importance of dancing and drinking; socially, the establishment of men's and women's roles, and those of appointed authorities (the sheriff), elected ones (the *grind* foremen), and ones whose standing is due to some particular skill or control over some particular resource (boat skippers, landowners); demographically, the bringing together of villagers and nonvillagers; linguistically, a somewhat distinct vocabulary for describing the hunt and its equipment; in terms of basic Faroese values and the tenor of everyday life, the threat, in the heat of the action, to common sense and practicality, self-control and egalitarianism, and the maintenance of these norms. All this is not to mention recollections of the Viking Age and appreciations of local and foreign perceptions of Faroese life, and of the Faroes' place in the Norse world, nor, generally and abstractly, the adjustment of such categories, presumably fundamental in any culture, as life/death and individual/group.

So let us go back to the *grindadráp*, taking it stage by stage and drawing together a few of these many threads as we go along. The slaughter and the less sanguinary customs associated with it are a particularly apt metaphorical guide to the "curious identity" of Faroese life because, as a *grind* is named and discussed, sighted, hunted and slaughtered, as its death is celebrated and the carcasses are divided up, they involve a concerted effort to make a thing Faroese.

Grindaboð: *The Language of the* Grindadráp

"*Grind*," when used of whales, has two main meanings in modern Faroese: a school of *Globiocephala melaena*, and the meat from these whales, either alone or with their blubber (*spik*). In a sense, the whole *grindadráp* represents a progression from one meaning (a school of whales) to the other (meat).

No one knows for sure just how, or when, "*grind*" came to mean "a school of *G. melaena*." The word surely derives, however, from Old Norse *grind*, "gate, lattice-work door"—hence also modern Faroese *grinda* ("to lay the foundation [*grind*] of a house"), *beinagrind* (literally "boneframe," skeleton), *duragrind* ("doorframe"), *grind* ("stile, gate"), etc.[2] Most scholars believe that the modern usage is derived from the verb *grinda*, because when whales *grinda* or *grindast*, pausing in a dense school, they resemble a barred gate (Petersen 1968:46; Hammershaimb 1891:95; J. H. Poulsen, personal communication). "*Grind*," in the sense of a school of whales, would thus be derived from *grindahvalir*—whales in the habit of *grinda*ing—while the sense of these whales' meat is in turn derived from it.

The meaning of "*grind*" itself is thus obscurely rooted in the Old Norse past, although its development in historical times as a local elaboration of Viking Age culture is fairly clear. The same is true of several other terms, which have political and military connotations. A *hvalvápn* or *hvalvákn* ("whale weapon"), for example, is the spear used in the *grindadráp*, and according to the *grind* laws of 1709/1710 "each man who had come and participated in the slaughter received two shares—one for himself and one for his weapon" (Petersen 1968:43). Similarly, "*sóknarongul*," the hook used to gaff the whales inshore, is derived from a combination of *ongul* (in everyday life a fishhook, from a root meaning something curved or angled) and *sókn*, which means both "district" and "attack." Its compounds include ones meaning "assailant" and "injury" (*atsóknarmaður, heimsókn*) on the one hand, and on the other hand "parish priest" and "local government" (*sóknarprestur, kirkjusókn, sóknarstýri*). This double meaning, like the old share for the hunter's weapon, derives from a time when legal assemblies were formed of the arms bearers of each district, who made up a military body as well as a political one.

The call to meet at such assemblies is (or was) called a *boð*: in "Øskdólgur," for example, it is said, translating literally, that "the king thought that he [Øskudólgur] could come also, when all the rest had come together: it was his right. So a *boð* was sent for Øskudólgur. . . ." In olden times, the *boð* for legal assemblies was the *tingakrossur*, a wooden cross brought round to villages and farmsteads. More recently, *boð* took the form of signal fires and sheets spread out, or have been brought verbally by runners, in order to announce such news as the arrival of merchant or pirate ships, a minister's coming to hold a service that Sunday in an isolated village, or a forthcoming parliament; to call back fishermen if bad weather threatened; or to ask if the men from one village had come safely ashore in another.[3] A *grindaboð* is thus one of many kinds of summonses to deal with urgent and extraordinary business involving widely separated communities: pirates, a merchant ship, the making and breaking of law, God, peril at sea, or, of course, a *grind*.

When the *grind* is dead, the whales are valued by *skinn* (literally "skins"). This is the smallest reckoning of areas or values in land, according to the traditional Faroese system: 1 *mørk* = 16 *gyllin*, 1 *gyllin* = 20 *skinn*. The reckoning by "skins" reflects the old Germanic agricultural base (cf. the Anglo-Saxon "hide"), but the *gyllin* measure is more recent in the Faroes, having reached the islands from the Hanse in late medieval times. A large *grind* whale, one measuring twenty *skinn*, is called a *gyllinsfiskur* or a *gyllinshvalur* ("*gyllin* fish" or "*gyllin* whale").[4]

Impressions of berserkness aside, then, the *grindadráp* is not, on the evidence of some of its most basic vocabulary, any more truly "Viking" than other aspects of Faroese life. "*Boð*" and "*skinn*," for example, recall very ancient practices, but ones which have been adapted over the centuries to new exigencies—the appearance of Hanseatic trading partners in the fourteenth century, and raids by Barbary pirates in the sixteenth century—as well as the enduring characteristics of life in the Faroes: difficult communications, a closely known land, and a continuing tradition of representative government. In short, this vocabulary bears witness to the extent to which ancient patterns have been modified as they have become enmeshed in the organization of a specifically Faroese culture. Purely local elaborations appear in other words—for example, *tólvtáttaband*, the "twelve-stranded belt" from which a *grind* knife is hung.

Yet a remarkably rich texture of associations characterizes both the ancient foundation and its modern superstructure. It is not clear just why "*grind*" itself should mean a pod of whales, but the basic idea is one of framing, founding, containing, or boundary-marking. It is not simply punning to suggest that this idea is extended in other terms to lay the foundations (*grinda*) of social life in concerted collective dealings—political and economic enterprises and communication among the Faroes' dispersed settlements.

Grindarakstur: *The Chase in Time*

A good deal of the literature about the *grindadráp* concerns the antiquity of the hunt, and its technique. It is not known, however, how old the *grindadráp* is in its present form, or in something like its present form.[5]

The earliest evidence is rather sketchy. In the Gulatingslóg, the late thirteenth-century Norwegian codification applied to the Faroes, "it says . . . that a man shall have the right to catch whales wherever he can. If a man catches a whale and the whale dies out on the sea, then he owns the whale, whether it be smaller or larger; and if the whale goes onto land, then he owns half and the land [i.e., the owner of the land, subject to taxation] owns half."[6] Since these laws reflect older customs, it seems likely that as early as the end of the Viking Age Norsemen probably hunted whales much as the Faroese do today: some might be killed at sea, and others might "go onto land." Still, J. Pauli Joensen concludes tentatively, but I think rightly, from a review of the literature that the Faroes' economic decline in the fourteenth and fifteenth centuries may have fostered greater interest in *grind*-whaling, so that by the middle of the sixteenth century Faroese "began to create an organization around the hunting of pilot whales so that [they] could fully utilize an economic resource surely known of earlier but not to any real extent needed" (1976:6).

The earliest fairly certain evidence suggesting that *grind* whales were customarily killed by driving them ashore dates from around 1600. The geographer Peder Claussøn Friis mentioned what sounds like a *grindadráp* in 1592, and used the word "*hualsgrind*" to mean a school of whales (J. P. Joensen 1976:1). Müller (1883:1) claims that the Faroes' first recorded *grindadráp* was in 1584; but as this involved only four whales found stranded on Lítla Dímun— a most unsuitable island—a more likely candidate for the earliest true *grindadráp* on his list occurred in 1600. According to Müller, the four whales of 1584 were called "Nuydengur."[7] Lucas Debes, writing in 1673, says that *grind* whales are called both "*Grindehval*" and, from the character of their meat, "*Sø-kvæg*" (sea cattle) (Debes 1963:74,77). In other words, although "*grind*" was evidently the most widely favored term, there remained some ambiguity about these whales' names until well into the seventeenth century. There seems likewise to have been some doubt, or debate, about the ownership of *grind* whales. In 1619 the Løgting decided a case in which a man had captured two *grind* whales at sea after a *grindadráp* had failed. The Løgting judged that he owned them without having to pay the tithe (Zachariasen 1961:88 n.; cf. Wylie 1978:15 n.). This judgment was clearly based on the ancient prescriptions of the Gulatingslóg, but it also indicates that as the customs of the *grindadráp* became more settled, some decision had to be reached about the status of whales killed outside the *grindadráp*. Müller reckons that over forty-one hundred *grind* whales were taken in thirty-nine *grindadráp* between 1600 and 1640 (Müller 1883:15–16).

It thus seems reasonable to conclude from admittedly scanty data that the *grindadráp*, in something like its present form and with something like its present importance, dates from the sixteenth century, perhaps even from the late sixteenth century. This was indeed a most critical period in Faroese history—a time, as I have argued elsewhere, when the readjustment of relations between the Faroes and the continent after the Reformation ushered in two centuries or more during which royal policy and the interests of the trade monopoly "entailed the preservation of the Faroes as a backward but culturally and economically distinct 'province within the realm' (*indenrigs Provints*), as [the eighteenth-century *løgmaður*] Hans Debes called it" (Wylie 1978:34). If there is something atavistic, to use Jørgen-Frantz Jacobsen's term, about the emotions and behavior in a *grindadráp*, we are more likely to find them in the sixteenth and seventeenth centuries than in the Viking Age. We must ask two questions. Why should the *grindadráp* be so exciting in terms of Faroese life after the Reformation? And on what basis did Faroese develop the skills they still use for driving and slaughtering a *grind*?

We shall take up the second question first. The Faroese technique of driving and slaughtering a *grind* obviously combines those of fishing and herding sheep, the two pursuits on which the economy was based. The answer to the first question will be, briefly, that the *grindadráp* is so exciting partly because it combines these two crucial pursuits, partly because of the degree of unpredictability of a *grind*'s arrival, and partly because a hunt produced a most welcome and most anomalous item, particularly in hungry times—an "imported" food that did not have to be bought with exports.

The Faroese method for driving a *grind* is to some extent dictated by the whales themselves. Japanese and, I am told, Gilbert Islanders (Bernd Lambert, personal communication) have found, obviously independently of the Faroese, that whales may be driven by casting stones behind them. So have Shetlanders, Orkney-men, and Newfoundlanders, perhaps not wholly independently, each of whom has had a *grind* whale fishery (Williamson 1945:134ff.; Sergeant 1953, 1962). The species is notorious anyway for beaching itself in large numbers without human encouragement (see, for example, Scott 1942). Debes says that in the Faroes "sometimes the school of whales comes into the fjords itself, in thick mist, and no one drives it in; sometimes on dark nights with the flood tide it runs in onto the sand, and when the ebb comes they lie dry on the sand, so that when people come out in the morning they see the sand lying full of dead whales, which happened recently a few years ago in Tjørnuvík" (1963 [1673]:76). No one knows why this happens; but when the whales find themselves close to shore they seem to orient themselves partly by sight, sticking their heads out of the water when they *grinda*, for example, as if for a look around. Svabo wrote in 1779:

> When the school has come a bit inside the whale-bay, it escapes less often even if it panics since most such bays appear cut off on the side facing the sea either by a protruding point or by another island. It happens, though, that the school will not enter the bay when it sights land; one must then try to trick the school by setting heavily smoking bonfires at the head of the bay so that the whales think that there can be a way out to open water there. [1779:44; the translation here follows J. P. Joensen 1976:12–13]

Similarly, a *grindamjørki* is a thick fog in which a *grind* may go astray between the islands.

Being keen students of the *grind*, Faroese have also noted that "when cuttlefish come ashore a *grind* is to be expected soon" (A.

Dahl 1931:52)—for *grind* whales feed on cuttlefish. The crane-fly (*Tipula oleracea*) is called a *grindalokkur* because, as it comes out in late summer, its appearance is said to presage the coming of a *grind*. I have been told that *grindir* most often appear in calm weather with a north wind, preceding a spell of bad weather. A *grindaregn* (properly *grimdaregn*, a violent rain) is held to "be associated with the arrival of a *grind*" (Jacobsen and Matras 1961).

Such close observations, matter-of-fact as they are, suggest one of the most important things about *grindir*—how unpredictably they come. There is a slight tension in the air in late summer, or whenever a *grind* has been sighted not far off. The first summer I spent in the Faroes, I stayed for ten days on Skúvoy. My host there spent his idle moments looking out the window over the fjord. I got to looking, too, and we would stand there silently together, not quite presuming to hope, as his wife set the table behind us. Jørgen-Frantz Jacobsen writes:

> *Grindir* are not always discovered from the sea. Often they are first seen from land. They can show themselves at all times of year, but most frequently in July and August. At these times it often happens that old enthusiasts of the *grind* undertake mysterious walks in the hills, preferably at night or in the early morning hours. Here they go alone—as it were by chance—and gaze out over the sea. But everyone knows what they are thinking of. They want to have the honor of being the first to discover a *grind*. It gives not only fame, but also a timely reward—if the finder can be the first to come out to the *grind* in a boat. Then he will get as pay the largest whale, the "*finningarhvalur.*" [1970:57–58]

A *grind*, then, may come at any time, and may touch any part of the Faroese world. Awaiting a *grind* today, one feels as never otherwise—except in winter storms, and then for different reasons—how isolated the Faroes are, how immense is the sea, and how broad the fjords between one island and the next. It is easy to appreciate how hopefully a *grind* must have been awaited in the days when a *grindadráp* meant a better chance of surviving the winter. In the seventeenth century especially, the winters were long and harsh, and there was always the chance that the merchant ships upon which life in the Faroes depended might not show up. The terrible winter of 1601/2 was followed by worse ones. "With few exceptions, the seventeenth century was a continuing series of bad fishing years" (J. S. Hansen 1966:113). Some years the crops failed too, or the sheep died, or all three things happened at once, so that everyone went hungry and the poor people died. Fishing for home consumption (and to a smaller extent for export) had always been important in the Faroese economy, and in these lean fishing years "the islands grew more dependent on imports of grain" (ibid.). But warfare on the continent made grain expensive or unobtainable, and Denmark was at war in the periods 1563–70, 1611–12, 1624–28, 1643–45, 1657–60, 1675–79, and 1709–20. The ships—perhaps one or two a year—might not be able to leave Copenhagen, which was the only legal port for the Faroe trade after 1619. And to make matters worse, the Faroes were oppressively administered from 1661 to 1708 by the Danish courtier Christoffer von Gabel and his son Frederik. According to Andersen, "the populace could not very well have been worse off, because the owners of the trade allowed the constant deficiency of what is, for a people whose main livelihood is fishing, just as necessary as grain-wares, namely timber for boats" (1895:79). But, as J. S. Hansen points out, "people had to live: the imports of grain increased, and now that there was no fish to pay for the grain with, wool-working had to do it, so that now became more and more the principal pursuit" (1966:113).

A *grind*, now, was a true anomaly in Faroese life—an import, as it were, for which nothing had to be traded. A *grind*, being a herd (*flokkur*, also "flock") of sea animals, also combines the characteristics of sheep and fish, and the *grindadráp* is carried out in much the same way, and in much the same language, as sheep herding and fishing, the twin foundations of, respectively, the Faroes' export economy and their subsistence economy.

Rakstrarmenn are either sheep herders or *grind* hunters, and as Svabo says, "it goes as a rule in the Faroes that a *grind* must be driven like a sheep into the pen, i.e., the boats must not row in front of it but only at the sides or behind" (1959:251). Sheep and whales both come in groups (*flokkar*), are herded in a drive (*rakstur*, *grindarakstur*, *seyðarakstur*), and are shared out in a division (*býti*, *grindabýti*, *seyðabýti*). Both are marked (*merkja*) for ownership, lambs by ear cuts and *grind* whales by incised numbers on their fins and head. Sheep and whales are further identified in the Faroese attitude toward killing them, namely, as mercifully as possible. The whales are killed as swiftly and efficiently as the circumstances allow, just as nowadays, when modern weaponry is available, sheep are usually shot in the brain before they are bled, although people say this makes the meat less good. (A similar technique has been tried on *grind* whales, but has "proved highly dangerous for the participating hunters and unnecessarily painful for the whales. It has, therefore, been long forbidden to use other weapons than the traditional" [J. P. Joensen 1976:19–20].)

The most prized part of both sheep and whales is the fat. Whale fat (*spik*, also, generically, the blubber of sea mammals) is a particular delicacy, reputed to act as an aphrodisiac and ward off sea sickness. But here the two species differ; sheep fat (*tálg*) is taken from around the internal organs, and is combined with meat or fish to be eaten. *Spik*, which blankets the whole animal, is eaten along with *grind* meat or fish, but is not combined with it in the preparation. *Grind* is perhaps more like fish than mutton in this way, for fish is also served with an accompanying fat—"dried" (i.e., salted) *spik*, cured tallow, or butter or margarine. *Grind* whales, of course, resemble fish in coming from the sea, and their kinship surfaces most clearly in the occasional use of -*fiskur* for -*hvalur* in such phrases as *finningarfiskur* for *finningarhvalur* ("finder's whale," the largest in the *grind*).

Otherwise, the use of fishing skills in chasing a *grind* needs little comment. Rowing is common to both, for example, though a *grindaróður* (*grind* rowing) is the especially hard rowing needed to pull up to a *grind* in time. A *grindaformaður* (*grind* foreman) leads the chase, while an ordinary *formaður* is the leader of any crew. A *kast* (cast, throw) is, among other things, the stone or weight thrown into the sea to herd a *grind*, and the cast of a fishing net. A *lína* is usually a line or rope used in fishing (or on the bird cliffs), while a *grindalína* is one used in the *grindadráp* (Hammershaimb 1891, 2:96).

In short, a *grind* and *grind* whales combine the characteristics of sheep and fish, and the *grindadráp* combines features of sheep herding and fishing, as these have been adapted to conditions set by the behavior of the whales themselves. At the same time, a *grind* represents in the unpredictability of its coming and in the need for it, the imports upon which life in the Faroes has always depended— and never more so than in the seventeenth century. It is, however, an anomalous arrival from the sea, since it need not be feared (like pirates) or paid for (like timber and grain).

Grindadráp: *Doing Everything Right*

The *grind* has been driven close to shore. There is a pause, an almost-silence. You watch the black fins rise smoothly above the waves, and sink down again. You pick out the foreman's boat, flying the Faroese flag. He chooses his moment, and spears the whale he hopes will lead the rest ashore. *Blóðið kemur inn*—"the blood comes in."

But let us leave the men to their work, and consider the people who are *not* here. Old people tell you "it's a custom" that women should not see the slaughter. In fact few women were present at either of the *grindadráp* I have witnessed, at Miðvágur and Húsavík. In the late eighteenth century, according to Svabo, pregnant women were forbidden to watch the chase or the ensuing slaughter, lest the whales "grow shy and wild" (1959:252). He goes on to say that after the failure of a *grindadráp* in 1781, in the bay by which Klaksvík has now been built up, "the men in this village have decided amongst themselves that, when a *grind* comes, it should be a responsibility for the old men in each farmstead, who could not be along [on the hunt] to prevent the womenfolk from seeing the *grind*."

This seems a curious belief. For one thing, it is clear that women do play an important part in the whole of the *grindadráp*— in those aspects of it which most obviously distinguish the Faroese activity from the Shetlanders' degenerate slaughtering and the Newfoundlanders' purely commercial enterprise. Women prepare the meal of fresh *grind* after the slaughter; they may take part in the dance, and such has been the men's haste to get to sea, the signal fires of the *grindaboð* "were most often lit by women" (J.-F. Jacobsen 1970:58). Moreover, women have occasionally taken part in the hunt itself, at least since the end of the nineteenth century. *Føringatíðindi* closed its report of a *grindadráp* in Tórshavn on 5 August 1896, in which a *grind* of 111 whales died, with the comment, "The women of Nólsoy also took part in the *dráp*—because too few of the menfolk were at home—, and it seemed to most people that they were just as strong and zealous as other *grindamenn*." Williamson (1970:115) tells a story about a *grindadráp* which took place in the mid-1930s in Hvalba. While the men of the village were off hunting a *grind* somewhere else, the cry of "*Grindaboð!*" went up in Hvalba itself. The women took to the boats and, led by the priest and a *grind* foreman, hunted and slaughtered a thousand whales by themselves. A Hvalba man confirmed this story to me, but said the *grind* was not so big.

As a rule, however, women do not take part in the chase or the slaughter, and though they are not now forbidden to help, they are not much in evidence in the lines of people hauling the whales to land. The old prohibition noted by Svabo was clearly exceptional; the second half of the eighteenth century was practically *grind*-less, and during that time such superstitions may have become more pronounced as people sought quasi-magical means to insure the success of a hunt. Still, why keep women away? I would suggest that just as the appearance of a *grind* calls into active, practical play all the most important organizational principles in Faroese society, so, by extension, the success of a hunt might sometimes have seemed to depend on fine-tuning the social order, even when this could have no immediate practical purpose. Thus, for example, since women's and men's work roles are strongly differentiated anyway, the hunt's success may have seemed to depend on keeping the eminently male work of herding, seafaring, and slaughtering out of women's sight.

A tendency to set matters just right on shore while the hunt goes on at sea also helps explain several other curious customs associated with the *grindadráp*. In at least one village, for example, it was once believed that "the priest should not be within the *grind*, because then it will not die. He should either row out around the *grind* or else go into the church, if he is in the place" (A. Dahl 1931:52). In other words, the priest must establish himself in one or the other of his two main identities; he must be a man "like other men" and take part in the *grindadráp*, or else he must be a priest and go inside the church. Similarly, it was long a custom—Svabo noted it in the eighteenth century—that if a *grindadráp* was going badly the church door would be opened to make the whales ground themselves faster. I have been told that in some places it was customary to open the little bell-door on the steeple. That is, the village should look as if it were a Sunday morning. Several other elements seem to enter into this belief. First, there is an element of fooling the whales, based partly on their reputation for good eyesight; if they "see" the village looking like a Sunday morning, when Faroese do no work, they may not "realize" the fatal significance of the splashing behind them. (Little do they know. As Norgate says, "a whale killing is the only thing which will persuade the Faeroese to raise their hands on Sundays"; and, as Jacobsen (1970:58) remarks, "If one were sitting in church [when the *grindaboð* was raised] and listening to the service, one would promptly shut up the hymnal and let the priest be a priest.")

Second, there seems to have been an association between priests and the success of a *grindadráp*, evidenced for example in the wryly humorous compounds *grindaprestur* and *grindatrøll*. A *grindaprestur* is a priest during whose tenure many *grindir* come, while a *grindatrøll* (literally, "*grind* troll" or "*grind* hex") is a priest or sheriff during whose tenure few *grindir* come. The priest, an exceptional person himself, is even more so in that he alone among all figures in Faroese society has no special part to play in the *grindadráp*, and may thus logically be linked with the exceptional occurrence of a *grind*'s appearance. Also, since he has oversight of the congregation's spiritual life, and mediates between life and death for the members of his flock, it might be felt risky for him to mingle with the "flock" of whales as they are driven to the kill.[8]

The hunt ends when the *grind* is dead. So far, the action has been mostly practical, devoted to passing the *grindaboð* about the land, herding the *grind* to a suitable bay, and killing it as expeditiously as possible. It has been a very exciting affair, from the elation of the *grindaboð* to the wild work of the slaughter, and one way or another it has been universally involving. The news has been passed far and wide. Crews have come and worked together. The sheriff is there. And, according to some old customs, women and the priest have been put in their places.

Culturally, however, the real drama is yet to come. For this universal mobilization has also provoked a crisis; after all the exaltation, how may things be returned to normal? It is a crisis on every level. Legally, the *grind* is dead, but it is not yet owned. It is no longer a collectivity of whales, but it is not yet a kind of food. There is an immediate emotional and practical problem; while the whales are being valued, what are we going to do all night with the cold, wet, armed, bloody, worked-up, and perhaps drunken men who have appeared in town? The *grind* will not be apportioned until morning. The men won't go home till then. So far, the hunters have dealt with creatures of the sea; now the state and church must be taken into account in the person of the sheriff and the institutions of taxes and tithes. There is an economic and social problem; who will get how many *skinn*? What claims does a landowner have as opposed to a landless crewman on one of the boats? How much meat will stay in the village and how much will go home with the hunters? Perhaps most basically, then, in terms of fundamental values, how may the general egalitarianism and cooperativeness of Faroese life be reconciled with the ranked categories of crewman and foreman, "Danish" official and Faroese peasant, ordinary *rakstrarmaður* and participants with special functions?

The hunt is over. The night's work now consists of recreating Faroese society. It has two parts, which go on simultaneously—the popular celebration and the official business of apportionment.

Grindadansur: *The Celebration of Self-control*

When the whales' carcasses have been dragged up beyond the reach of the tide, people begin to drift away from the shore. They may do various things: most drop in on friends for a rest, a chat, or a bite to eat and drink; some men may begin drinking heavily; and, in times past, some would engage in contests of strength. Within a couple of hours everyone, strangers and village folk alike, will partake of a meal of fresh *grind* from the *matarhvalur* ("food whale"), which has been set aside and butchered at once. The meal, and to some extent the visiting around, are institutionalized, and are calming. The drinking and the contests of strength are neither.

Nowadays, at least, the drinking at a *grindadráp* is sometimes so common that it might be called epidemic. As a rule, only men drink in the Faroes, and they drink to get drunk. Particularly at festival times, they go from house to house and bottle to bottle, proclaiming their inebriation by walking wildly and unsteadily, bursting into song and becoming exaggeratedly friendly. It is a far cry from the usual methodical gait and quietspoken reserve of Faroese. Men often act drunk after only one or two drinks—long before I, at least, could even feel the effect of the alcohol, let alone think, in accordance with the prescriptions of my own culture, that I should show how well I hold my liquor. A drunken man is almost literally not himself; "beer is another man," as the old saying has it (Hammershaimb 1891,1:321). A drunken man is irresponsible—not always pleasantly so. In the village where I did field work, quarreling (which is studiously avoided) is often blamed on there being "liquor involved in it" ("*tað var brennivín uppi í*"). This is an old way of thinking. In 1622, for example, a lawsuit involving a farmer named Mikkjal and the representatives to the Eysturoy spring parliament was partly resolved after the representatives "admitted to the Løgting that they had said these hard words about Mikkjal under the influence of liquor and thoughtlessly, and asked for forgiveness. . . . [They] said, then, that they had been drunk at the Selatrað spring parliament in 1622; but the Norwegian lawbook required that representatives should be sober in their functions" (Zachariasen 1961:299).

Most drinking is social and celebratory, and thus often takes place on the same occasions as dancing: over Christmas and New Years, for example; before Lent; and, especially, at Ólavsøka, or Saint Olaf's Wake, the holiday on 29 July at the opening of the yearly parliamentary session. Sometimes there are institutional checks on the effects of alcohol—as when wedding guests are offered a single welcoming glass of liquor when they come to the wedding feast—but otherwise things tend to get a little out of hand. As Debes wrote, "They do not use to make any debauch in drink among themselves; except about Christmas, and then here, as in other places, they chear themselves with a joyfull and merry cup; yet we cannot say that they are all free from drunkenness with Brandy, which is lately come to *Feroe*, but specially among the less understanding, and those that have scarce wherewith to pay" (1676:272–73).

Drinking thus resembles dancing in some ways. Both involve changed gaits and kinds of speech; both are done rarely, and then in binges; and both take place mostly at times when Faroese are brought to face the world outside everyday village life: the arrival of a *grind*, religious holidays, the opening of the parliamentary session, and such festivals of transition as weddings. But drinking is, for all this, the opposite of dancing; it entails a loss of self-control, and marks the discontinuity of transitional times rather than the passage over them. Nor, in a practical sense, do drinking and dancing mix. However "primitive," "wild," or "monotonous" it seems to foreigners—opinions differ; the young Englishman James Wright noted in his diary in 1789 that he "did not relish it much, as the music is detestable and no variety in the measure" (West 1970:43)— Faroese dancing is an exercise in continuity and self-control. It links the dancers with their legendary past, mingles all members of the community and focuses their activity. It removes conflicts from the realm of everyday life to a story realm, while the dancers coordinate their voices and movements. "What, moreover, should be well looked after in the ballad singing is to 'get the word under the foot,' as the old ones used to say. One gets the word under the foot when one stresses one word or syllable at the same time that one steps along with the foot" (Jakobsen 1906). But drinkers are only men, and women are not interested in dancing with drunks or fending off their attentions. Their movements are uncoordinated. And although liquor may have blurred whatever hostility among men is left over from the hunt, it fails to direct their attention to any common enterprise except discovering another bottle and sharing its contents.

These comments on drinking at a *grindadráp* are drawn partly from my notes on one I attended at Miðvágur. I also got the impression that night that the general excitement spills over in a sexual direction—another potential source of discord, which is otherwise undercut by the male camaraderie and the nonpairing of sexes in the ballad dancing. I was kidded the next morning for having accepted an invitation to breakfast at the house of a woman whose husband had been away fishing for months, and on the way home I was told indecent stories and taught obscene words. This was the only time I found Faroese to be anything but circumspect and matter-of-fact in sexual matters.

The hunters' general excitement is thus potentially threatening in many ways. But in the normal course of events it is channeled and eventually attenuated by the customary meal of fresh *grind* and, especially, by the dance. Both these activities involve women, and the meal, of course, involves them in their culturally central roles—mistress of the household and purveyor of hospitality. In the great visiting-about after a *grindadráp* most men probably call on kinsmen and old friends. In theory, however, anyone is welcome at any house. This accentuates the usual Faroese customs of visiting, and except for the number of men about from other villages, and the fact that many of them may be drunk, the village ambience rather resembles that of a Sunday, or of a funeral day when visitors have come to *fylgja* ("follow" the coffin to the graveyard).

The dance begins in the evening. Traditionally, dances are held on transitional occasions; often, therefore, since some transitions are also marked by church services, dances provide a kind of counterpoint to religious ceremonies. The dances after Christmas, and at the new year, and each Sunday until Lent, are a popular counterweight to the Christian God's coming and going, which are celebrated in church. "At many places in the Faroes . . . in the old days when one went to church where it was ice-cold during the winter, one traditionally danced oneself warm [*'dansa seg heitan'*] when the church service was over" (J. P. Joensen 1976:21). There is a wedding dance—a social joining of the couple's family and friends after the church ceremony and a festive meal, but before they consummate their marriage privately. People also danced, traditionally, at parties for those who had helped to get the hay in, for men who had gone to fetch the doctor, for a young man who had landed a halibut in his first season as a full-fledged fisherman, and so forth.

I have mentioned a somewhat tense *grindadansur* I attended at Miðvágur. The *grind* had been very small, many men were very drunk, and the townspeople knew that most if not all of the *grind* would go to the hunters—many of them, including myself, hunters only nominally, in that they had been present when the slaughter took place and had given their names to the sheriff. The stabilizing function of the ballad dancing was illustrated by the increased tension that nearly broke through in fights when some adolescents played pop tunes for "English dancing" on a record player. At a more neighborly *grindadansur* at Húsavík later in the year, an accordion player led some more popular "English dancing." This *grind* had also been very small, but there were more women at this dance, and so far as I know everyone came from the island of Sandoy. Men drank less than the hunters had at Miðvágur. Despite some disappointment at the *grind*'s size, the dancers' familiarity with each other and their closeness to home called more informal social controls into play. The dance broke up some time after two in the morning, and the people went home to snatch a few hours' sleep before the division of the spoils in the morning. Traditionally, it would have gone on all night long.

It may be worth recapitulating some of the things a *grindadansur* does. It keeps the hunters busy, while wearing off the excitement left over from the hunt. It links the day of the slaughter and the day of the division of the spoils. It reunites men and women. It mingles visitors and villagers, and hunters and those who, come morning, will own some of the *grind* meat from the hunted *grind* whales. It also mingles in a common activity all grades of hunters, while shifting the focus of attention from their differing specialties to those of the leaders of the ballad singing—and the leaders of the singing shift from one ballad to the next. Its regular and repetitious steps and refrains offer a collectively enjoyable way of attenuating with vigorous but controlled movement the more individualistic exertions of the hunt. The ballads recall the ancient past, about which no one disagrees—in contrast to the present. The ballads link the legendary past and the outside world, establishing the Faroes' place in a wider world. Dancing is, moreover, one of the few activities in which all Faroese—and only Faroese—may participate fully; foreigners may learn the steps, but are unlikely to learn the words, let alone become *skiparar* (leaders). The dancing thus distinguishes the popular culture from the official management of Faroese affairs, as represented by the sheriff and his appointees. In short, it is a controlled and self-controlling exercise, which, as it effects the passage from one meaning of *grind* to another, goes a long way toward reconstituting Faroese society.

Grindabýti: *The Division in Time*

We have gone off visiting, had a bite to eat and a drink or two, danced all night, and left the sheriff by the shore. And in leaving him to his business we have also lost sight of the *grindadráp*'s place in Faroese history.

The office of sheriff (*sýslumaður*) in the Faroes probably dates from the late twelfth century, when the Norwegian king began appointing local men to oversee the administration of justice in each small district in the realm. In the Faroes, at least, the sheriffs were responsible to the bailiff (*fúti*), an office that had been established around 1035. The bailiff was originally a tax collector. The sheriffs and the bailiff were part of a system of royal administration complementing the even older system of judicial parliaments (*ting*), whose independent powers and prerogatives they increasingly circumscribed.[9] The bailiffs were foreign—Danish, since Copenhagen took over directly the oversight of Faroese government at the Reformation—while the sheriffs have always been Faroese, although until 1948 the law they represented was largely promulgated abroad.

The sheriff takes charge of the *grind* when it has been killed. He has two main duties: to guard the whales, and to measure them and decide their apportionment. In addition, he must see to the grappling-up of any whales that died in the water and sank. Since most of his time is taken up with the measuring and apportionment, he delegates watchman's authority to local men.

There is of course a practical purpose behind setting a watch over the whales; thievery is not unknown in the Faroes, and it seems from Svabo's comments that in the late eighteenth century it was "not considered thievery but, rather, pluck or manliness to steal *grind*" (1959:256). Jørgen Landt, following Svabo, similarly decried the pilferage of *grind*, and lamented that there was inadequate policing of the shore (Landt 1800:398–99; cf. J. P. Joensen 1976:25–26; I can find no such passage in the 1810 English translation of Landt).

The problem of thievery is something we may come back to in

a moment, when we take up the rules of distribution. Today what strikes the observer is how unconcernedly the hunters seem to abandon their catch on the shore. For conceptually as well as legally it is a critical time; the whales are no longer a wild and unowned sea-*grind*, but they have not yet become apportioned pieces of *grind* meat. The ritual danger of this time is partly obviated by the socializing, the meal of fresh meat, and especially the dance; but the sheriff's oversight of the dead *grind* also has a ritual element. The *grind* is not really abandoned, but left under the care of the official arm of Faroese culture, which thus takes its place in the recreation of the social order even as most people are recreating it unofficially in the dance.

I do not want to suggest that the ritual danger of this intermediate period is acute; but the sense that a *grind* must not be left unattended between its death and its final apportionment also comes out in less common customs that seem at first glance to have as purely practical an intent as the watch set by the sheriff. Sámal Johansen describes what happened to the *grind* brought back from a *grindadráp* in Miðvágur as the share for the villagers of Vík:

> Then the *grind* was unloaded, but nothing was done about its distribution before the men had slept. The boats were drawn up and washed, and when that was done [the crew of] sixteen tired men went to bed.
>
> But the *grind* could not lie unattended, and thus it was sat up over. They "sat up over *grind*" or "watched up over *grind*" when the *grind* came to the village late in the evening, or, as on this occasion, at night. It was not because they were afraid that people were going to take some of it, but so that animals— rats, cats, and the birds of the sky [or, birds of heaven: *himmalsins fuglar*]—would not disturb it. It was mostly children, boys and girls, and then some older people who sat up over *grind*. [1970:102]

The "older people" are all women in this account, and it seems, as Johansen remembers it, that this was more a time for games and storytelling than of anxious lookout for rats, cats, and the birds of the sky. The underlying fear seems to be that part of an unwatched *grind* might pass beyond control. This obviously parallels the fear of thievery, and it could be dealt with in much the same way; that is, by setting over it a watch of people so far not involved in the hunt (the old people and children; the sheriff) and by expressing obliquely (in stories and ballads) the enduring norms of social life.

The basic principle of distributing the catch is an application of old Norse law to the peculiar nature of whales, which can be hunted at sea but slaughtered on shore. A man owned whatever he could get from the sea; but the owner of a piece of land owned its produce and whatever washed up on his beaches. The catch thus had to be divided somehow between the hunter and the landowner. This "somehow" has changed considerably over the centuries. We need not take up each little change, but we should note that in general the rules for distributing the *grind* provide a kind of Faroese social history in miniature.[10]

I have already cited the late medieval Norwegian codification, the Gulatingslóg, whereby the hunter of a whale that was driven ashore was entitled to half the catch, while "the land" owned the other half. According to the Seyðabræv, an official version of customary Faroese law set down in 1298 which in effect established acceptable local deviations from continental practice, the hunters' share was one quarter of the catch, while the landowner's share was three quarters (Petersen 1968:295). There is now a long gap in the records, but Zachariasen (1961:96) surmises that the Seyðabræv's proportion was used until about the time of the Black Death around 1350; between then and the early seventeenth century, customs evidently came to vary considerably from place to place and from time to time (cf. Petersen 1968:42).

What is certain is that by 1673, when Debes described the system in some detail, a fairly simple elaboration of medieval practices had been worked out, which took into account both the discoverer of the *grind*, and the church, as well as the hunters and the landowners: "When all the whales are thus pulled up onto dry land and are counted, the tithe is first taken out; next the finding-whale for him who first saw it; the remainder is divided into two parts, the one part for the people, the other to him who owns the land, whether this be the king, a noble, or a freehold-farmer" (1963:76). Debes does not say who "the people" were—presumably they were the hunters—nor who was in charge of the hunt or the distribution, but "it is apparent from our earliest sources that after the school was dead the [sheriff] assumed leadership for the affair" (J. P. Joensen 1976:20).

The laws received further codification and elaboration in 1709/10, when the Danish king took over the trade monopoly and attempted to regularize, and so improve, the lot of his Faroese subjects.[11] What might be called governmental shares now increased. First the finder's whale, the largest in the school, was set aside, and the rest were marked by men appointed by the bailiff—in practice probably most often by the sheriff and his own appointees. Then the tithe went to the church, while five whales went to officials or institutions of the church and state: the leprosarium outside Tórshavn, the dean of the Faroes' church, the bailiff, and the parliamentary secretary (*sorinskrivari*). One whale was sold to repay damages to men and equipment during the hunt. The remainder was divided equally between the hunters and "the land." The hunters' share was subdivided according to the extent of the hunters' participation in the hunt. It is not quite clear, at least to me, what happened to the land's share. If the land—that is, the shore where the whales were killed—was freehold, or to the extent that it was, the land's share was taken by the farmer or farmers who owned it. But just over half of the land in the Faroes was owned by the crown, and thus the king often owned all the land's share. It seems from Svabo's comments that toward the end of the century, at least, the sheriff sold off the crown's share; I cannot make out what recompense tenant farmers received.

It is clear, however, that during the eighteenth century the customs for dividing up the catch diversified again, and may even have grown rather haphazard. This may have been due in part to the virtual disappearance of the *grind* between 1745 and 1795. It may also have accompanied an increase in the disorder of the hunt itself; certainly, Svabo at the end of the eighteenth century and Landt at the beginning of the nineteenth give impressions of the hunt and distribution of the spoils far removed from the apparent unanimity of action described by Debes in 1673. Some competition and rivalry has perhaps always been associated with the *grindadráp*—Johannesen (1976:8) records an undated but apparently modern case in which the men of one village tricked those of another into arriving too late at a *grindadráp*. But according to Svabo, the size of the land's share led to attempts to drive the whales into bays where one or another faction among the hunters might receive larger land shares. "One argues and complains vigorously about this instead of paying attention to the hunt, and it is certainly not always the best advice which is followed" (Svabo 1779:52; Joensen's translation [1976:23]).

The law was changed in 1832, with supplementary modifications in 1837 and 1839. The new laws took the form of royal decrees, since at this time the Faroes had no home government. In this as in other matters, however, the king was evidently moved to try to improve the lives of his subjects in this backward new county (*amt*), and in doing so he followed the advice of the enlightened if sometimes condescending governors (Danish *amtmænd*) with whom the Faroes were now blessed, after centuries of arbitrary rule and misrule. Surely the Danish bailiff, Christian Pløyen, a great afficionado of the *grindadráp* who became governor in 1837, was among the "knowledgeable men" referred to by Petersen:

> The king had taken into consideration how it was best to manage this occupation, which had no fast rules in law, and how it would be fitting to set forth fast rules about the drive, the shares, and the distribution. Then it should be added that the king made use of previously valid arrangements with appropriate changes which a majority of Faroese had desired, and after consultation with knowledgeable men he put them together in a regulation. [1968:83]

The new laws reflect both the diminishing importance of agriculture in the 1830s, and the crown's and governors' desire to stimulate the Faroese economy. The main change was that the land's share was reduced to one quarter of the catch. All or part of the king's own share was put up for sale "within decided areas," while the rest, "after officials, teachers, and for example the poor [in Tórshavn] had gotten [shares], was put back in the whales to be shared by hunters" (Petersen 1968:81). As of 1839, the proceeds from the sale went into what Müller, later in the century, called "an economical fund for the Faroe *amt*," to be used in such projects as building bridges and landing places.

The laws of 1832 were modified several times later in the century. As pauperism declined with the growth of the commercial fishery, the paupers' part of the king's share was abolished; and as the royal administration ceased to be paid in kind, with a cut of Faroese products, the officials' whales were no longer set aside. The tithe on fish was abolished in 1892, and on whales and other products in 1908. But the crucial modification in the law of 1832 was to enlarge the definition of *rakstrarmaður* ("pursuit man," hunter) to include all the inhabitants of the district where the *grindadráp* took place. As Müller says, "by Ragstemand is understood not only the men that have been at the butchering, but the entire population of the district which is regulated as belonging to the whale voe [bay], with a view to which a census is taken once every year" (1883:13). The actual hunters, however, continued to receive a special share.

Further modifications were proposed by "an old *grindamaður*" in a letter published on the front page of *Føringatíðindi* on 16 March

1899. Pointing out that "the *grind* regulations have often been changed in such a way as the times have pressed men to," he argued that "the catch and profits of the *grind* catch could be [used] for universal advantage." His recommendations included diminishing the landowners' share. This foreshadowed new regulations put forth in 1909, whereby the state bought out the landowners' share with the proceeds from the sale of those whales which had previously gone to the tithe. In 1935 the landowners' share was abolished outright.[12]

Two more changes in the law of 1832 should be mentioned. From 1832 to 1909, and then in theory until 1948, the governor was nominally in charge of the *grindadráp*. From 1832 to 1857, the actual leaders of the chase and slaughter, the *grindaformenn*, were appointed by the sheriff in each district; since 1857 they have been elected. The importance of special *grind* districts has increased, however, since their first formal definition in 1832. *Grind* districts, of which there are nine in the Faroes, do not necessarily coincide with administrative districts (*sýslur*). They overlap, so that a given village may be part of two or even three *grind* districts. The districts are censused each year, and their populations are reckoned in "boat's shares" (*bátspartar*) of about fifty people each.

Thus the present system has grown up, and has most recently been codified in laws passed in 1955 and 1970. Rights to shares of the *grind* are determined by (1) participation or special duties in the *grindadráp*, and (2) residence in the *grind* district where the kill took place. Here is the modern version, as the sheriff of Vestmanna explained it to me in the summer of 1970.

The first sighter of the *grind* gets the largest whale, which he may exchange for two smaller whales totaling the same weight or less. The two measuring men appointed by the sheriff get one *skinn* per one hundred whales marked. The four *grind* foremen in the district each get 1 percent of the *grind*, no matter which of them led this particular hunt. The sheriff gets 2 percent. These are the fixed shares.

Then the sheriff, having heard all claims for damages to boats and equipment—and injuries to men—auctions off enough whales to pay for repairs. A maximum sale price is set by law (it was twenty-five *krónur* per *skinn* in the summer of 1970), to which 14 percent is added—10 percent for the sheriff and 4 percent for a state tax. (A *skinn* generally runs about 150 pounds.)

The rest of the division depends on the size of the *grind*. If it is large enough, each hunter who has given his name to the sheriff receives a fixed amount of *grind* (and blubber) for each day spent on the hunt. The sheriff tries to arrange things so that each crew gets a whole whale to divide up. The captains of each boat are responsible for sharing out their crewmen's share and their own. The rest is divided equally among all the "boat's shares" in the *grind* district. In addition, following an old custom, any visitors who have registered with the sheriff before the slaughter are granted a share.

If, however, the *grind* proves too small to provide at least one *skinn* for each "boat's share," half of the catch remaining after the fixed shares have been apportioned is divided among the hunters, while the other half is auctioned off. The proceeds of the auction go into what Müller, the present sheriff's predecessor in Vestmanna, would have called an "economical fund" for the town.

It will be appreciated that the sheriff is very busy with paperwork through the night. The result of his labors is the slips of paper (*seðlar*) which "come out" in the morning, on which each representative of groups entitled to receive a share of *grind* reads the number of his whale. The men gather to receive their slips, and then walk down to the shore to butcher their whales.

The *grindadráp* has its own history, as the development of the system of sharing out the *grind* suggests. This history in many ways mirrors Faroese history as a whole: in the adaptation and elaboration of ancient ("Viking") ways to the circumstances of life on these islands, in the establishment of a more isolated and more peculiarly Faroese culture in the late sixteenth and early seventeenth centuries, in the increasing importance of the Danish officialdom, in the role of local figures, and in the shifting relative importance of sheep herding and fishing as the twin foundations of the Faroese economy. The *grindadráp* has remained a mirror of each stage of Faroese cultural development largely because, although *grindir* come often enough that traditional patterns of dealing with them can grow up, persist, and be changed as need be, they come seldom enough that the *grindadráp* must remain an exceptional business. The *grindadráp* requires a concerted effort to make something Faroese, and entails a concentrated and heightened enactment of the norms of everyday life, and of those by which the Faroes' relations with the "outside" worlds of nature, foreign overlords, and the heroic past are adjusted.

At times, however, the *grindadráp* has been a rather poor mirror. During the late eighteenth century few *grindir* came; it seems from Svabo's and Landt's comments, that the *grindadráp* became a quite degenerate undertaking. And during the middle of the nineteenth century so many *grindir* came that the *grindadráp* nearly became a commercial enterprise, which may even have contributed to the decisive beginnings, from about 1830 on, of Faroese modernization. In the 1840s "the value of exports of oil [tried from the whales] was greater than that of fish" (Petersen 1968:47; cf. Degn 1929, Patursson 1961:14, and Müller 1883:12–13). It may have been around the same time that, according to an undated clipping from a (Scottish?) paper called *John O'Groat's Journal*, "during the last six weeks the inhabitants of the Faroe Islands captured no fewer than the extraordinary number of two thousand eight hundred whales. A whole cargo of whalebone has been despatched from that island to England. It is intended for manure." There were not so many *grindadráp* in the second half of the century, but on 17 August 1889, after a remarkable week in which some two thousand whales were killed on Vágar and another three hundred in Vestmanna, *Føringatíðindi* commented disapprovingly that "there is now considered to be a surplus of *grind*, so that much is not rightly used, but lies and spoils, some whales with the blubber on, and many with the meat." In other words, surplus as well as dearth may diminish the *grindadráp*'s aptness as a cultural text. The crucial legal and cultural problems of distributing the catch disappear if no whales are ever caught, and become trivial if so many are caught that there is more than enough for everyone. Also, if *grindir* came regularly the *grindadráp* would join the round of ordinary pursuits, while their coming would be less characteristic of the general precariousness of conditions for life in the Faroes. As a rule, as Debes said, "God . . . taketh care [the Faroese] should not have satiety of all things at one time" (1676:163).

Appreciations of the Grindadráp's *Importance*

We have now followed the course of the *grindadráp* as a single event and as it has developed over several centuries of repetition. We have traced some of its associations to other aspects of Faroese life. Let us conclude by looking at the modern *grindadráp* in a rather different light—as a self-consciously organized event, and as a literary one.

I have already quoted a man who in 1899 wrote to the editor of *Føringatíðindi* that "the *grind* regulations have often been changed in such a way as the times have pressed men to." He was right, of course—but by whom, in recent times, have the regulations been changed, and in accordance with what pressures and sentiments?

The most detailed and precisely datable changes in the *grindadráp* have been in the rules for distributing the catch. Ancient and in principle fairly simple, these were given their first modern codification in 1832 by the Faroes' Danish administrators, who around this time were exceptionally able and well-intentioned men; they were not only the virtual rulers of the Faroes but also—what was new—career civil servants with no interest in using their position to enter the upper levels of traditional Faroese society.[13] They respected the Faroese, though perhaps rather condescendingly by modern standards. Much of their work was directed toward the creation of a more modern Faroese economy. Thus the reforms of 1832 and their later codicils in a way resemble their predecessor, the codification of 1709/10, in establishing an official, standard version of already existing local customs. The reforms go further, however. The diminishment of the land's share, the use of monies made by selling some whales to sponsor such social services as bridge building and the construction of landing places, and the provisions for the poor of Tórshavn reflect quite modern notions of the responsibilities of the state. These innovative variations on ancient themes also reflect the diminishing importance of agriculture in the 1830s and, especially, the governors' desire to stimulate the Faroese economy.

The governors' programs and reforms of these years seem almost pathetically modest today—the foundation of a savings bank in Tórshavn in 1832, the opening of three branch stores of the royal trade monopoly in the period 1836–39, the Monopoly's purchasing of fresh fish to process for export in 1845, the new *grind* regulations, and so on. Some, indeed, were before their time. Christian Pløyen, who was bailiff from 1830 to 1837 and governor from 1837 to 1848, favored the abolition of the Monopoly, which did not occur until 1856; in 1839 he sent several Faroe men to Shetland to learn long-lining techniques—but long-lines were not really used in the Faroes until about 1850, and it was many years before they were common (Patursson 1961:13–14). Some reforms were decried, or were poor bets to begin with. Christian Tillisch, governor from 1825 to 1830, failed to persuade Faroese farmers to use plows, and in the 1840s the law for compulsory schooling in Danish was openly resisted. But modest as they were, some reforms proved timely and decisive, particularly insofar as they favored the development of an export economy based on fishing. For as Pløyen saw, "the future of Faroe lay on the sea" (West 1972:83).

It is significant, then, that in providing greater shares for the hunters and a regular means of distributing shares about the newly defined *grind* districts, the regulations of 1832 began to treat *grind* more like fish than like sheep. As Petersen suggests, "the fellowship of fishing in so many villages must have had its part in these universal rights" (1968:83). This change was not radical; rather, it shifted the emphasis to those parts of the oldest Norse basis for distributing *grind* that apparently derived from rules for sharing out fish among a boat crew and a village. It is a system of apportionment probably older than Faroese society, and it resembles that of other fisherfolk. First, in the Faroes, certain varieties of fish—halibut, for instance—went to the individual crewmen who caught them, and special shares went to men who played special roles: the foreman, the man who kept the boat steady with his oars while the others worked their lines, and the man who had wakened the others to go out fishing. Then the tithe was taken out and the rest divided "so that each man got one share and the boat got one"—that is, the owner of the boat got a share to pay for use of the boat and for wear and tear on equipment (Patursson 1961:17).

> There were also departures from these customs of sharing out the catch. In some villages it was the practice to share out in such a way that each house in the village got a share. It is probable that these village customs are ancient. Often alms were given from the catch. In some villages the sharing was such that fishermen who couldn't work were given the same share as those who had been out. It was also the practice in many villages where more than one boat went fishing, that the whole catch was combined and then shared out among all the fishermen. [ibid.]

Sámal Johansen describes such a local variation, as applied to *grind*, in the village of Vík:

> The whole village was together in the distribution. There were then two hundred and forty shares in the village, and the whole *grind*, including the whale which [in the case Johansen is describing] had been bought [at auction] was shared out—it came to only a few pennies to pay for each share of the bought whale. Then men who had been west in Vágar [to fetch back Vík's share, since the village was in Miðvágur's *grind* district] owned

a third of the whole *grind* as a workers' share, and this third
was first put aside. Then the other two-thirds were shared out
to all the village. [1970:103]

The reforms of the later nineteenth century and those of the
present century have accentuated the trend to treat the whales more
like fish. These have, however, been the work of Faroese legisla-
tors; the days when paternalistic Danish oversight of the Faroes was
acceptable were numbered even before the advent of free trade in
1856.

Problems persist nonetheless, and one finds "a continual process of integration. New situations generate new practices which
eventually are adopted as provisions in the whaling regulations" (J.
P. Joensen 1976:31). The Faroese population is now much larger,
and technological advances—power boats; modern communications
equipment; fine roads, bridges, and ferry services—have made it an
easy matter for far more people to hear the *grindaboð* and go to the
slaughter. A good many men now go to the *grindadráp* without
actually taking part in the hunt, and hundreds of people may come
by car just to watch. Both, if they give their names to the sheriff,
are entitled to shares, as hunters or as "visitors." Moreover, a *grind*
must be very large, even without the presence of such supernumer-
aries, to provide enough meat for all the residents of a *grind* district.
It has thus been proposed to limit the hunters' share to those men
who actually took part in the hunt in open boats (I believe such a
rule is already in effect in Tórshavn), and to define "visitors" more
exclusively. J. P. Joensen (1976:30–31) recounts some innovations
introduced by the sheriff of Vágar, which, however, have not yet
found their way to full legal recognition. He has, for example, introduced a new fixed deduction of special shares for the men who
hunted the whales. This rather resembles a wage, and is in keeping
with the modern Faroese economy. Men are rewarded for what they
actually do; barter has virtually disappeared, while the careful, reciprocal exchange of services is also disappearing; and so far as I
know, no village shares as a whole in the catch of all its fishermen.
The sense of community is increasingly mediated by cash, and by
full-time work at specialized pursuits.[14]

The *grindadráp* is thus becoming a specialized pursuit in its
own right. Still, it retains an exceptional place in Faroese life. This
is due not only to the fact that even in this relatively certain age
grindir still naturally come at unpredictable intervals, but also precisely because the *grindadráp*'s economic importance has dwindled.

As it is an exceptional event, and one whose performance recalls the Faroes' olden culture, it has come to serve, in the hands of modern specialists—writers, for example, and purveyors of touristic mementos—as a symbol of Faroese culture.

Just when slaughtering whales was first found to be typically Faroese is unclear. But "it is interesting to note that the words 'In dese Voort comen veel Walvisken' ('In this part come many whales') are written between the islands of Borðoy and Kunoy on the maps produced by Lucas Waghenaer in 1592 and Joris Carolus in 1634. . . . Earlier, in 1539, two men carving up a whale were figured on the map of Olaus Magnus" (Williamson 1970:112). Debes described the *grindadráp* in the seventeenth century, as did Svabo in the eighteenth; but these descriptions are for the most part taken up with practical matters.

The recognition of the *grindadráp*'s symbolic significance—or, rather, the creation of the *grindadráp* as a symbol—began in the early nineteenth century and was part of that age's search, here as elsewhere in Europe, for regionally typifying traits in customs and manners of speech already being rendered obsolete by the industrial revolution. This symbolic recreation of the *grindadráp* was also, at first, the work of non-Faroese. Although written in Danish, Governor Pløyen's "Grindevise" ("Ballad of the *Grind*"), with its refrain of "Hardy lads, to kill a *grind*—that's our desire," is in a sense one of the first works of modern Faroese literature. (It was published in 1835.) Traditional ballads were still being composed, but for the most part they looked back to the heroic Norse age; lyric poetry was shortly to be written in Faroese, but it dealt mainly with natural events and pastoral scenes. The "Grindevise" long stood nearly alone as a celebration of contemporary human activity in the Faroes.[15]

Few foreign descriptions of the Faroe scene since then have failed to include some mention of the *grindadráp*. Thus, in 1885 an anonymous writer for the *Saturday Review* of London wrote:

> If you were to ask the boys of Thorshavn (Thorshavn is the capital of the Faroes) what they would like best to see, ten to one they would reply 'a herd of grind.' Their fathers would, without a doubt, echo their preference. And if the leading publicist of Faroe (Sysselmand Müller) were consulted as to the chief factor in the prosperity of the isles and the happiness of the inhabitants, he would affirm unhesitatingly that nothing could promote these more effectually than a catch of 'grind.' In brief, the 'grind' may be said to give the tone to life in Faroe.

This is not wholly unreasonable despite its tone—and Müller's more practical view of things is at least given due notice.[16] Fuller, more serious treatments follow the tenor of Williamson's comment: "Should this very remarkable practice ever vanish from the Faeroe scene, then this small nation will have lost an integral part of its nationhood, and one of the most significant factors in the curious identity of its life" (1970:96).

The *grindadráp* has not disappeared, but its significance has changed—for it has become a mooring of self-conscious self-description. Hammershaimb included a description of the *grindadráp* in his *Færøsk Anthologi* (1891), as one of his lovingly drawn "Pictures of Folk Life"—"Evening," "Springtime," "Haymaking," "*Grindaboð*," "Wedding," "Fishing," etc. Jørgen-Frantz Jacobsen devoted a chapter to the *grindadráp* in his *Færøerne: Natur og Folk*, first published in 1936. This book is still popular in the Faroes, but it was written partly to introduce the Faroes to foreign travelers. It is written in Danish. The chapter on the *grindadráp* begins: "The Faroese are the old Vikings' descendants. But few places in the North has this old character so dwindled as among these sober and peaceful folk"—except, he goes on, when a *grind* comes! He does explicitly what the *grindadansur* does implicitly— joins the Faroes to the wider Norse world through the *grindadráp*. In the most recent full treatment of the *grindadráp*, J. P. Joensen does much the same thing, but in anthropological style, and in English. His article begins, "The pilot whale hunt is today a distinctive cultural characteristic for the Faroe Islands even though it has a long history and has earlier been practiced by other peoples in the North Atlantic" (1976:1).

Curiously enough, then, the *grindadráp*, traditionally a part of the internal subsistence economy, has come to provide a common ground between Faroese and foreigners. On the level of tourism, shops in Tórshavn sell to both Faroese and foreigners *grind* knives and jewelry depicting whales, and postcards of the slaughter, along with fishermen's sweaters worked in traditional patterns, articles of old-fashioned clothing, and models of old-style carrying baskets and spinning wheels. When an actual *grind* is sighted, Faroese hurrying to watch the *grindadráp* are joined by tourists lucky enough to be around. On the literary level, writings about the slaughter, and especially its aftermath, provide a kind of *grindadansur* in which both foreigners and Faroese may find a "cultural text" for discovering both their own and this society's temper at the same time.

Articulating their place in the world has always been a critical matter for the Faroese, and is now becoming a more complex one. Founded on a common West Scandinavian repertoire of habits of action and thought, the Faroes' culture has been cast and recast to fit the exigencies of life on these small islands. The Faroes, distant though they seem to outsiders, have never been cut off from the outside world with which, indeed, the Faroese not only have cultural ties, but also have had for survival's sake to maintain regular relationships. Faroese self-recognition has thus always been complicated. On the one hand, it is of an immediate, unreflecting sort: how do we know our homeland, and how do we know each other? But it has also depended on recognizing others—principally Danes—not only as different from Faroese but also as members of the Faroese world. Thus to be Faroese has entailed a reflected sort of self-recognition—a trick of seeing oneself in outsiders' eyes, or through outsiders' institutions. And most recently it has entailed the self-conscious domestication of outsiders' institutions and the establishment of local ones to provide a formally indigenous official culture to give meaning to everyday life.

The Faroese are hardly unique in much of this. Most peoples have neighbors with whom they must adjust relations without losing their own integrity. Many peoples must do so despite their neighbors' greater economic and political power. In such cases a culture has sometimes been lost. The Faroes' has not been; it has changed, but not discontinuously. Perhaps the most important factor in the survival of an identifiably Faroese culture has been the redeployment of the language in a written form. Here as elsewhere in Scandinavia, there is a strong sense that a written language unifies people by lending them an official identity. In gaining a written form, however, neither the language nor the culture it expresses has remained unchanged. A theme of our later chapters has been that, just as the language itself has become something formal as well as vernacular, so elements of the traditional culture have become fixed as symbols of the modern culture's integrity—mirrors, as distant as a Danish officialdom once was from the run of everyday events, in which one discovers the integrity of contemporary life. In a sense, the ballads are more resonant now than when they were still being composed, the *grindadráp* more typifying than when it meant a full drying shed all winter, the language more telling than when it was only spoken. Tórshavn, by the same token, has taken on a new importance in Faroese life. Always the Faroes' political center and long the only place where foreign trade might be carried on, it has now also become the center of the modern internal economy and the place where specialists articulate a self-consciously Faroese culture.

Our discussion of all this has been embodied in studies of diverse aspects of Faroese life, and has become now rather abstract and impersonal. As a corrective, let us conclude with a scattering of more concrete personal examples. The Faroese is a living culture and a changing one, and its articulation is not automatic. In December 1974, one of us spent part of a return visit to the Faroes in Tórshavn, acquainting himself with the "city" by interviewing people whose work gives the Faroes their "national" character.

6
Tórshavn, December 1974

I walk to the end of the Tinganes to reorient myself. The Tinganes is the rocky spit between Tórshavn's "Eastern" and "Western" harbors, where the Løgting used to meet, and where some of the Monopoly buildings still stand, renovated to serve as government offices. Last night I came in on the weekly plane from Reykjavík. In the summer, when there are three flights a week from Iceland, the plane flies direct from Reykjavík; but yesterday it put down first at Hornafjörður in southern Iceland, dropping in over a black volcanic shore onto an unpaved airstrip. There were not many passengers; in summer, the planes are always full. We got out to stretch our legs, and looked past the tiny airport building to abrupt, brown-green mountains and the dead gray ends of glaciers squeezing to the sea.

The Faroese landscape is more modest, less austere. The plane skims over a low place—only fifty meters high—in the cliffs of Vágar and over a long lake to land suddenly in an empty bowl of the hills near the village of Sørvágur. The British army built the Faroes'

Plate 8a. Tórshavn: the Eastern Harbor and the Tinganes about 1900. (From A. v. Geyr-Schweppenburg, *Meine Reise nach den Färöern* [Padernborn: J. Esser, 1900], frontispiece)

Plate 8b. The same scene today. (Photograph: Kalmar og Alan, Tórshavn) ·

first airstrip here during the war. It is as large a stretch of flat land as there is in the Faroes. The air is cool but soft, and even at this time of year the breeze has a moorland tang. We are thirty kilometers from Tórshavn as the crow files, but the trip takes two hours by bus, ferry, and taxi.

The bus is stuffy; Faroese like to keep the windows shut, and the passengers are starting to work on their duty-free cigarettes. A couple of men break out a small bottle of duty-free liquor. The bus takes us "over" Miðvágur and Sandavágur to a ferry landing on Vestmannafjørður. "Sam," the ferry, crosses the fjord to Vestmanna. From here we go by taxi to Tórshavn. It is early afternoon, but the winter days are short. Night has fallen when, just before climbing the hills north of Tórshavn, the road bends suddenly around a lurid gas station at a crossroad in the empty landscape. To the left, below the road, the lights of several little villages straggle around the shores of Kollafjørður and Kaldbaksfjørður. Across the sound, there is a glow from the lights of the towns on Eysturoy. Tórshavn finally appears below us as a vast collection of lights, brightest by the harbor.

Tórshavn is new to me, in a way. Of course I know people here, and several times I've lived here for a few weeks. But I know it mostly from my readings in Faroese history, and as "the city" to which, while I was doing field work, I would come in every month or so, weather permitting, to shop and see the sights. What strikes me now, from the Tinganes, is the newness of the city, and its sprawl.

A couple of fishing boats are unloading their catch or taking on ice on the far side of the "Western Harbor," at Bacalao, Tórshavn's fish-processing plant. Bacalao is flanked by the slipway of the shipyard and a cluster of oil-storage tanks emblazoned "ESSO" and "SHELL." The hill behind Bacalao is dominated by the great square-built buildings of the Seamen's School, a radar aerial turning on its tower. A little lower, to the right, are the fieldstone National Library and the modern buildings of Fróðskaparsetur Føroya, the Faroese Academy, its walls stained black and its roof done in some green asphalt material in memory of the traditional style of tarred siding and sod roofs. Farther around to the north, modern suburbs reach up the slopes to the Vestmanna road, which climbs along the hill topped by the antennas of Útvarp Føroya, the Faroes' radio station. This hill closes the northern horizon; to the west, the low noonday sun will soon set behind the ridge of Kirkjubøreyn.

At the base of the Tinganes in the "Eastern Harbor," open boats are moored behind a jetty where the interisland ferries come and go. From there, beneath the ruins of a fort first built to guard the harbor in the sixteenth century, the commercial quay reaches out past a long row of warehouses to a breakwater stretching nearly across the harbor mouth. Tórshavn is a poor natural port. Trucks and fork-lifts shuttle back and forth. One freighter is unloading a cargo of little Christmas trees. Forty years ago, a man in the village told me once, people used to make Christmas trees with scraps of wood, wrapping them in moss.

Tórshavn was not a prepossessing town near the end of the last century. Old photographs show narrow, irregular streets—really just alleyways between houses—paved, if at all, with lumpy-looking stones. Even a horse-cart was a rarity in those days. The town (its population was about thirteen hundred in 1890; today it is ten times that) was clustered by the waterfront, and was only just beginning to spread back up the hills from the Tinganes. Few of Tórshavn's public buildings are a century old. The Lutheran church at the base of the Tinganes was built on the outskirts of town in ·1788, and extensively rebuilt in 1865. A few steps away, across the little square from H. N. Jacobsen's bookstore (in a building once housing the Latin School), the Løgtingshús, or parliament-house, was built in 1856 and rebuilt fifty years later. Up the street, the present offices of the Savings Bank date from 1904; a block to the west, beyond their modern (1958) home, the former offices of the Føroya Banki, the national bank, were built in 1906. This building now houses the technical high school. Most of Tórshavn's buildings suggest how new is its place in modern Faroese life. The national theater dates from 1926, and the national library, which seems so old, from 1931. There was little or no industry in Tórshavn until the 1920s. It had no drying house for cod until 1920, and no shipyard until 1936. The Faroes already had many drying houses and several shipyards. Bacalao was founded in 1953, and the harbor-works have been under construction, off and on, since 1921. Tourists—there have been many since the late nineteenth century, mostly traveling singly, often on their way to greater vistas and adventures in Iceland—might put up in private homes, an informal "inn," or the seaman's hostel (built 1923, enlarged in 1954). The Faroes' first real hotel, the Hafnia, was built in 1951.

There is not much for tourists to do in Tórshavn. You may buy a sweater or a cap, browse in Jacobsen's bookstore and pick up some postcards, go to the art gallery up the hill or to the tiny museum in the national library, maybe watch a freighter unload; or you may take a bus or boat tour to see several sights outside town, or ride the ferries round the islands. The city seems slow, small, and provincial, less remarkable for its busy port and headlong traffic than for touches of the picturesque. Two summers ago I met a small crowd of Frenchmen off a big liner that anchored here for a day on a cruise around the Northlands. They asked me what language the people spoke—Danish? Icelandic?—and happily photographed a few old houses and boats and an old man dressed in traditional costume: *"Ah, c'est bien typique, ça."*

Leif Groth, Danish High Commissioner for the Faroes

Since the passage of the Home Rule Law in 1948, Danish interests in the Faroes have been looked after by an official called the high commissioner (Danish *rigsombudsmand*, Faroese *ríkisumboðsmaður*). His residence is that of his predecessor, the governor (Danish *amtmand*), built in 1880–81 a stone's throw from the Løgtingshús. It stands in a small park boasting some of the Faroes' rare trees, looking like a bourgeois country home. Its slate roofs still look outlandish, and must have seemed more so ninety years ago, when almost all Tórshavn's roofs were sod. The most visible token of the arrival, in 1972, of its present tenant, Mr. Groth, was a coat of off-white paint on its fieldstone walls.

Mr. Groth first came to the Faroes in 1961 as assistant high commissioner. He returned as high commissioner after a stint as secretary in the prime minister's office in Copenhagen. He is a young man, an up-and-coming type in Copenhagen, I am told, and his appointment was widely taken to indicate that the Danish government was going to take Faroese affairs "quite seriously." So was the fact that the queen made a carefully prepared little speech in Faroese when she visited here in 1971.

A copy of Lockwood's *An Introduction to Modern Faroese* lay on Mr. Groth's desk as we talked, and I asked if he spoke the language; most Danes here cannot. He said he can understand it, but not speak it; he finds it "a very foreign language." We spoke in English.

Our conversation was interrupted once, when I chatted briefly with the girl who does housework for him. She is from the village where I had done field work, and a couple of summers ago I had lived with her family. She came to Tórshavn to work and to be near her boyfriend, who is studying at the Faroese Academy. When I went back to the village I found that she was planning to quit this job soon, finding herself overworked and underpaid.

I asked Mr. Groth about his duties here. He finds his job has two parts. He is an ambassador to an essentially foreign country, responsible for reporting back to Copenhagen on the details and circumstances of decisions made by the local government. But he is also practically an *amtmand* in the old style, charged with seeing that local laws do not conflict with national ones, and with representing the interests of the state. "Of course I have my own views, but I try as much as possible simply to explain to Copenhagen." He "normally" recommends projects to Copenhagen, "but sometimes I have had to say no."

I asked about a current topic of conversation, the first issue of "Faroese" stamps. The post office here is only a branch of the Danish postal service, but according to the present arrangement with Denmark, the Løgting may vote to take it over at any time. In fact it did vote to do so in 1948, but the *løgmaður* never signed the bill, so that it never became law. Now this year the Danish postal service decided out of the blue to print stamps with the Danish name "Færøerne" on them, showing local scenes and paintings by local artists. This was essentially the conservative counterproposal in 1948 to the nationalists' move to take over the post office—a state of affairs both moderate and radical nationalists find galling. An Italian stamp dealer I met on the plane told me that the stamps are sure to attract international philatelic attention, and may earn the post office as much as five million *krónur* a year—about $900,000. Faroese politicans have protested, and a compromise has been worked out; the stamps will say "Føroyar" (Faroese) instead of "Færøerne" (Danish). But the post office remains a branch of the Danish postal service, which will pocket the profits from the stamps. A move is afoot to take over the post office, but the Løgting has just begun to settle down to work after the elections in November, and no consensus has emerged as to whether such a bill might pass.

Mr. Groth knows that taking over the post office is as much a symbolic matter as a practical one, since it calls into question the whole range of the Danish government's obligations and services here according to the Home Rule Law. As to taking over the post office, he says simply, "They can if they will." He goes on to stress that the Home Rule Law is only "a framework law," and that "the Faroese are to have as great a part of self-government as possible."

He is diplomatically silent about how great this "part" will be, but I have the impression he thinks the Faroese might do well to manage more of their home affairs. Since 1961, he says, "the Faroes' status has changed a great deal—not formally, but really." He finds that Faroese politicians are "better educated" than they used to be, and "participate better" with each other and in negotiations with the Danish state.

Erlendur Patursson, Politician and Journalist

I met Erlendur Patursson over a cup of coffee at the Hotel Hafnia, across the street from Mr. Groth's residence. He was sorry, he said, not to be able to give me more time, but, at sixty-one, he finds it difficult to do all the work he has undertaken. He has written a series of history books, many articles, and a two-volume history of the Faroese fishing industry. He is head of the nationalist Republican Party (Tjóðveldisflokkur), which he helped to found in 1948, and a member of both the Løgting and the Danish parliament. He edits the party organ, *14 September*, the only Faroese newspaper that comes out, as its advertising puts it, "every day except Sunday and Monday." The paper is named after the day in 1946 when a slim plurality voted for complete independence from Denmark. (The referendum was annulled by the Danish government.) In 1906 his father, Jóannes Patursson (1866–1946), had been a founding member of the then radical Self-Rule Party (Sjálvstýrisflokkur).

Mr. Patursson explains the Republicans' nationalism. The Faroes, he says, must make themselves as independent as possible, economically as well as politically. They stand a good chance of prospering as an independent state because they are a food-producing country in an overpopulated world. The Republican Party thus favors the greatest and most reasonable exploitation of the Faroes' natural resources, and, perhaps surprisingly, Mr. Patursson looks forward in the distant future to a revival of Faroese agriculture, which currently accounts for less than 3 percent of the GNP. The Faroese, he says, cannot hope to be completely self-sufficient, but they could certainly supply more of their own meat and dairy products. (Except for fish and for some potatoes, lamb, and milk, the Faroes import almost all their food.)

In the meantime, fishing is the foundation of the Faroese economy. The Republican Party favors extending the fishing limit

to 200 miles, unilaterally if need be, for both economic and ecological reasons. As Iceland has extended its limits, the fish stocks
around the Faroes have been more heavily exploited, and it is
widely felt that, as in Iceland's case, regulation by the Faroese state
would ensure their survival. The Republicans also favor establishing
a "pollution limit," so that the seas themselves will not be contami-
nated by passing ships. All this would involve extending existing
claims and regulations, since current laws already control the exploitation of fish stocks within a twelve-mile limit and prohibit
dumping waste. This limit is, however, embodied in a Danish treaty,
and, modest as it is, is threatened by Danish membership in the
European Economic Community. The Republican Party opposes
Faroese membership in the EEC, while realizing that refusing to
follow Denmark in this regard might entail complete independence.
(As matters turned out the next year, a special accommodation was
arranged; the Faroes are not members of the EEC, but they remain
a Danish dependency.)

I told Mr. Patursson I had read a good deal of Faroese history
and was interested to know what he thought of the modernization of
Faroese life. Yes, he said, the most decisive turning point came in
1953, when the hydroelectric station was built in Vestmanna. People
could now light their homes and businesses cheaply, and use modern
appliances and machines. Together with the rapid postwar modernization of the fishing fleet, electricity literally powered the rapid industrial growth of both Tórshavn and the Faroes as a whole.

I asked what makes Tórshavn such a special place. He said that
it has been built up as the islands' seat of government, the site of
the biggest schools and businesses, and the forum for cultural
events. It is the home of the Faroes' intellectual community.
Tórshavn, he adds, is unlike Klaksvík, the main deepwater fishing
port on the northern island of Borðoy, and the villages, because here
so many people's work is directed beyond "just making a living."

We had finished our coffee, and Mr. Patursson recommended
to me an article in a several-days-old *14 September*. As we walked
back to the newspaper office to pick up a copy, we met Eyvindur
Mohr, the painter, coming out of Jacobsen's bookstore. "Well, Jonathan," Eyvindur asked me in English, "did you meet that *rebel?*"
He asked Erlendur about the role of the Self-Rule Party in the formation of the Landsstýri, the Løgting's executive committee. A few
yards down the street a man I didn't know asked about that day's
editorial in *14 September*, which criticized the "conservatism" of
the programming and news broadcasting of Útvarp Føroya, the Far-

oes' radio station. Erlendur would not be drawn out on either subject—especially, perhaps, with a foreigner listening in.

Útvarp Føroya, Faroes' Radio

Útvarp Føroya has nine or ten employees, who work in cramped quarters next door to the offices of *14 September*. Jógvan Arge tells me that the station needs a new building and some new equipment. He received training in journalism in Denmark; his father, Niels Juul Arge, is "foreman" at Útvarp.

Útvarp was founded by the Løgting in 1956. Five *løgtingsmenn* and a listeners' representative oversee its affairs, but the station is otherwise privately managed. It is financed from several sources: a tax on radio ownership (90 *krónur* per household per year), announcements ("The Klaksvík Young Women's Christian Association will hold a meeting tonight at eight o'clock . . . "), greetings-and-music programs on Wednesday and Sunday afternoons ("Peter Thomsen, dear father and husband, happy birthday this Tuesday— Andreas, Suni, and Elisabeth. Jóan Zachariasen on board *Sjúrðaberg*, have a good and short trip—the wife and children. And now we will hear Charley Pride sing. . . ."), and the "V-4" lottery-and-variety program on Saturday evenings.

Útvarp is on the air about five hours a day, and except on Sunday (when there is only a long afternoon program) it comes on the air at mealtimes with the weather forecast and the news. The station's plaintive electronic identifying tones, drawn from a ballad tune, are repeated for several seconds, and one imagines children being hushed and conversations faltering all over the Faroes' scattered villages. "Útvarp Føroya, good day. The weather: a deep low pressure area over southern Greenland is driving slowly eastwards. Another low pressure area. . . ." The style is conversational and matter-of-fact. Discussions of the weather are a serious part of Faroese conversation.

"Our most important program is probably the news," Jógvan says. "We use the Norwegian and Danish wire services, and steal a few things here and there." About half of Útvarp's broadcast time is devoted to music, however, and the rest largely to sports events, interviews, and various cultural programs. He says he does not know how much difference Útvarp makes in Faroese life—"maybe not much, except out in the smaller places where people have few experiences."

I ask about Útvarp's language policy. "Yes, we're supposed by law to be apolitical. At first we just wanted to *use* the language, you know, but then we also had to renew it. We try to speak as good Faroese as possible. Some foreign words are too well established to do anything about, but we have worked up a new terminology; we used to speak half-broken Danish, but now when emigrants come back to the Faroes they often find they cannot understand Útvarp very well. We make up words, translate them, or find them in the ballads."

I try to avoid being interviewed myself: "American? Speaks Faroese? Let's tape it. . . ." A young technician wanders in. "Here's a man in your line of work," Jógvan tells him. "See if you can convince him to speak on the air." The technician, it turns out, is studying folklore at the University of Oslo, where he is finishing a master's thesis about tales of seeing the ghostly crews of ships that had gone down. We swap stories, since we have done field work on the same island. We agree it is difficult to do research in a country so intimate that it is almost impossible to protect one's informants.

Jóhan Hendrik Poulsen, Philologist and Teacher

Jóhan Hendrik Poulsen is from the same island, where his father was a schoolteacher. He is married to Erlendur Patursson's sister, and both men live in Kirkjubøur, from which they commute over to Tórshavn.

Jóhan Hendrik is heir to the Faroes' small but distinguished philological tradition, whose leading lights have been V. U. Hammershaimb, Jakob Jakobsen, and, most recently, Christian Matras. He studied in Iceland from 1960 to 1962, and in 1966 received a master's degree in Norse philology from the University of Copenhagen. After teaching for a year at the University of Illinois, he returned to the Faroes in 1971 to become head of the Department of Language Study at the Faroese Academy, Fróðskaparsetur Føroya.

Philology, he explains, has always been a political as well as a practical pursuit in the Faroes. The immediate problem has been to try to clear out the Danish loans and neologisms which accompanied the arrival of a new way of life, and to build up a "clean" written language, capable of describing the larger world in which the Faroese have rather suddenly found themselves. An important achievement was the publication, in 1928, of a Faroese-Danish dictionary edited by Christian Matras and M. A. Jacobsen. A supplement to this dictionary, which has been Jóhan Hendrik's principal work for several years, will come out in a few weeks. In 1967 his senior colleague, Jóhannes av Skarði, brought out a Danish-Faroese dictionary. This work, he says, is perhaps more important than the Faroese-Danish dictionary, "because most people read more of Danish," and older people learned only Danish in school. "We live by two languages, Danish and Faroese, and we try to mix them as little as possible."

Work on the language is now largely centered at the Faroese Academy. It was established by the Løgting in 1965, around a learned society, founded in 1952 by a group of intellectuals, to encourage scientific research in the Faroes. The Academy tries, he says, "partly to build up Faroese from what it already is," advising Útvarp Føroya, for example, on neologisms, and answering requests for "real" Faroese words. He smiles: "We do not always have the answer." Jóhan Hendrik has a weekly radio program, in which he discusses a few words each time, and reads letters from listeners and solicits their help on the dictionary project.

In linguistic as well as political matters, Faroese find themselves inspired by Icelanders and Norwegians. The Academy follows their example—particularly the Icelandic one ("That is my specialty," Jóhan Hendrik says, smiling again because he knows I know that some people find his "pure" Faroese too Icelandic)—of building new terms on old West Scandinavian roots, in the hope that they will weather the Danicizing tendency. He hopes the language will grow through the introduction of more Faroese textbooks; the Academy has recently backed the publication of textbooks in physics and natural history. Since "Danicizing" often means adopting English, Greek, or Latin words through Danish, these texts go to what seems, to an English-speaker who takes for granted a scientific vocabulary drawn from Latin and Greek, the extreme of giving "purely" Faroese names to biological and physical concepts.

The Academy is also a teaching institution. It offers year-long programs in Faroese language and literature, a two-year program that may be used for credit toward degrees in Scandinavian universities, and a series of courses in Latin, Greek, and Hebrew. It sponsors an evening lecture series, summer programs for foreign students, and a number of courses open to the public: the reading and evaluation of old documents, Icelandic, archeology, anthropology, English, French, German, and Faroese—including a special course in Faroese as a second language. The Academy building houses the offices and laboratories for fisheries research and product testing, which will, however, be moved in a few months to a building still under construction across the street.

Jóhan Hendrik explains all this modestly—appropriately so, since the Academy's achievements may seem unimpressive to a foreigner, and many of its courses are undersubscribed. But he points to comparable situations elsewhere; the Shetlandic Norse language, Norn, for which Jakob Jakobsen published an etymological dictionary in 1928, died out, although the Shetlands had long been more populous and less poverty-stricken than the Faroes. He shows me with some pride an Irish government report on the Gaeltacht, which holds up Faroese as an example of a regional language reviving with economic growth. He concludes: "The Faroese language has a strong position. It is strong enough to serve in the future as a symbol of our nationality. The interest in the language is alive among the people. It would be a sad loss to forget our language the way the Shetlanders did."

As we walked to the door it was 4:30—already well after dark—and the winter's first, light snow had fallen. A little girl called out to her playmate, "It'd be *skæg* to go indoors!" The girls eased past us (Faroese are very tolerant with children). "Did you hear?" Jóhan Hendrik asked me. "'*Skæg*,' that is Danish for 'fun.' That is the way new words come into the language." Jóhannes av Skarði came up the steps, and the two men fell to talking about a dialect word for part of a feather.

Marius Johannesen, Teacher and Journalist

I met Marius and his wife, Jóna, a couple of summers ago, through Jóhan Hendrik's parents, with whom they are good friends. The two men were both teachers, and are both members of the Self-Rule Party. Marius, like many Faroese, is a man of great energy and varied achievements. He retired as principal of the Folk High School when he turned sixty-five in 1970, but he still teaches Faroese at the Seamen's School. He edits *Tingakrossur*, the weekly newspaper that is the organ of the Self-Rule Party. He has written several books, including a pretty little edition of the satirical ballads, and he and some friends have recently formed their own publishing company. Together he and his daughter-in-law have written a cookbook of modern and traditional Faroese food—the Faroes' first—which reached the bookstores last week; and when I came by the house this evening he was correcting galleys for a children's book. He is working on a dictionary of modern Faroese slang, much of which, he says, turns out to come from English—like *bumma*, to beg, as in *bumma eina sigarett*, "bum a cigarette." Like many men of a generation who sailed young to the Iceland fishery, he is heavy-shouldered from the eighteen hour days working handlines in deep water.

He hails from the tiny village of Funningur, in the north. How did he happen to come to Tórshavn? "Well, as you know, I was the teacher north there in Mikladalur on Kalsoy, and it happened then that the Folk High School was having difficulties. Well, so the five-man committee in charge of the school asked me if I could come south to Tórshavn to look into matters. They were looking for a new principal, and I got the job. That was in 1953." How has Tórshavn changed since then? "Well, you, I'll tell you a story. It was in 1920—I was fifteen then, since I was born in 1905—that I went to sea for the first time. My father and I were paid off at Advent with a check for our shares of the haul, from Mortensen's, south on Suðuroy. Of course we couldn't cash the check north there. So we went over to Norðskáli—that was on December 11—and spent the night there, and the next day we came south to Tórshavn. Then we went back the same way. Well, so we were four days cashing a check. There were only two monetary institutions in the Faroes then, the Faroes' Bank and the Savings Bank. Now there are sixty-seven. I think it's sixty-seven, counting branches of the banks—I've just written an article about it for *Tingakrossur*. That's maybe too many, don't you think? Well, so then in 1923 I came south to the Teachers' School here to become a teacher. There were two thousand people in Tórshavn then, about that anyway. . . . Yes, Tórshavn's spirit has changed a great deal, and its significance has maybe changed too. Now you can cash a check in your home village, if you want." He used to think, he says, that the Faroes' commercial capital should have been established around Skálafjørður, a fine natural port. But Tórshavn was too important.

I ask about the Self-Rule Party, which, some people say, has become gradualist to the point of immobility. "Well, I want to be free from Denmark, but gradually, step by step—that has been our slogan." He has little patience with what he considers the precipitous nationalism of the Republicans. He agrees that his party's strength is being able to support now one party, now another; for years it had only one member in the Løgting, but in the recent elections it has picked up an additional, at-large seat. "But we want independence, too—that is what we are aiming for."

Útvarp's classical music program (a concerto grosso by Corelli) ended at this point in our conversation. The announcer said we were now going to hear the third part of a trip with Marius Johannesen and Niels Juul Arge around the island of Kalsoy. The program had been taped during the summer. "Wait a moment," Marius said, "I didn't hear myself the other two times." I had the disconcerting impression when our conversation resumed of hearing him in stereo, one half describing Kalsoy, the other half talking about Tórshavn. His northern accent seemed stronger on the radio. His live voice said, "Well, so Tórshavn is the midpoint in the Faroes. It was a *brimpláss*—there was a lot of surf here—but it was a natural center. The ballads tell us that the settlers chose it as a place to hold their parliament. . . . You know, the Folk High School was first built outside of Klaksvík, in an open field. Then after about ten years, in 1909, it was moved to Tórshavn, because conditions were better here than elsewhere (*tí tað lá betri her enn aðrastaðni*)."

Eyvindur Mohr, "Mechanic" and Artist

Mohr is an old Tórshavn name. It evidently came to the Faroes in the early eighteenth century when, like a number of foreigners who married into Faroese society, a certain Nicolai Fr. Mohr who worked for the Monopoly married a local widow. Her son by her first marriage was one Peter Jensen, who also worked for the Monopoly and is said to have been a joiner. Peter's son, Nikolai Mohr, was a distinguished naturalist. He published a book on Icelandic natural history in 1786, and was a friend and collaborator of Jens Christian Svabo and of the Icelander þorður Thoroddsen who had, in turn, studied with Linnaeus. Craftsmanship and a certain internationalism seem to run in the family. Eyvindur's cousin Kjartan Mohr is director of the Tórshavn shipyard and the leader of the small, Tórshavn-based Progress Party (Framburðsflokkur). Eyvindur himself is one of the most accomplished young Faroese artists, and is gaining considerable recognition abroad.

We talked in his kitchen over a cup of coffee, looking out over the lights of Tórshavn. He designed and built his house himself. We spoke a singular mixture of Faroese and English. He learned English as a boy from the British soldiers who occupied the Faroes during the war. He also speaks German and some Italian, and, like most Faroese, can make himself understood in Icelandic and Norwegian, partly by changing his accent and intonation, and partly by using a somewhat modified grammar and vocabulary. His elder daughter sat folding decorations for the Christmas tree.

"I wanted," he says, "to be an artist ever since I was a kid— ever since I was a kid." But he began his career as an electrical engineer, first in Tórshavn, where he was born and raised, and then after the war in a factory in Copenhagen. In the early 1950s he survived a long bout with tuberculosis, and "then I began to work as an artist, up here in the Faroes, but I kept a mechanical shop for a living." In his shop Eyvindur made an invention of his own, a radar-reflector for longline buoys. He first exhibited his paintings here in 1948, but did not have his first one-man show until 1969. He has painted full-time since 1970, when he received a grant from the Landsstýri and the Faroes' Art Association (Listafelag Føroya) to study in Rome under Professor Pappaguzzi at the Scuola Libera of the Accademia Bell' Arte. He was invited the next year to Voss, Norway, to study under the English abstract painter Jeremy Moon. (Eyvindur's own paintings are representational.) He has, with several others, exhibited his work in Iceland and several times in Norway, including a show that toured the country, ending triumphantly at the National Gallery in Oslo. He visited Italy again in 1972, and hopes to return to Rome next year to live for a while with his family. He likes Rome itself, he explains, and the teachers and critics he finds there, but he also wants his daughters, now eight and twelve, "to learn something of the world's culture quite apart from Denmark, so when they grow up they will not think Copenhagen is all there is. Quite apart from Denmark—do you understand me, Jonathan?"

Like other Faroese painters, Eyvindur is almost entirely self-taught. He asked me once how artists are trained in America. I said they often work at life drawing with nude models. Ah, he said, that would be impossible here; everyone would know who the model was. What he misses most, however, is informed criticism of his work. "It seems as if people are afraid to have an opinion about art at an exhibition here—it is as if they are looking for a friend who knows something more than they do, so they can repeat what he says. People buy, but they do not know what they buy, if it is good or bad." Still, as he says, "The Faroese are very arts-minded." There are ten or a dozen full-time artists here, including two sculptors, and many people who paint only part-time.

Work in the fine arts is centered in Tórshavn, and is supported by a mixture of private and government enterprise. Aside from its several private galleries, Tórshavn has the Faroes' Art Association, the Faroes' Art Collection (Listasavn Føroya), and the Faroes' Art Gallery (Listaskáli Føroya). The Art Association was founded in Copenhagen during the war by Faroese wanting to help some of their artists who were trapped there—Mikines and the sculptor Janus Kamban, among others. The idea was "taken home," as Eyvindur says, after the war, and the association has continued to buy works. The Art Collection buys pictures for the Landsstýri out of public funds. Its purchasing committee is made of up one representative from each political party, together with several members of the public. The Art Gallery is run by the municipal government, the national government, and the Art Association. It built and maintains a gallery on the edge of town, up near the soccer field. Eyvindur finds the edifice scandalous. "Yes, I'll tell you what. I said in an interview with *14 September* that the building itself doesn't inspire respect for the arts; it looks like a factory for assembling three-legged wooden horses with tails. It should be a real museum, not store any of its paintings, but show some of the best ones all the time so that people can always see them, and let the others hang in banks and offices and places where people come in. Oh yes, I got a big reaction from the arts establishment when I said that."

Eyvindur delights in controversial statements. He is a fervent nationalist, but a couple of years ago he did a series of cartoons mocking people of all political persuasions, for the conservative newspaper *Dimmalætting*. He signed his cartoons "ð"—a letter which, in Faroese, has many values, but never quite the one you expect. Sometimes it is silent. He complains that Faroese are "absolutely" uncritical of Danish artists. "Danish artists come here, stay a few weeks—they can have a show whenever they want, just call up—and then they tell *us* how the Faroes should be painted. We cannot paint Denmark; why do they think they can tell us?" One of his paintings, a landscape owned by a Danish museum, will grace one of the new "Faroese" stamps.

I ask about Tórshavn. "Yes, Jonathan, I will tell you. If you meet an American, or a German, or a Dane, and you meet him in China, and you ask, 'Are you longing home? Yes? What for?' He says, 'I miss my city—New York, Copenhagen—my brothers, family, so on.' Ask a Faroese in China, 'Are you longing home? What for?' He says, 'The Faroes . . . the Faroes.' *All* the

Faroes. . . . Tórshavn, yes, Tórshavn is the world's smallest but most cosmopolitan capital—that's my meaning. You can get every variation here." He cocks an amused eye at me to see if I will believe him.

New Year's Eve, 31 December 1974

Josefina Smith invited me to a New Year's Eve party with her husband. They had recently been married down in Denmark, where he is studying gymnastics and history. She works in the airline office in Tórshavn, next door to the Hafnia. Smith is a Suðuroy name, and her aunt Ruth was a well-known artist. One of Josefina's brothers, Sonny, is a disk jockey at Útvarp. The crowd at the party was mostly young, and vaguely bohemian. We sat around and talked, and drank a bit, and then listened to a very funny program on the radio.

The program was in honor of the old year, but it purported to be about Rockall, not the Faroes. Rockall is a singularly godforsaken rock in the middle of the Atlantic. No one cares much about the rock itself, but it *is* a piece of land, and so whoever claims it might also be able to claim territorial waters around it. Just now the British are claiming it, having sent out a helicopter with a flag. But the Danes protested formally, saying that the Faroese had been there first, though they neglected to bring a flag along. Last night the radio reported that the Irish have also laid claim to Rockall. Útvarp's fantasy, now, is that Rockall is inhabited—in fact, inhabited by settlers from various *un*inhabited islets in the Faroes. It turns out to be a prosperous little place, quite a lot like the Faroes. Radio Rockall turns out to be quite a lot like Útvarp Føroya.

We are introduced to Rockall by a man with a voice like Marius Johannesen's, who rows around the island with Niels Juul Arge telling obscure tales about each cleft and pinnacle. Ashore we hear about traffic problems and listen to what local politicians have to say. Then a dictionary program comes on, and a man with a voice like Jóhan Hendrik Poulsen's tells about an important old word he has discovered for the left offside teat of a cow. Each vignette is followed by a catchy little tune with the refrain "Rockall, Rockall, Rockall. . . ."

At midnight the party retired to the roof of the apartment building where our host lives. Huddled against a cold wind, we set off fireworks—the New Year's custom in Scandinavia—and looked out over the harbor and the half-darkened city, where here and there other parties were shooting up Roman candles. I did not get home until 3:30. The next evening, still nursing a hangover, I didn't feel up to seeing if I could find some ballad dancing in the city. Three days later I flew home.

Notes

Chapter 1. Introduction

1. According to the Irish monk and scholar Dicuil, writing in 825, a "set of small islands"—undoubtedly the Faroes—had been inhabited "for nearly a hundred years by hermits sailing from our country, Ireland." But now, he went on, "because of the Northman pirates they are emptied of anchorites, and filled with countless sheep and very many diverse kinds of sea-birds" (Tierney 1967:74–77). Lacking more direct evidence than Dicuil's comment and a few local traditions and place names, it has until recently been believed that the Irish settlement was sparse as well as short-lived. Now, however, radiocarbon dating of pollens from peat beds in the northern, mountain-dimmed village of Tjørnuvík—an unlikely site, but it was fernier and dotted with small lakes at the time of its Viking settlement—has indicated that the place was occupied as early as the first half of the seventh century, presumably by Irish. It may be that the Irish settlement was earlier and more extensive than has usually been thought.

2. Some land in the Faroes had been owned by foreign noblemen and by such institutions as the cathedral minster in Bergen. By the end of the seventeenth century most of this land had become locally owned freehold. Since 1937, rents for king's farms have been paid to a Faroese agricultural council whose administration was assumed by the Løgting following the Home Rule Law of 1948.

3. By "Scandinavia" here we mean Iceland, Faroe, Norway, Denmark, and Sweden, excluding Finland and the (multinational) Lapps. Haugen, in the quotation below, means by it Iceland, Norway, Denmark, Sweden, and Finland.

Chapter 2. A Sense of Place

1. Words written in small capitals represent direct translations of Faroese. I have hoped in this way to avoid burdening the text with a large Faroese vocabulary. The Faroese words so translated are:

ABOUT: *um* (see note 7, below)

EAST: *eystur* (direction), *eysturi* (place)

FJORD: *fjørður*

HOME: *heim* (direction), *heima* (place)

IN: *inn* (direction), *inni* (place)

NORTH: *norður* (direction), *norðuri* and *norðri* (place); also *norðari* (comp. adj., more northern)

OUT: *út* (direction), *úti* (place)

OVER: *yvir* (direction), *yviri* (place)

SOUND: *sund*

SOUTH: *suður* (direction), *suðuri* (place)

WEST: *vestur* (direction), *vesturi* (place).

Faroese regularly creates adverbs of place by adding the suffix -*i* to adverbs of direction. Following English usage I have collapsed this distinction and written, OUT, for example, to represent both *út* (direction) and *úti* (place). Faroese also has adverbs meaning "from a place," formed by adding the suffix -*an* to the root: thus, *norður* (NORTH), *norðan* (from-NORTH); *heim* (HOME), *heiman* (from-HOME), etc. These simply reverse the direction of the root adverb, and are used to give a slightly different emphasis to already established idioms. A trip from Sandur to Skopun, for example, might be described as "*eg kom heiman*" ("I came from-HOME") or as "*eg kom norður*" ("I came NORTH"). Such formulations are not treated below, since their meaning derives from the meaning of the idioms from which they are formed.

Other suffixes are also possible, but are not treated here for the same reason: *Norðeftir* (NORTHward), *norðaneftir* (from-NORTHward), *norðanfyri* (NORTH of), etc.

On Faroese adverbs and prepositions generally, see Lockwood (1964:53–62, 90–101).

2. Other combinations of prepositions include: *í*, *í*, *úr* (into, in, out of), *til*, *við*, *frá* (to, along, from), and *til*, *á*, *av* (to, on, off).

3. "Up" (*upp*) describes movement up a steep slope, while "down" (*niður*) describes movement down a steep slope. "From-below" (*niðan*) describes movement up a gradual slope, while "from-above" (*oman*) describes movement down a gradual slope. These are used, mostly within very restricted areas, to indicate movement toward the sea or toward the hills. The only idiomatic use of *niður* I know of is "down to Denmark [from the Faroes]." Denmark is often called just "*har niðri*," "down there." For some idioms based on *oman* and *niðan*, see notes 6 and 9, below.

4. The "s" in English "island" is a late, Latinized spelling, probably influenced by "isle" (from Latin *insula*, through the French).

5. The etymology of SOUND is obscure. It may indicate a sundering passage or a swimmable one. The basis of its Faroese sense in West Nor-

wegian thought may be reflected in Icelandic *sundaleið*: "the 'sound-passage,' the course through the islands along the coast of Norway" (Cleasby 1957).

6. You might also say "*oman á kaiuna*" ("from-above onto the dock") if you were approaching it by land. This is a general Faroese expression, noteworthy in Sørvágur only because, exceptionally, Sørvágur's dock is not actually on the shore below the village.

Oman and *niðan* ("from-above" and "from-below") are also used for travel to and from the hamlet of Gásadalur, out along the FJORD past Bøur. One goes "*niðan* to Gásadalur" from Bøur, and returns from Gásadalur "*oman* to Bøur." This special usage reflects an occasional practice of describing a journey in terms of its most spectacular leg—and Gásadalur is cut off by a spectacular mountain from Bøur.

7. I have glossed *um* as ABOUT since it carries both main senses of English "about": around (*venda um, venda seg um*: turn around, turn oneself around) and concerning (*tosa um*: talk about). More idiomatic translations depend on the context: "during," "through," "past," "across," "upon," etc. Some illustrative usages given by Jacobsen and Matras are as follows: "sail ABOUT the headland" and "row ABOUT the spit" (around, past); "reach ABOUT the table" and "jump ABOUT the stream" (over, across); "ABOUT the day" (during); "ABOUT the same time" (at); clouds "drive ABOUT the moon" (across); and the time is "gone ABOUT midnight" (past). Combined with other words, ABOUT gives such senses as: "OUT ABOUT the door" (through, out through); "up ABOUT one's knee" (over, up over); and "through ABOUT" (right through, across).

Unlike the other words considered in this chapter, ABOUT may be used prepositionally as well as adverbially in idioms of orientation.

8. Compass terms were traditionally also used to tell the time of day according to the position of the sun: "it is EAST" (six in the morning), "it is half-WEST" (four-thirty in the afternoon), etc.

9. It is possible that Tórshavn's peculiar nature may underlie a series of highly exceptional idioms based on *oman* and *niðan* ("from-above" and "from-below"). *Oman* and *niðan* usually indicate movement down or up a fairly gentle slope, toward sea level or away from it. But travel along the shore between Skansanes and Holm just outside Tórshavn's harbor is "*oman við Strond*" or "*niðan við Strond*," and, perhaps by extension, "*niðan á Sund*" and "*niðan til Kaldbak*." My collection of terms for the important but extremely complicated area between southern Streymoy and Eysturoy is unfortunately too small to make much of this. One key is perhaps the role of Skálafjørður as the entry point from Tórshavn to Eysturoy ("IN to Strendur," "IN to Nes"). A more tantalizing notion is that one goes "from-above" and "from-below" along the coast outside Tórshavn because Tórshavn, like the places where other, regional parliaments met, is (conceptually) a large rock (the Tinganes) in a depression in the hills. In any case, as the logic of the compass system suggests, Tórshavn is in a way not on the shore at all.

10. A northeast shore is an anomalous thing anyway from a West Norwegian point of view. The sea lies west of Norway. In Faroese (and Icelandic), northwest and southwest are accordingly *útnyrðingur* and *útsynningur* (literally, "out-northerly" and "out-southerly"), while northeast and southeast are *landnyrðingur* and *landsynningur* (literally, "land-northerly" and "land-southerly"). So far as I know, these two words represent the only such uses of *út* in Faroese, where it otherwise means simply OUT to sea, whichever way the sea happens to lie. But the problem of fitting this picture of an outward, westward sea to circumstances in which the sea lies to the east appears in a curious use of *fram* in the northeastern parts of Iceland and the Faroes. Here, for example, the adverb of place *frammi* (outward, forward, seaward) has come to mean up a valley, away from the actual sea. The reason, perhaps, is that in these anomalous parts of Iceland and the Faroes, the "real" sea—real, that is, from a West Norwegian point of view—lies not toward Norway to the east, but upcountry over a considerable stretch of land to the west.

11. Matras 1933:11. The historical parts of the following paragraphs rest largely on Matras's work. The idioms of orientation under discussion are partly his and partly from my collection.

12. Unlike *almost* every other FJORD, that is. Leirvíksfjørður is also curious in being named after a feature on the shore nearer to Streymoy. It "ought" to have been named "Kalsoyarfjørður" for the outlying island of Kalsoy, or perhaps "*Norðoyarfjørður" for the whole outlying archipelago. It may be named as it is for several reasons: because the name "Kalsoyarfjørður" was already taken; because Leirvík, cut off by steep mountains from the rest of Eysturoy, was felt to be part of the Norðoyar; because it is the only settled spot on the FJORD; or because of some combination of these.

13. "The Deeps" (*Djúpini*) may also be a kind of upland depression in that they lie along the actual way, over the mountains of Eysturoy, to the westward sea (cf. note 10, above).

Chapter 3. *Øskudólgur, Social Change, and the Meaning of Faroese Folklore*

1. *Føringatíðindi*, 4 May 1899. *Føringatíðindi* was published from January 1890 until December 1901. (Two further issues appeared in 1906.) A facsimile edition has recently been published, with introductory material by Hans Jacob Debes and Christian Matras.

2. At least one attempt has been made to discover some basic significance in the very similar Norwegian Askeladden tales. Brunvand (1959) discusses two of its characteristic features, the prominence of the youngest of three sons and his habit of sitting by the hearth, in light of the custom of inheritance, noted in various cultures, whereby the youngest son inherits his parents' house. Brunvand suggests that the figure of Ash-

lad may be a remnant of earlier Germanic custom, but the evidence is slim, and the argument largely speculation. In any event, such an analysis does not explain why the tales were of interest to anyone in historical times.

3. This is not true, strictly speaking, of the representatives (*løgtingsmenn, løgmaður*) of the ancient political-judicial assemblies. But these figures' independent standing had long since been eroded, and the old parliament (Løgting) had been abolished in 1816. (It was revived in a slightly different form in 1852, but was for many years nearly powerless.) For recent treatments of the Faroese political system in English, see West (1972) and Wylie (1974, 1978).

4. Faroese did not keep horses. The few ponies in the Faroes were used primarily as pack animals.

5. An unmarried woman is called a *gomul genta* ("old girl"). The princess is not a central figure in this tale, and her ambiguity is less marked than Øskudólgur's. Female but unmarried, her transition to adulthood is relatively simple—a matter of choosing a husband. Unlike real village girls, she is constrained in her choice by her father's setting a fantastical contest for her hand; but even so the final decision is hers, and, looking him up and down, she finds Øskudólgur a suitable groom.

6. Anciently—which is to say, in the time of ballad kings— Øskudólgur would indeed have had this right to appear at the king's court. Before the days of kings, such assemblies were judicial as well as political bodies, and, in the Faroes at least, the king's role was only, in theory, to legitimize them and to confirm the election of their chief spokesman. The Faroes had local, "spring" parliaments (*várting*) as well as the national parliament (Løgting). These were abolished in 1896 (Petersen 1968:245).

7. This transmission of office from a man to his daughter's husband recalls the common practice, after the Reformation, of the post of *løgmaður* passing to the incumbent's son-in-law (cf. Wylie 1978:49–50).

8. For an analysis of the demographic effects of the growth of the export fishery, and an account of the strains caused by the passing of informal labor exchange in one village, see Wylie (1974).

9. *Føringatíðindi*, 2 February 1899. For a detailed history of the Faroese fishery, see Patursson (1961).

10. As "Øskudólgur" is a tale of socialization, it represents a kind of process like the one proposed by van Gennep (1960) for rites of passage. But Douglas's ideas (1966, chap. 6) and Leach's (1966, dealing with symbolic representations of time) provide the basis for expanding van Gennep's model, whereby the story (or the rite) embodies a "loop mechanism" for (1) removing abnormalities, (2) holding them in a "symbolic charging area," and (3) reintroducing previously abnormal figures into an appropriate level of the system. A mechanism of this type may remove individuals from their ordinary level, hold them in a "liminal" position, and return them to their previous level. This is the process Leach discusses. Or it can remove them from their normal level, hold them, then introduce them at

a different level, as is the case for initiation rites. Third, individuals can be removed from *between* well-defined levels or categories, to be introduced on a level they were not previously associated with; Øskudólgur's transformation from ash-lad to king is clearly of this type. Finally, there is the type that removes individuals from between categories in order to reintegrate them in the category to which they previously belonged; this is the course of typical curing rituals.

These four basic types of ritual (and literary) process may be represented in diagrams loosely based on Leach's model (see figure 13).

A. General ritual progress (adapted from Leach)

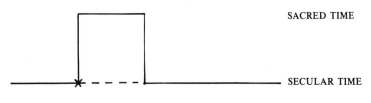

B. Initiation rites

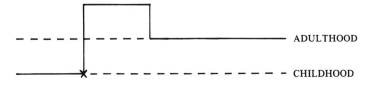

C. Øskudólgur

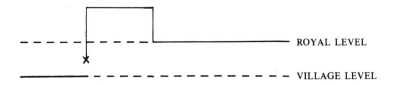

D. Curing rites

Figure 13. Symbolic transformation mechanisms

Time moves from left to right. The solid line represents the progress of a given individual, while the dotted line represents that of other individuals; *X* marks the position of the actor at the beginning of the transformation process. The general pattern of progress is from the course of everyday life through some kind of removal from it (for example by sickness or removal to an initiation ground, or in Øskudólgur's case, by an inability to fit the locationally defined male sex role). Then the subject passes through a liminal period, often under the aegis of sacred or semisacredly endowed figures (doctors, talking birds, shamans, etc.), and is finally reintroduced to the secular course of events. I want to suggest that the plot of this tale, and perhaps of folktales generally, represents a variant of a common ritual pattern.

In the case of "Øskudólgur," at least, it is clear that the sources of power for reinforcing a conceptual system are as potentially dangerous as they are useful. Whether they derive from a figure's lack of definition within the system (Øskudólgur's ambiguous masculinity), or from outside it (the external power of the talking bird, the king's ability to build a glass castle atop a mountain), they consist by definition of all that is beyond mundane control, hence potentially unclean and chaotic. This "power" and its associated "interstitial" and "external" positions are not, in the tale, mere figures of speech; they are precisely represented in the characters' attributes and in the settings in which incidents take place. The tale might be mapped more completely, as in figure 14.

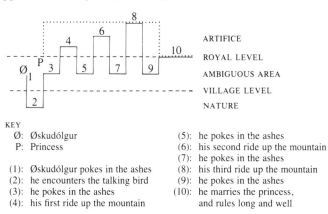

KEY
Ø: Øskudólgur
P: Princess

(1): Øskudólgur pokes in the ashes
(2): he encounters the talking bird
(3): he pokes in the ashes
(4): his first ride up the mountain

(5): he pokes in the ashes
(6): his second ride up the mountain
(7): he pokes in the ashes
(8): his third ride up the mountain
(9): he pokes in the ashes
(10): he marries the princess, and rules long and well

Figure 14. "Øskudólgur" mapped

Outside the system is the inherent chaos of Nature, in reality separated from the village only by the shoreline and the walls of the village center and infield. Øskudólgur is placed between the village and the royal level of society. He is finally integrated on the latter level after his encounter with the talking bird and his expeditions up the mountain into Artifice— an area that represents the extreme case of qualities that define the royal level as opposed to the village level (for example, the untempered individualism possible there) and that represents a superhuman source of power analogous to Nature.

11. Counting separately the two quite different versions of tale 28, there are eight-one folktales in Jakobsen's collection. Of these, thirty-two (nos. 1, 3, 9, 14–18, 24–26, 34–42, 45, 46, 51, 56–58, 61, 65, 69, 72, 73, and 78) deal with boys like Øskudólgur who succeed unconventionally, while two (nos. 29 and 30) deal with boys who do not succeed. Eighteen (nos. 2, 4, 19, 20, 28b, 31, 32, 43, 44, 47, 48, 60, 62, 66, 67, 70, 71, and 77) have female central figures. Three (nos. 8, 10, and 11) have a boy hero and a girl heroine, and three (nos. 12, 21, and 22) concern a mother and her son. In one way or another, all fifty-eight of these tales concern the dangerous fortunes and ambiguous successes of boys and girls away from home. The remaining twenty-three (nos. 5–7, 13, 23, 27, 28a, 33, 49, 50, 52–55, 59, 63, 64, 68, 74–76, 79, and 80) are unrelated, or deal with this theme only peripherally.

The tales with the most variants are "Øskudólgur" (five variants) and the related "Pápaleysi" (no. 1, four variants) and "Lítla Gráa Aftanfyri Hurðarbak" (no. 41, three variants), and the girls' tales "Risans Klóta" (no. 2, five variants) and "Gentan í Risahellinum" (no. 4, four variants). The "unrelated" tales have no more than a single version each; the rest have one or two.

There is some evidence that while both men and women were concerned with what we have loosely called Øskudólgur's problem, men were disproportionately *unconcerned* about the problems of Øskudólgur's female counterparts. Jakobsen collected, in all, 116 tales and variants of tales—in a few cases, the same variants from more than one informant. Breaking down the tales by the types noted above and by the sex of his informants, we get the chart in figure 15.

Figure 15. Jakobsen's tale-"types" and sex of informants

	INFORMANTS			
TALE-"TYPE"	MEN		WOMEN	TOTAL
Øskudólgur, etc.	22 (46%)		26 (54%)	48
Failed lads	1 (33%)		2 (67%)	3
Girl heroines	7 (24%)		22 (76%)	29
Boy and girl	1 (20%)		4 (80%)	5
Mother and son	3 (43%)		4 (57%)	7
Other	12 (50%)		12 (50%)	24
Total	46 (40%)		70 (60%)	116

That is, given the general ratio of 40 percent told by men to 60 percent told by women, the proportions of male and female informants is more or less what one would expect (well within ten percentage points) for all types of tales except girls' tales and ones dealing with a boy and a girl (e.g., "Hansel and Gretel"). (The very miscellaneous "Other" category is split evenly between men and women.) These two types were told very largely by women—76 percent and 80 percent, respectively—suggesting that, like Øskudólgur's brothers, most men did not trouble themselves with the concerns of women's life, while problems like Øskudólgur's were of more even and widespread interest. It is worth noting, too, that six of the seven girls' tales told by men were told by Jóhan Hendrik Matras.

12. A full translation of this tale is as follows:

The Beautiful and Clever Queen

A king wanted to have a wife who was both beautiful and clever, but he found no woman who pleased him. So he dressed himself like a poor boy and went out traveling in order to search for a wife. He came to a poor house and asked the people to put him up. The couple said they had no bed to put him in, unless they put him in their own bed and lay down on the floor themselves. No, the stranger said, he would lie down on the straw himself. He saw no one except those two, and asked if no other people were there. But they concealed [the truth] from him and said there was no one. In the morning he heard someone spinning on a wheel in the attic. They should let him see this person who was at their house, the guest said: for a person *is* there. The couple then had to let him see their daughter—for it was she who had been spinning—and, now, she was the most beautiful of girls to see. The king takes a fancy to her, but thinks it would be too vulgar for him to have a poor man's daughter for his wife. So he goes home and says nothing. But when he got home, he could not rest easy: he thinks about her beauty all the time, but he doesn't know if she might be clever or not. He wants to test her, writes her a letter, encloses a twist of silken thread and asks her to weave it into a rug. She writes him back, encloses a peg in the letter, and asks him to make it into a loom: then she will weave him a rug. Now the king sees that the girl is clever as well as beautiful, fetches her home and makes her his queen, but sets the condition that she not concern herself with affairs of state.

One day a poor man comes to the king's place with a pregnant mare, and the mare is put in the stable where the horses stood. In the morning the mare had foaled; the foal stood among the horses, and thus the men who owned the horses thought the foal belonged to them. The man did not want to go away with no foal, and he presented his case; but it availed nothing. Then he went to the queen and asked her counsel. She told him to take a fishing line, go out to a sand-bank and hold the line down in the sand, and, to each person who came to him and asked why he was sitting like that, he should answer that impossible as it was for him to pull fish from the sand—so it was impossible for horses to foal. The man does so.

People gossip together about him and ask why he is sitting like that; but he answers as the queen had advised him to do. Now he was taken and asked who had taught him that; but he didn't want to say. So he is imprisoned and tortured until he confessed. Now the king hears that the queen had counseled him; he rejects her, because he had forbidden her to concern herself with affairs of state. She says, that before they separate both of them should have a feast first, and she wants to have a treasure with her for remembrance before she leaves the realm. He grants her this: she shall get what she wishes. So they hold a feast; the queen puts sleeping drops in the king's drink, so that she gets him to sleep; then she takes a cart, harnesses a horse, puts the king in the cart and drives away with him to the house where her parents live. Then she lays him down up in the attic in the bed where she herself had been accustomed to sleep. Now when the king awakens in the morning, he is really mad—he asks her why she has done this with him. But she answers that he permitted her to take a treasure with her, whatever she might choose—and she had no greater treasure than himself: so she took him away with her. Then the king saw that there was nothing to do about her, so clever she was. She should come home again with him, he said, and thereafter have the right to give counsel, at her discretion, in all affairs of state as she wanted.

13. The most complete collection of the heroic ballads is Djurhuus and Matras (1951–72). A collection of satiric ballads has recently been published in an attractive little series by Marius Johannesen (1966–74).

14. *Føringatíðindi*, 17 November 1898. The article goes on, "This is worth bearing in mind, not least because, as the speaker said, he is not among those who want to have Faroese be absolutist (*einaráðandi*) in the Faroes." Dr. Jakobsen did not want Faroese to become what Danish had been. He thought its use should be limited to purely local matters, and he objected to the artificiality of the by now nearly established etymological orthography, which was difficult for children to learn (cf. pp. 89–90 and note 5 to chap. 4).

Chapter 4. Language Roles and Culture Contact

1. The following discussion rests partly on Haugen (1976); see also Lockwood (1964:5ff.).

2. The classic account of Faroese dialect differences is Hammershaimb's (1891:lvii ff.); see also O'Neill (1963).

3. The former duchies of Slesvig (German Schleswig) and Holstein lie at the base of the Jutland peninsula. The immensely complicated "Slesvig-Holstein Question" exercised European diplomacy throughout the nineteenth century. It led to war between Denmark and Germany in 1848–49 and in 1864, and triggered the outbreak of the Austro-Prussian War in 1866. The fighting in 1848–49 was inconclusive, but Denmark

was defeated handily in 1864. Since 1866, Slesvig and Holstein have been part of Germany, except that North Slesvig was returned to Denmark in accordance with the results of a plebiscite held in 1920.

Legally, the Slesvig-Holstein Question centered around the issues of their union and the form of their connections with Denmark, the Danish king, and the German Confederation. It was also a constitutional, nationalist, and linguistic question. Some Slesvig-Holsteiners were German speaking while some were Danish speaking. Liberal and nationalist opinion in Denmark held that language was "the primary distinguishing feature of a people who, it was claimed, should be granted the right of political self-determination" (Oakley 1972:172–73).

The gist of Grundtvig's argument is that a Danish government that protested against the use of German as the language of instruction in Slesvig-Holstein could not logically insist that Danish be the language of instruction in the Faroes. His booklet has recently been republished along with Hammershaimb's article and one by his fellow Faroese Niels Winther, an afterword by Hans Bekker-Nielsen, and bibliographical and biographical matter. The quotation below is from pp. 16–17 of this edition, pp. 3–4 of the original.

4. The similarity between written Faroese and written Icelandic was of course unavoidable once an etymological orthography for Faroese had been decided on. There was evidently some disagreement later in the century, when the question of modifying Hammershaimb's orthography arose, as to how closely Faroese should resemble Icelandic. Some people felt that making the orthography more phonetic would have the undesirable effect of estranging Icelanders and Faroese (e.g., *Føringatíðindi*, 3 June 1897), while others were prepared to go so far as to say: "If the plan is to push our mother tongue so far that we, by using it, can come so near Icelanders that Icelanders and Faroese can use the same language, then for my part I must say: Rather a thousand times have Danish church, school and legal language than Icelandic—and [this] although I certainly feel myself to be as Faroese in disposition as any man" (*Føringatíðindi*, 2 March 1899).

5. The course of the controversy may be followed in detail in *Føringatíðindi*.

Jakobsen first published pieces in his more phonetic orthography in the Faroes' other newspaper, *Dimmalætting*. These were derided by *Føringatíðindi* (December 1890), although Hammershaimb himself seems to have taken Jakobsen's efforts more seriously (Hammershaimb 1891:lvi). In August 1892, however, *Føringatíðindi* reported a formal proposal "to try to institute an acceptable change of Hammershaimb's orthography, which might be expected to be easier to learn to read and especially to write." It published the proposed changes in detail in January 1893, and in September announced the formation of a special committee to look into the issue.

Matters now apparently hung fire for about two years. Then in October 1895 the proposed changes (with some further modifications) were again brought up; *Føringatíðindi* published these on 2 January 1896, along with the committee's comments. Some changes were accepted, but these were mostly minor. Such major changes as abandoning ð were rejected. The Føringafelag's membership now found itself badly split; on 20 September Jóannes Patursson resigned from the society, remaining only to edit *Føringatíðindi's* edition for 1 October, which is almost entirely taken up with a long review of the language issue and a history of the society. He, like many others, disapproved of the changes. Matters were brought to a head again by a proposal from society members in Copenhagen to drop the changes. This was done in March 1898, and confirmed in December. By now, however, the Føringafelag's hold on its membership was slipping badly, and in 1901 it passed quietly out of existence.

Reading through the old newspapers, one has the impression that although the Føringafelag "died of quarreling" (H. J. Debes 1969)—and Faroese avoid quarreling whenever possible (cf. Wylie 1974)—its journal did provide a testing ground for Faroese as a language of debate. It was all the more important, then, that its language be, or look, as "high" as possible, since everyday speech is not a language for disagreement. As one correspondent who favored the more etymological orthography wrote to *Føringatíðindi* at the height of the debate, "If they will not recognize our writing system, then the language will travel a very short path—then it will not be honorable—no, then it will come no farther than everyday use among us, and it [this result] will befall each part of the society,—this [a return to Hammershaimb's orthography] must also be the best way of returning compromise and peace to our society, which the change [in orthography] has divided" (*Føringatíðindi*, 21 January 1897).

The language question was the main reason for the Føringafelag's dissolution, but not the only one. A related problem was organizational—its division into "village societies" as opposed to a single society centered in Tórshavn. In an organizational way, this is of course much the same problem as that of rural dialects versus urban standards.

Chapter 5. Grindadráp

1. For an account of real mayhem—enough to appall a Faroese *grindamaður*—on a "porpoise" hunt on the Blasket Islands in Ireland, see Ó Crohan (1951:8–12).

Hebrideans, Orcadians, and Shetlanders have hunted *grindir* much as the Faroese do. As Williamson says, however, the hunt in the Scottish islands "had nothing like the same sociological significance" (1970:117), although in the Shetlands, at least, the arrival of a *grind* did generate considerable excitement until the early twentieth century. By this time the Shetland *grindadráp* had become quite degenerate. For a description, see Sandison (1895). For a discussion of laws governing ownership of the whales which offers a most interesting contrast to Faroese laws and suggests why the Shetland *grindadráp* may have degenerated, see Edmondston (1809, 2:154–74).

I translate below a description of how the last stages of the *grindadráp* should be carried out, according to an unsigned article in *Føringatíðindi*, 7 July 1898:

> A proper man makes no thrust without thinking what it will achieve. He knows how to stab where he plans, and as hard as he wants.
>
> When it happens in the first rush forward to strike in such a way that the whole *grind* or a large part of it runs aground, then the slaughter will be ended most quickly, the whales suffer the least pain, and the meat will be the least cut into with infectious matter, which can cause it to become "burned" or spoiled.
>
> Sometimes the *grind* has turned out again or is milling about before it is right to strike. Then it is right to strike hard the whales who are on the way outward, and otherwise to "make blood in the *grind*" as quickly as possible. At the same time, it must not be forgotten that there are stupid people who waste their strength by slicing the blubber apart instead of making fewer stabs, which likewise cause bleeding.
>
> When "blood has come in" and there is a proper milling about, it is right to strike a great deal, so that the *grind* is pushed nearer to land, where it is shallower—so that the whales have little room to be under the water—and it is a shorter way of bringing to land those whales that are killed out on the water. Men unused to the work stab the *grind* as much away from the land as toward it. Such men should be driven out of the slaughter by the foreman or leaders.
>
> The whales may be stabbed hard, so that they die with the first stab. When this is done thoroughly and the *sóknarongul* is at hand, so that the whale does not sink, then the whale will not be hurt unnecessarily and the slaughter will go on quickly.
>
> A proper man does not attack a living whale except for this reason: lest it get free to run with the boat with the risk of causing damage to boats or men.

2. The Old Norse word had supernatural connotations as well. A *grind*, in the Old Norse sense of a gridwork, is used magically in a critical passage in the *Færeyingasaga*, which describes the advent of Christianity in the Faroes. Tróndur í Gøtu, the leader of the pagan faction, places some kind of square frame or wickerwork—a *grind*—in front of a fire and draws nine circles around it in order to call forth the shade of his Christian rival Sigmundur, to discover who Sigmundur's murderer had been. "It may be noted in this connection that the word *grind* figures in the names of the barriers which enclosed the worlds of the dead in early Norse belief"

(Foote 1964:94). The Arab traveler Ibn Fadlan, who in about 922 visited Swedish encampments on the Volga and had the dubious privilege of witnessing a funeral, describes how a "thing like a door-frame" was held up three times for a slave girl who was about to be sacrificed to look through; through it she saw the dead (Garmonsway, Norman, and Simpson 1968:343).

3. On the various boð, see R. Joensen (1961).

4. On the *gyllin* measure, see Zachariasen (1961:392ff.).

5. Certainly men of the North have long hunted whales. A Neolithic rock carving at Strand, in North Trøndelag, Norway depicts a whale with—curiously—a mysterious latticework pattern over its tail (Ellis Davidson 1967:19, 26). Toward the end of the ninth century, the Norwegian traveler Ohthere spoke matter-of-factly to King Alfred's court about large, even commercial fisheries for narwhals and great whales (Bright 1935:38–39).

6. Peterson (1968:42, 82). The laws referred to are those of King Magnus, Ch. VII, Art. 64. For a modern Norwegian translation, see Taranger (1968:158–60). On "the land's" ownership of a portion of a *grind*, see below, pp. 120–21. Faroese law was codified in the *Seyðabræv* of 1298, in which articles 8 and 11 deal with whaling. Article 8 reads: "Now if a farmer's farm-hands meet a whale out on the sea and cut a boat-load from it, then they have the seventh part of it; but if they bring the whale to land uncut, then they have from it as the lawbook says. Now if men drive a whale onto land, but do not own the land below, chase and save it beyond the high-tide mark, they shall have the fourth from it. It is the same with wood. But if men find cows or sheep or other cattle out on the sea and bring them to shore, then they shall own the fourth from it" (Jakobsen 1907:15; cf. Petersen 1968:294–95).

7. In modern Faroese, a *nýðingur* is a large *grind* whale. A young *grind* whale is called a *leiftur* or a *grindahvølpur* ("*grind* whelp").

There are said to be two kinds of *grind* whales. One is distinguished by a broader dorsal fin and a thicker shape; the other has a thinner and higher fin, and its body is leaner (Müller 1883:2; Williamson 1949:70–71; J. P. Joensen 1976:1). Williamson and Joensen agree that the high-finned type is more easily driven.

8. Cf. Williamson (1970:115): "The sporting parson, apparently, is no rarity in the Faeroes but it is considered most unlucky for the boat containing him to get between the *grind* and the shore. It is also very unlucky to have a woman bearing an unborn child present at the slaughter." The stress on pregnant women may be related to the fact that pregnant whales sometimes abort spontaneously during the slaughter. On the other hand, in keeping with the generally matter-of-fact Faroese attitude toward the *grindadráp*, young whales and fetuses nearly fully formed are eaten, but are not thought to be particularly good (or bad). It is also said that the blubber of milking whales takes salt badly—it tends to be thin and rather runny. This is of course negative evidence; but surely other peoples might

be inspired to build myths or taboos on these observations about mother whales.

9. See Wylie (1978) for a detailed treatment in English of the Faroese legal-political system after the Reformation.

10. For detailed descriptions in English of changes in the rules of distribution, see Debes (1676), Landt (1810), Müller (1883), Williamson (1945, 1970), and J. P. Joensen (1976); Joensen has a comprehensive bibliography for Danish, Faroese, and other sources.

11. My account here follows Petersen (1968:43 et passim); cf. J. P. Joensen (1976:21ff.).

12. Petersen (1968:46); J. P. Joensen (1976:22, 25) says 1934.

13. On Danish officials' incorporation into traditional Faroese society, see Wylie (1978). West (1972:79–84) describes the work and character of these governors: Christian Tillisch (1825–30), his brother Frederik Tillisch (1830–37), Christian Pløyen (1837–48), and the rather less well-liked, or less well-appreciated, Carl Emil Dahlerup (1849–62).

14. Today, of course, fishermen are paid their shares out of the proceeds of the whole catch, though it is customary for them to reserve a few fish for themselves for household use. The whole system of payment by shares presupposes a labor-intensive fishery. For an account of its uneconomical aspects in the more modern and capital-intensive sectors of today's fishery, see í Jákupsstovu (1972).

15. In a sense, the modern equivalent of Pløyen's "Grindevise" is the terrific series of paintings of the *grindadráp* by the Faroese artist S. J. Mikines (b. 1906). One of these hangs in the meeting room of the Løgting in Tórshavn.

16. The prize for a ridiculous appreciation of the *grindadráp* must go to John Buchan, in whose adventure story *The Island of Sheep* the role of (as it were) the U. S. Cavalry is played by an "army" of *rakstrarmenn*, "men shaggy and foul with blood, and each with a reeking spear . . . ; their hair and eyes were like the wild things of the hills; the cries that came from their throats were not those of articulate-speaking men. . . ." (1956:237). The baddies are routed. Had the men been articulate, they might have been singing a close runner-up for the prize—a martial air (sung to the tune of "*La Marseillaise*") called "Grindavysa" published in Copenhagen in 1892. To translate this would be to perform a disservice to Faroese letters; but it, and the volume of verse in which it appeared (Jakobsen 1892), are of some interest in being written according to the orthography favored by Jakobsen, not the one developed by Hammershaimb and shortly adopted as standard.

A Note on Sources

The Faroes support a very large literature which is, however, somewhat diffuse. We list below, along with references from our text, some of the more important works about the Faroes, particularly ones in English or with English summaries.

1. *Bibliography*. Large bibliographies will be found in Dansk-Færøsk Samfund (1958) and Trap (1968), and in West (1972), Williamson (1970), and Wylie (1974, 1978). Whitaker (1978) reviews recent anthropological literature. The annual catalogue from H. N. Jacobsen's bookstore in Tórshavn is as good a guide as any to books in print.

2. *Language*. The standard dictionaries are Jacobsen and Matras (1961; with supplement, 1974) and av Skarði (1967). Svabo's eighteenth-century Faroese-Danish-Latin dictionary has recently been published (1966–70). Hammershaimb (1891) contains a large Danish-Faroese glossary. The standard comprehensive grammar is Lockwood (1964). Hammershaimb (1891) contains the classic description of Faroese dialects; see also O'Neill (1963).

3. *History*. On "Viking" Faroe, see S. Dahl (1971) and scattered references in general studies of Viking times (e.g., G. Jones 1968; Foote and Wilson 1970). For translations of the *Færeyingasaga* see Powell (1896), Press (1934), and Young and Clewer (1973), and for properly skeptical appreciations of its historicity, see Foote (1964, 1965, 1970).

Primary sources for later periods—particularly after the mid-sixteenth century—include: Jakobsen (1907; the late Middle Ages), Evensen (1908–14; sixteenth century), and E. Joensen (1955, 1958, 1961, 1969; 1615–90); and Debes (1673, 1676), Svabo (1959), Landt (1800, 1810), and West (1970). N. Andersen (1895) excerpts many seventeenth-century documents. Degn (1933, 1945) provides a starting point for any historical consideration of land tenure in the Faroes. The recent facsimile edition of *Føringatíðindi* is a gold mine for the crucial period 1890–1900.

The literature on special topics is large but mostly in Faroese. See Degn (1929) and Joensen, Mortensen, and Petersen (1955; with English summary) on commercial history; Petersen (1974; with English summary) on the Løgting; Nolsøe (1963–70) on maritime history; Patursson (1961) on fishing; Zachariasen (1961) on the period 1535–1655, and N. Andersen (1895) on the period 1600–1709.

The only full-length history of the Faroes in English is West (1972), which is particularly devoted to political developments since the mid-nineteenth century. On the period following the Reformation, see Wylie (1978). Wylie (1974) surveys Faroese history, with particular attention to demographic developments since about 1800.

Histories of Denmark (e.g., Oakley 1972; W. Jones 1970) sometimes mention the Faroes, or Faroe-Danish relations.

4. *Surveys of the Faroe Scene.* See Debes (1673; English translation, 1676), Svabo (1959), and Landt (1800; in a somewhat abridged English translation, 1810) for earlier periods. For modern times, see for example J.-F. Jacobsen (1970; sometimes with an English summary), Heinesen (1966; in Danish), and Williamson (1970; in English). Trap (1968) and particularly Dansk-Færøsk Samfund (1958) are indispensable. Both are in Danish.

5. *Travelers' Accounts, Human Geography, and Anthropology.* Works in these categories rather overlap, and vary immensely in quality. For a guide to works in English, see the annotated bibliography in West (1972). In forming a preliminary assessment of both casual and scholarly accounts, one should of course note how long a visitor was in the Faroes and what language he spoke with Faroese. Many—even most—books and articles are based on a summer stay of only a few weeks, and commonly evince a conviction that the writer has been among the first to "discover" the Faroes. Sometimes, however, even a brief stay has been reported with keen observation (e.g., Panum 1940). These comments naturally do not apply to works by Faroese.

The properly social-scientific literature is rather small. Wylie (1974) is the only full-length ethnography of a Faroese village. J. P. Joensen (1975) is a remarkable study of life on board the smacks, sloops, and schooners that were once the backbone of the Faroese fishing industry. See also his account of the *grindadráp* (1976). M. Andersen (1971) considers the fate of Faroese girls who emigrate to Copenhagen. Í Jákupsstovu (1972; in Faroese and English) considers the economic sociology of commercial fishing. Hermansson (1972; in Swedish), E. Vestergaard (1974; in Danish), and T. Vestergaard (1974; in Danish) are ethnographic accounts of aspects of village life. Two articles by Blehr (1963, 1964) have gained a certain currency in the anthropological literature. Otherwise, see Adams et al. (1966), Brimnes (1971), John (1971), Meesenburg (1971), Neve and Nielsen (1971), Nielung (1971), West (1977), and Williamson (1970), among the more recent literature.

6. *Folklore and Folk Literature.* The standard collection of ballads is Djurhuus and Matras (1951–72). The standard collection of legends and folktales is Jakobsen (1898–1901). For satirical ballads, etc. (*tættir*), see Johannesen (1966, 1969, 1974). For an excellent brief introduction to Far-

oese folkways, see Rasmussen (1968; in Faroese), and for a good deal of rather miscellaneous material in English see Williamson (1970). For a compendium (in Faroese) of customary law see Petersen (1968). In general, of course, one can hardly do without Dansk-Færøsk Samfund (1958).

Faroese folklore supports a wide secondary literature, little of which is in English.

7. *Periodicals.* The Faroes support an immense periodical literature in many fields, most of which is naturally in Faroese or Danish. The scholarly journal *Fróðskaparrit* often has articles in English, and those in other languages have English summaries. Statistical data are available in the *Årsberetning* put out each year by the office of the Rigsombudsmand på Færøerne; in an occasional journal called *Faroes in Figures* put out at irregular intervals by a group of Tórshavn businesses; and in the Danish Government's *Statistiske Årbog* and the United Nations' *Demographic Yearbook.* The local *Varðin* is a distinguished historical, literary, and folkloric journal. The Faroese-Danish *Fra Færøerne/Úr Føroyum* contains articles of historical, artistic, and sometimes political interest. The tourist publication *Welcome to the Faroes* often has excellent articles and always has beautiful photographs. Finally, an English-language journal devoted to Faroese subjects, *The Faroe Review*, has begun to be published in Tórshavn.

Bibliography

Aarne, Antti, and Thompson, Stith. 1964. 2d revision. *The types of the folktale*. FF Communications no. 184. Helsinki: Suomalainen tieakatemia (Academia scientiarum fennica).

Adams, D. R., et al. 1966. *Expedition to Vidoy, the Faroe Islands 1966*. Newcastle: University of Newcastle Upon Tyne Exploration Society. Mimeographed.

Andersen, Maria. 1971. *Føroyskar gentur í Keypmannahavn*. Copenhagen: Hitt føroyska studentafelagið.

Andersen, Niels. 1895. *Færøerne 1600–1709*. Copenhagen: G. E. C. Gad. Reissued 1964, edited by John Davidsen. Tórshavn: Justinssen.

Anonymous. 1885. Faroe whales. *Saturday Review of Politics, Science, and Art* 60:474–76.

Blehr, Otto. 1963. Action groups in a society with bilateral kinship: A case study from the Faroe Islands. *Ethnology* 2:269–77.

———. 1964. Ecological change and organizational continuity in the Faroe Islands. *Folk* 6:29–33.

Blöndal, Sigfús, ed. 1908. *Æfisaga Jóns Ólafssonar Indíafara samin af honum sjálfum (1661)*. Vol. 1. Copenhagen: Hitt Íslenska Bókmentafelagið, and S. L. Möller.

Bradford, Dernle, and Woolfit, Adam. 1970. Denmark's Faroes, isles of maybe. *National Geographic Magazine* 138:410–42.

Bright, James W. 1935. *Bright's Anglo-Saxon reader*. Revised and enlarged by James R. Hulbert. New York: Holt, Rinehart and Winston.

Brimnes, Ole. 1971. Tanker omkring en tyveårig dagbog. *Bygd* 2 (4):18–23.

Brunvand, Jan. 1959. Norway's askeladden, the unpromising hero, and junior-right. *Journal of American Folklore* 72:14–23.

Buchan, John. 1956 [1936]. *The island of sheep*. Harmondsworth: Penguin.

Cleasby, Richard. 1957. 2d ed. *An Icelandic-English dictionary*. Revised, enlarged, and completed by G. Vigfusson, with a supplement by Sir William Craigie. Oxford: Clarendon.

Dahl, Adolf. 1931. Gomul trúgv úr Sandoy. *Varðin* 11 (1–2):46–54.

Dahl, Sverri. 1971. The Norse settlement of the Faroe Islands. *Medieval Archaeology* 14 (1970):61–73.

Dansk-Færøsk Samfund. 1958. *Færøerne*. 2 vols. Copenhagen: Dansk-Færøsk Samfund, Dansk-Færøsk Kulturfund, and Det Danske Forlag.

Debes, Hans Jacob. 1969. Formæli: Tjóðskaparrørslan og føringafelagstíðin, in *Føringatíðindi* [facsimile edition]. Tórshavn: Emil Thomsen.

Debes, Lucas. 1673. *Færoæ et Færoa reserata*, [etc.]. Copenhagen: Mattias Jørgensen. Republished 1963, with an introduction by Einar Joensen. Tórshavn: Einars Prent og Forlag.

———. 1676. *Færoæ et Færoa reserata: that is a description of the islands and inhabitants of Foeroe[. . .]*, englished by J[ohn] S[terpin], doctor of physic. London: W. Isles.

Degn, Anton. 1929. *Oversigt over fiskeriet og monopolhandelen paa Færøerne 1709–1856*. Tórshavn: Varðin.

———. 1933. Kongs-, ognar- og prestajørð í Føroyum. *Varðin* 13 (3–4):65–83.

———. 1945. *Færøske kongsbønder, 1584–1884*. Tórshavn: Varðin.

Djupedal, Reidar. 1964. Litt om framvoksteren av det færøyske skriftmålet, in *Skriftsspråk i utvikling: Tiårsskrift for norsk språknemnd 1952–1962*. Edited by Alf Hellevik and Einar Lundeby, pp. 144–86. Oslo: J. W. Cappelen.

Djurhuus, N., and Matras, Christian, eds. 1951–72. *Føroya kvæði: Corpus carminum Færoensium a Sv. Grundtvig et J. Bloch comparatum*. 6 vols. Copenhagen: Einar Munksgaard [vols. 1–3], Akademisk Forlag [vols. 4–6], and Universitets-Jubilæets Danske Samfund [all vols.].

Douglas, Mary. 1966. *Purity and danger: An analysis of concepts of pollution and taboo*. London: Routledge & Kegan Paul.

Edmondston, Arthur. 1809. *A view of the ancient and present state of the Zetland Islands [. . .] in two volumes*. Edinburgh and London: John Ballantyne, and Longman, Hurst, Rees and Orme.

Ellis Davidson, H. R. 1967. *Pagan Scandinavia*. New York: Praeger.

Evensen, A. C., ed. 1908–14. *Savn til føroyinga sögu í 16. öld*. Tórshavn: Hitt Føroyska Bókmentafelagið.

Foote, Peter G. 1964. Færeyinga saga, chapter forty. *Fróðskaparrit* 13:84–98.

———. 1965. *On the Saga of the Faroe Islanders*. London: H. K. Lewis.

———. 1970. On legal terms in *Færeyinga saga*. *Fróðskaparrit* 18:159–75.

Foote, Peter G., and Wilson, D. M. 1970. *The Viking achievement*. New York: Praeger.

Garmonsway, George Norman, and Simpson, Jacqueline, trans. 1968. *Beowulf and its analogues*. London and New York: Dutton.

Geertz, Clifford. 1972. Deep play: notes on the Balinese cockfight. *Dædalus* (Winter 1972):1–38.

van Gennep, Arnold. 1960. *The rites of passage*. Translated by Marika B. Vizedom and Gabrielle C. Daffee. Introduction by Solon T. Kimball. Chicago: University of Chicago Press.

Grundtvig, Svend. 1845. *Dansken paa Færøerne, sidestykke til Tysken i Slesvig*. Copenhagen: C. A. Reitzel. Republished 1978, C. C. Rafn-Forelæsning nr. 5. Edited, with an afterword, by Hans Bekker-Nielsen. Odense: Odense Universitetsforlaget.

Hammershaimb, Venceslaus Ulricus, ed. 1851. *Færöiske Kvæder I: Sjúrðar Kvæði*. *Nordiske Oldskrifter*, vol. 12. Copenhagen: Det Nordiske Literatur-Samfund.

———. 1891. *Færøsk Anthologi*. 2 vols. Copenhagen: S. L. Møller (Møller and Thomsen). Facsimile edition 1969. Tórshavn: Hammershaimbsgrunnurin.

Hansen, J. Símun. 1966. *Havið og vit. 2. partur: Minniligir dagar*. Klaksvík: privately published.

———. 1971. *Tey byggja land. 1. partur: Fugloyar sókn*. Klaksvík: privately published.

Haugen, Einar. 1957. The semantics of Icelandic orientation. *Word* 13:447–60.

———, ed. 1965. *Norsk Engelsk Ordbok. Norwegian English Dictionary*. Oslo and Madison: Universitetsforlaget and University of Wisconsin Press.

———. 1966. Semicommunication: The language gap in Scandinavia, in *Explorations in sociolinguistics*. Edited by Stanley Lieberson, pp. 152–69. Bloomington and The Hague: Mouton.

———. 1968. The Scandinavian languages as cultural artifacts, in *Language problems of developing nations*. Edited by Joshua A. Fishman, Charles A. Ferguson, and Jyotirinda Das Gupta, pp. 267–84. New York: Wiley.

———. 1976. *The Scandinavian languages: An introduction*. London and Cambridge, Mass.: Faber and Faber, and Harvard University Press.

Heinesen, Jens Pauli, ed. 1966. *Føroyar í dag (Færøerne i dag)*. Tórshavn: Norrøna Felagið.

Hermansson, Nanna. 1972. *Nólsoy: En färöisk bygd i omvandling*. Lund: Etnologiska institutionen, Lund Universitet. Mimeographed.

Jacobsen, Jørgen-Frantz. 1965. *The farthest shore*. Copenhagen: Royal Danish Ministry for Foreign Affairs.

———. 1970. *Færøerne: Natur og folk*. 3d ed. Tórshavn: H. N. Jacobsens Bókahandil.

Jacobsen, M. A., and Matras, Christian, eds. 1961. *Føroysk-donsk orðabók* (*Færøsk-dansk ordbog*). 2d ed., revised and expanded. Tórshavn: Føroya Fróðskaparfelag.

———, eds. 1974. *Føroysk-donsk orðabók* (*Færøsk-dansk ordbog*): *Eykabind* (*Supplementsbind*). Prepared by Jóhan Hendrik W. Poulsen. Tórshavn: Føroya Fróðskaparfelag.

Jakobsen, Jakob, ed. 1892. *Føriskar vysur írktar o sungnar äv Føringun y Kjøpinhavn (1876–92)*. Copenhagen: S. L. Møller.

———. 1898–1901. *Færøske folkesagn og æventyr*. 2 vols. Copenhagen: Samfund til udgivelse af gammel norsk litteratur. Republished in 3 vols. 1964–72. Tórshavn: H. N. Jacobsens Bókahandil.

———. 1906. Dansur og kvøðing. *Føringatíðindi* 13 (2) (28 February 1906):2.

———, ed. 1907. *Diplomatarium Færoense: Føroyst fodnbrævasavn.* [Vol. 1.] *Miðalaldarbrøv upp til trúbótarskeiðið.* Tórshavn and Copenhagen: H. N. Jacobsen, and Vilh. Prior.

———. 1928. *An etymological dictionary of the Norn language in Shetland*. London and Copenhagen: David Nutt, and Vilhelm Prior.

———. 1974. *Sagnirnar um Óla Jarnheys og Snæbjörn*. Illustrated by Barður Jákupsson. Tórshavn: Bókagarðurin.

í Jákupsstovu, Jákup. 1972. *Kor fiskimanna í Føroyum* (*Wage determination and working conditions for fishermen in the Faroe Islands*). Tórshavn: Marius Ziska.

Joensen, Einar, ed. 1955. *Tingbókin 1615–54*. Tórshavn: Landskjalasavnið.

———, ed. 1958. *Løgtings- og vártingsbókin 1655–1666*. Tórshavn: Landskjalasavnið.

———, ed. 1961. *Løgtingsbókin 1666–77*. Tórshavn: Landskjalasavnið.

———, ed. 1969. *Vártings- og løgtingsbókin 1667–1690*. Tórshavn: Landskjalasavnið.

Joensen, Jóan Pauli. 1975. *Færøske sluppfiskere: Etnologisk undersøgelse af en erhvervsgruppes liv*. Lund: Gleerup.

———. 1976. Pilot whaling in the Faroe Islands. *Ethnologia Scandinavica 1976*:1–42.

Joensen, Jóhan K.; Mortensen, Arnbjørn; and Petersen, Poul. 1955. *Føroyar undir fríum handli í 100 ár: Minnisrit um frígeving Føroya handla 1 januar 1856*. Tórshavn: Føroya Landsstýri.

Joensen, Robert. 1961. *At glaða og at brenna vita*. Klaksvík.

Johannesen, Marius. 1966. *Tættir I: Nólsoyar Páll*. Tórshavn: Tingakrossur.

———. 1969. *Tættir II: Hoyberatáttur, Brókartáttur, Lorvíkspáll, Ánaniasartáttur*. Tórshavn: Tingakrossur.

———. 1974. *Tættir III: Símunartáttur og 10 aðrir tættir*. Tórshavn: Tingakrossur.

———. 1976. *Eitt sindur um Kalsoynna og nakrar sagnir knýttar at henni*. Tórshavn: Grønalíð.

Jóhansen, Johannes. 1971. A paleobotanical study indicating a pre-Viking settlement in Tjørnuvík, Faroe Islands. *Fróðskaparrit* 19:147–57.

Johansen, Sámal. 1970. *Á bygd fyrst í tjúgundu øld.* Tórshavn and Vágur: H. N. Jacobsens Bókahandil.

John, B. S., ed. 1971. *Village studies from the Faroe Islands.* University of Durham Department of Geography, Occasional Papers 12. (Mimeographed.)

Jones, Gwyn. 1968. *A history of the Vikings.* New York: Oxford University Press.

Jones, W. Glyn. 1970. *Denmark.* New York: Praeger.

Labonne, Henry. 1888. *L'Islande et l'archipel des Færoer.* Paris: Hachette. First published in *Le Tour du Monde* 54 [2d semester, 1887]:385–416.

Landt, Jørgen. 1800. *Forsøg til en beskrivelse over Færøerne.* Copenhagen: Tikjøbs.

———. 1810. *A description of the Feroe Islands [. . .] translated from the Danish.* London: Longman, Hurst, Rees and Orme.

Leach, Edmund. 1966. Two essays concerning the symbolic representation of time, in *Rethinking anthropology,* pp. 124–36. London: Athlone.

Lévi-Strauss, Claude. 1968. *Tristes tropiques.* Translated by John Russell. New York: Athaneum.

Lindbergh, Anne Morrow. 1974. *Locked rooms and open doors: Diaries and letters of Anne Morrow Lindbergh, 1933–1945.* New York: Harcourt Brace Jovanovich.

Lockwood, W. B. 1964. *An introduction to modern Faroese.* Copenhagen: Munksgaard.

Lützen, Christian. 1958. Undervisning, in *Færøerne,* vol. 2 (Dansk-Færøsk Samfund), pp. 33–55.

Margolin, David. 1970. Øskudólgur and Faroese society. Unpublished senior honors thesis, Harvard University, Cambridge, Mass.

Matras, Christian. 1932. Stednavne paa de færøske Norðuroyar. *Aarbøger for Nordisk Oldkyndighed og Historie* 22: 1–322.

———. 1933. *Stednavne paa de færøske Norðuroyar.* Copenhagen: H. H. Theiles.

———. 1968. Sproget, in *Trap, Danmark.* Edited by N. Nielsen et al., pp. 167–74.

———. 1969. *Føringatíðindi og móðurmálið,* in *Føringatíðindi* [foreword to facsimile edition]. Tórshavn: Emil Thomsen.

Meesenburg, H. 1971. Tanker omkring et liniediagram. *Bygd* 2 (4):29–31.

Müller, A. C. 1883. Whale-fishing in the Faroe Isles, in *Fish and fisheries: A selection of prize essays of the International Fisheries Exhibi-*

tion, Edinburgh 1882. Edited by Daniel Herbert, pp. 1–17. Edinburgh and London: William Blackwood and Sons.

Neve, Hanne, and Nielsen, Leif. 1971. Der var engang en bygd, der hed Næs. *Bygd* 2 (4):3–16.
Nielung, Ole. 1971. Klaksvík—en færøsk storbygd. *Bygd* 2 (4):25–8.
Nolsøe, Páll J. 1963–70. *Føroya siglingarsøga*. 7 vols. Tórshavn: privately published.
Norgate, Sidney. 1943. *"Kanska" or the land of maybe*. Tórshavn: H. N. Jacobsen.

Oakley, Stewart. 1972. *A short history of Denmark*. New York: Praeger.
Ó Crohan, Tomás. 1951. *The Islandman*. Translated by Robin Flower. Oxford: Clarendon.
O'Neil, Wayne. 1963. The dialects of modern Faroese: A preliminary report. *Orbis* 12 (2):393–97.

Panum, Peter Ludvig. 1940. *Panum on measles: Observations made during the epidemic of measles on the Faroe Islands in the year 1846*. Translated by Ada Sommerville Hatcher. New York: Delta Omega Society.
Patursson, Erlendur. 1961. *Fiskiveiði fiskimenn*. 2 vols. Tórshavn: Einars Prent.
Petersen, Poul. 1968. *Ein føroysk bygd*. Tórshavn: privately published.
———. 1974. *Føroyar í søguni I*. Funningur: privately published.
Phillpotts, Bertha S., ed. and trans. 1923. *The life of the Icelander Jón Ólafsson traveller to India* [etc.]. *Vol. 1: Life and travels: Iceland, England, Denmark, White Sea, Faroes, Spitzbergen, Norway 1593–1622*. Works issued by the Hakluyt Society, Second Series, no. 53. London: The Hakluyt Society.
Powell, F. York. 1896. *The tale of Thrond of Gate*. London: D. Nutt.
Press, Muriel A. C. 1934. *The Saga of the Faroe Islanders*. London: J. M. Dent and Sons.

Rasmussen, Rasmus. 1968. *Føroysk fólkamenning*. Copenhagen: Føroyska Studentafelagið.

Sandison, A. 1895. Whale hunting in the Shetlands. *Saga Book of the Viking Club, or Orkney, Shetland, and Northern Society* 1 (1):42–53.
Schrøter, J. H. 1951–53 [1819]. *J. H. Schrøters optegnelser af Sjúrðar Kvæði*. Edited by Christian Matras. Vol. 3. Copenhagen: Munksgaard.
Scott, E. O. G. 1942. Records of Tasmanian Cetacea: No. II: A large school of the pilot whale, *Globiocephalus melas* (Traill, 1809), stranded at Stanley, Northwestern Tasmania, in October, 1935. *Rec-*

ords of the Queen Victoria Museum, Launceston, Tasmania 1 (2): 5–34.

Sergeant, D. E. 1953. Newfoundland's pothead whale industry. Canada Department of Fisheries *Trade News* 5 (9):3–4.

———. 1962. *The biology of the pilot or pothead whales* Globiocephala melaena *(Traill) in Newfoundland waters*. Fisheries Research Control Board of Canada, Bulletin no. 132.

Skaale, Óluva, and Johannesen, Marius. 1974. 2d ed. *Matur og matgerð*. Tórshavn: Grønalíð.

av Skarði, Jóhannes. 1967. *Donsk-Føroysk orðabók (Dansk-Færøsk ordbog)*. Tórshavn: Føroya Fróðskaparfelag.

Svabo, Jens Christian. 1779. Om den færøske marsviin-fangst. *Det Almindelige Danske Bibliothek: Et Maaneds-Skrift* (Copenhagen) 3.

———. 1959. *Indberetninger fra en rejse i Færøe, 1781–1782*. Edited by N. Djurhuus. Copenhagen: Selskabet til Udgivelse af Færøske Kildeskrifter og Studier.

———. 1966–70. *Dictionarium Færoense. Færøsk-dansk-latinsk ordbog*. 2 vols. Færoensia, Textus et Investigationes, vols. 7 and 8. Edited by Christian Matras. Copenhagen: Munksgaard.

Taranger, Absalon, ed. and trans. 1968. *Magnus Lagabøters Landslov*. 4th printing. Oslo, Bergen, and Tromsø: Universitetsforlaget.

Tierney, J. J., ed. 1967. *Dicuili liber de mensura orbis terræ*. Scriptores latini Hibernæ 6. Dublin: Dublin Institute for Advanced Studies.

Trap, J. P. 1968. *Trap, Danmark. Bind 13: Færøerne*. 5th edition. Edited by Niels Nielsen, Peter Skautrup, Therkel Mathiassen, and Jóannes Rasmussen. Copenhagen: Gads.

Vestergaard, Elisabeth. 1974. *En beskrivelse af religiøse ritualer i bygden Sand på Færøerne og deres ændring eller ophør i løbet af de sidste hundrede år*. Etnografisk Institut, Århus Universitet, Studenterfeldrapport nr. 3. Århus: Moesgård.

Vestergaard, Torben. 1974. *Færøsk odelsbønder: En etnografisk analyse af resterne af et nordisk stammesamfund*. Etnografisk Institut, Århus Universitet, Studenterfeldrapport nr. 2. Århus: Moesgård.

West, John F., ed. 1970. *The journals of the Stanley Expedition to the Faroe Islands and Iceland in 1789. Vol. 1: Introduction and diary of James Wright*. Tórshavn: Føroya Fróðskaparfelag.

———. 1972. *Faroe: The emergence of a nation*. London and New York: C. Hurst, and Paul S. Eriksson.

———. 1977. The edge of Europe. *Natural History* 86(10):40–47.

Whitaker, Ian. 1978. Recent anthropological studies of the Faroe Islands (1971–1975). *Folk Life* 16:78–84.

Williamson, Kenneth. 1945. The economic and ethnological importance of the caaing whale, *Globiocephalus melaena* Traill, in the Faeroe Islands. *Northwestern Naturalist* 20:118–36.

———. 1949. Notes on the caaing whale. *Scottish Naturalist* 61:68–72.

———. 1970. *The Atlantic islands: A study of the Faeroe life and scene.* 2d ed. With an epilogue by Einar Kallsberg. London: Collins.

Wylie, Jonathan. 1974. I'm a stranger too: A study of the familiar society of the Faroe Islands. Ph.D. dissertation, Harvard University, Cambridge, Mass.

———. 1978. *The Faroese Reformation and its consequences.* Antropologisch-Sociologisch Centrum, Universiteit van Amsterdam, Papers on European and Mediterranean Societies no. 10. Amsterdam: Universiteit van Amsterdam.

Young, G. V. C., and Clewer, Cynthia R., trans. 1973. *The Faroese Saga freely translated with maps and genealogical tables.* Belfast: Century Services.

Zachariasen, Louis. 1961. *Føroyar sum rættarsamfelag 1535–1655. Annales societatis scientiarum Færoensis supplementum IV.* Tórshavn: Føroya Fróðskaparfelag.

Index

administration, Danish: offices, 118; role of high commissioner, 9, 138; social reforms and, 5–6, 126–27

adverbs: in idioms of orientation, 23–28, 31; of place and direction, formation, 152 n. 1

ævintýr. See folktales; "Øskudólgur"

Arge, Jógvan, interview, 141–42

Ashlad. *See* Øskudólgur; "Øskudólgur"

Ashlad tales, Norwegian, and "Øskudólgur," 154 n. 2

assemblies, in ancient times, 155 n. 6. *See also* Løgting

bailiff (*fúti*), history of office, 118

ballad dancing: at *grindadráp*, 99–100; drinking and, 115–16; role in *grindadráp*, 117–18; traditional contexts, 116–17. *See also* "English dancing"

ballads, heroic (*kvæðir*): genre of oral tradition, 68; modern contexts, 70; modern role, 71; normative function, 69. *See also* Faroese oral tradition

ballads, satirical (*tættir*): genre of oral tradition, 68–69; modern counterparts, 71. *See also* Faroese oral tradition

"Beautiful and Clever Queen, The": "Øskudólgur" and, 68; translation, 159–60 n. 12

Bergen: administrative center, 3; writing tradition, 77. *See also* Faroe Islands, Norway and

boð, contexts, 104. *See also grindaboð*

boundaries, sea, idioms of orientation and, 22, 25–28

Christianity, introduction, 76–77

commissioner, Danish high, role, 9, 138

compass terms: in idioms of orientation, 27–31, 40–43; usage, 158 n. 8. *See also* idioms of orientation

Copenhagen, Faroese culture and, 8, 89

dancing. *See* ballad dancing; "English dancing"

dancers, ring of (*dansiringur*), image of Faroese culture, 12

Danish constitution of 1849, Faroese reaction, 82

Danish in the Faroes, by Svend Grundtvig, 82

Danish language: Faroese and, 80, 85; learned by Faroese, 79; role A.D. 1550–1900, 77–82; role after World War II, 91–92

"Deeps, The" (*Djúpini*): idioms of orientation and, 39; symbolic meaning of, 154 n. 13

Denmark, Faroe Islands and, 4–6, 9, 57–64 passim, 77–94 passim, 118, 120–22, 126–27, 138

distribution rules: of *grindadráp*, as social history, 120–24; of *grindadráp*, modern, 123–24, 128

division of labor, traditional, 54–56. *See also* sex-role differentiation; women; work

drinking: ballad dancing and, 115–16; in Faroese culture, 115; at *grindadráp*, 114–15

economic change, Faroese culture and, 63–64

education, formal: beginnings, 81; changes, 89–90; Danish influence, 81; politics and, 81–82; resistance, 81

education, higher, institutions of, 90, 143

"English dancing," *grindadráp* and, 99, 117. *See also* ballad dancing

etymologies: FJORD, 19–20; *grind*, 103; *hvalvákn* (*hvalvápn*), 103; implements used in *grindadráp*, 103–4; -*oy*, 18–19; *sóknarongul*, 103–4; SOUND, 152–53 n. 5; *streymur*, 18

farm, traditional household composition, 53

farmers, tenant (*kongsbøndur*), 7. *See also* land tenure

Faroe Islands: conceptual map, 21, 22–23; Danish county, 5–6, 81–82; Denmark and, 4–6, 9, 57–64 passim, 77–94 passim, 118, 120–22, 126–27, 138; *grindadráp* in descriptions, 129–30; Norway and, 3, 75, 76, 80, 105, 120; population, 6; settlement by Irish, 3, 151 n. 1, chap. 1; settlement by Scandinavians, 3

Faroese Academy (Fróðskaparsetur Føroya): role in language planning, 143; teaching institution, 143

Faroese culture: A.D. 850–1000, 74–76; A.D. 1100–1530, 76–77; A.D. 1550–1900, 77–82; conceptual elaboration, 94; Copenhagen and, 8, 89; Danish citizenship and, 81–82; definition, 93–94; drinking, 115; economic change and, 63–64; effects of Reformation, 77–82; fine arts, 147–48; Føringafelag and, 89; *grindadráp* as symbol, 128–29, 130; intellectuals and, 8; language role development and, 93; National Romantic movement and, 82, 83; ring of dancers as image, 12; role of *grindadráp*, 102, 113; role of "Grindevise," 129; self-recognition, 131–32; two levels, 62–63

Faroese economy: *grindadráp* and, 128; modern, 6; "Øskudólgur" and, 63; traditional, 52–53

Faroese Folk High School: Faroese language and, 90; founding, 90

Faroese history: *grindadráp* as mirror, 124–25; overview, 3–9

Faroese language: character during Reformation, 79–80; controversy after 1900, 90; cultural implications of orthography, 88; Danish and, 80, 85; development, 80; dialect distinctions, 80; Faroese Folk High School and, 90; Føringafelag and, 162; growth of written form, 90–91; Svend Grundtvig and, 82–83; V. U. Hammershaimb and, 82, 84, 85; "high" variety, 92–93; Icelandic and, 79, 84, 85, 161 n. 4; Jakob Jakobsen and, 89, 160 n. 4; loanwords, 92–93; Jákup Nolsøe and, 84; Napoleon Nolsøe and, 84; orthographic controversy, 89, 161–62 n. 5; orthographic samples, 85; orthography, 8–9, 83–84, 85, 86–88; orthography and dialects, 85–86; N. M. Petersen and, 84; phonetic divergence, 80; policy of Faroes' Radio, 142; C. C. Rafn and, 84; role A.D. 1550–1900, 79–82; J. H. Schrøter and, 83–84, 85; significance of study, 142–43; Jón Sigurðsson and, 84; Slesvig-Holstein Question and, 160–61 n. 3; social boundaries and, 94; South Streymoy dialect, 89; status, 9, 144; J. C. Svabo and, 83–84; symbolism of written form, 89; teachers college and, 90; Tórshavn and, 88–89; translation of New Testament, 83–84; translations from Danish, 93; use A.D. 1100–1530, 77

Faroese nationalism, World War II and, 91

Faroese oral tradition: decline, 70; genres, 68–70; modern counterparts, 70–71; modern role, 71–72; normative function, 69; performance, 69–70; role in nineteenth century, 68–70

Faroese society: A.D. 850–1000, 74–76;

Grundtvig, Svend, Faroese language and, 82–83
Gulatingslóg, *grindadráp* and, 105, 120

Hammershaimb, V. U.: Faroese language and, 8, 84, 85, 88; formal education and, 82; *grindadráp* and, 130
HOME, in idioms of orientation, 39–40, 41, 42, 43
Home Rule Law (1948), 9, 91
horses, in Faroe Islands, 155 n. 4
hvalvákn (hvalvápn), etymology, 103

Icelandic language, Faroese and, 84, 85, 161 n. 4
idioms of orientation: ABOUT in, 153 n. 7; adverbs in, 23–28, 31, 152 n. 3; alternatives in constructing, 35–37; areas of reference and, 32–33; as history, 32, 39–40; Christian Matras and, 39; coherence and complexity, 15–16; combinations of prepositions in, 152 n. 2; compass terms in, 27–31, 40–43; conservativeness, 44; contexts, 13–15; equivalence of land and sea in, 18–22; Faroese terms, 151–52 n. 1; FJORD in, 23, 24–28, 35–36, 154 n. 12; forms, 17; HOME in, 31–32, 39–40, 41, 42, 43; in Norðoyar, 37–40; *oman* and *niðan* in, 153 n. 6; on Sandoy, 40–43; pervasiveness, 44–45; prepositions in, 23–28, 31; regional sets, 37–43; rules governing, 31–32; sea boundaries and, 22, 25–28; SOUND in, 23, 24–28; Tórshavn and, 153 n. 9; *um* in, 153 n. 7; waypoints and, 33–34; West Norwegian usage and, 154 n. 10
intellectuals, Faroese culture and, 8, 89, 139–41, 142–49
interviews: Jógvan Arge, 141–42; Leif Groth, 137–39; Marius Johannessen, 144–46; Eyvindur Mohr, 146–49; Erlendur Patursson, 139–41; Johan Hendrik Poulsen, 142–44
Irish, settlement of Faroe Islands by, 3, 151 n. 1, chap. 1
island, English spelling, 152 n. 4

Jacobsen, Jørgen-Frantz, *grindadráp* and, 130
Jakobsen, Jakob: Faroese folktales and, 158 n. 11; Faroese language and, 9, 89, 160 n. 14, 161–62 n. 5; Faroese oral tradition and, 46–48
Jákupson, Jákup. *See* Jakobsen, Jakob
Joensen, J. P., *grindadráp* and, 130
Johannessen, Marius, interview, 144–46

Kirkjubøur: church school, 77; seat of bishopric, 3, 76
kvæðir. See ballads, heroic

Landsstýri (Faroese executive committee), Home Rule Law and, 9
land tenure: by foreigners, 151 n. 2; *grindadráp* and, 120–23; types of, 7, 53
land use, 7
language use: A.D. 850–1000, 75–76; A.D. 1100–1530, 76–77; A.D. 1550–1900, 77–82; after World War II, 91
Latin: role A.D. 1100–1530, 76–77; role A.D. 1550–1900, 79
legends (*sagnir*): genre, 68; modern counterparts, 71
Løgting (parliament): in early medieval period, 75; elementary education and, 90; history, 3; Home Rule Law and, 9. *See also* assemblies
Lutheranism, effects of introduction, 77–79

marriage law, traditional, 53–54
marriage patterns, traditional, 67
Matras, Christian, idioms of orientation and, 39
Matras, Jóhan Hendrik, folktale informant, 53, 54, 159
Mohr, Eyvindur, interview, 146–49

National Romantic movement, Faroese culture and, 82, 83
nobles, role in "Øskudólgur," 60
Nolsøe, Napoleon, Faroese language and, 84
Nolsøe, Jákup, Faroese language and, 84

Norðoyar, idioms of orientation in, 37–40

Norway, Faroe Islands and, 3, 75, 76, 80, 105, 120

Norwegian language, role A.D. 1550–1900, 77–78

Old Norse, role A.D. 850–1000, 75–76

Old West Scandinavian, role A.D. 1100–1530, 76–77. *See also* Old Norse

Øskudólgur: ambiguous male, 56–57, 61–62; cultural ambiguity, 60–61, 62

"Øskudólgur": analytic approach to, 52; analytical implications, 65; "The Beautiful and Clever Queen" and, 68; Faroese economy and, 63; folktales with female figures and, 66–67, 68; Norwegian Askeladden tales and, 154 n. 2; other folktales and, 65–66, 68; rites of passage and, 155–58 n. 10; role of nobles, 60; royal level of society and, 57–60; status of princess, 155 n. 5; symbolic map, 157; tale type, 51; translation, 48–51

parliament. *See* assemblies; Løgting

Patursson, Erlendur, interview, 139–41

Petersen, N. M., Faroese language and, 84

Pløyen, Christian: *grindadráp* and, 99, 122; social reforms and, 126, 127

political office, transmission, 155 n. 7

political parties, beginnings, 9. *See also* Republican Party; Self-Rule Party

postal service, political issue, 138–39

Poulsen, Jóhan Hendrik, interview, 142–44

prepositions, in idioms of orientation, 23–28, 31, 152 n. 2

priests, role in *grindadráp*, 112–13

princess, status in "Øskudólgur," 155 n. 5

Rafn, C. C., Faroese language and, 84

Reformation: effects, 4, 77–82; *grindadráp* and, 106. *See also* Faroe Islands, Denmark and

Republican Party (Tjóðveldisflokkur), nationalism, 139–40

rites of passage, "Øskudólgur" and, 155–58 n. 10

ritual danger, in *grindadráp*, 119

royalty: representatives in Faroe Islands, 58–59; traditional village culture and, 57–60. *See also* administration, Danish

Runic alphabetic, role A.D. 850–1000, 75–76

sagnir. See legends

Sandoy, idioms of orientation on, 40–43

Scandinavia, meaning in present work, 151 n. 3

Scandinavians, settlement of Faroe Islands by, 3

Schrøter, J. H., Faroese language and, 83–84, 85

Self-Rule Party (Sjálvstýrisflokkur), position, 145–46

separatism, development, 8–9. *See also* Faroe Islands, Denmark and; Faroese language, Danish and

sex-role differentiation, reflected in folktales, 66–67. *See also* division of labor; women; work

sexual attitudes, *grindadráp* and, 116

Seyðabrӕv, *grindadráp* and, 120, 164 n. 6

sheriff (*sýslumaður*): history of office, 118; role in *grindadráp*, 98–99, 100, 118, 119, 124

Sigurd, Ballad of. *See* Sjúrðakvӕði

Sigurðsson, Jón, Faroese language and, 84

Sjálvstýrisflokkur. *See* Self-Rule Party

Sjúrðarkvӕði, orthographic samples, 85

Slesvig-Holstein Question, Faroese language and, 160–61 n. 3

social history, distribution rules of *grindadráp* as, 120–24

social problems, reflected in folktales, 68

social reforms, Danish administration and, 5–6, 126–27

sóknarongul, etymology, 103–4

SOUND: etymology, 152–53 n. 5; usage, 22, 38

Svabo, J. C., Faroese language and, 83–84

SYMBOL AND CULTURE

Jonathan Wylie and David Margolin, *The Ring of Dancers: Images of Faroese Culture*

Ruth Gruber Fredman, *The Passover Seder: Afikoman in Exile*

Gillian Feeley-Harnik, *The Lord's Table: Eucharist and Passover in Early Christianity*